BEST BLACK PLAYS

BEST BLACK PLAYS

THE THEODORE WARD PRIZE FOR AFRICAN AMERICAN PLAYWRITING

Edited by Chuck Smith

With a foreword by Woodie King Jr.

NORTHWESTERN UNIVERSITY PRESS
EVANSTON, ILLINOIS

Northwestern University Press
www.nupress.northwestern.edu

Printed in the United States of America

10   9   8   7   6   5   4   3   2   1

ISBN-13: 978-0-8101-2390-8
ISBN-10: 0-8101-2390-8

LIBRARY OF CONGRESS CATALOGING-IN-PUBLICATION DATA
Best black plays : the Theodore Ward Prize for African American
    Playwriting / edited by Chuck Smith ; foreword by Woodie King Jr.
        p. cm.
    ISBN-13: 978-0-8101-2390-8 (pbk. : alk. paper)
    ISBN-10: 0-8101-2390-8 (pbk. : alk. paper)
    1. American drama—African American authors. 2. African
Americans—Drama. I. Smith, Chuck, 1938– II. Lee, Leslie,
1944– Sundown names and night-gone things. III. Southers, Mark
Clayton. Ma Noah. IV. Euell, Kim. Diva daughters Dupree.
V. Title: Sundown names and night-gone things. VI. Title: Ma
Noah. VII. Title: Diva daughters Dupree.
PS627.N4B47 2007
812.54080896073—dc22
                                                    2007006118

♾ The paper used in this publication meets the minimum requirements
of the American National Standard for Information Sciences—Permanence
of Paper for Printed Library Materials, ANSI Z39.48-1992.

*This volume of plays
is dedicated to the memory of August Wilson,
Lloyd Richards, and Benjamin Mordecai.*

CONTENTS

FOREWORD

Woodie King Jr.

Traditional theatergoers who go to see plays by black playwrights often have the misconceived notion that the playwright, like Topsy, just grew. However, across America, in small black theaters, workshops, and contests, they are sought, encouraged, and often produced. So, ten or fifteen years after the *mainstream* "discovers" Ntozake Shange, or George C. Wolfe, or August Wilson, we *discover* in their journey Nuyorican Poets Cafe, New Federal Theatre, Inner City Cultural Center, Plowshares Theatre, Crossroads Theatre, Kuntu Rep, Black Horizon Theatre, and Penumbra Theatre.

In the 1940s and 1950s, when Theodore Ward wrote *Our Lan'* and *Big White Fog,* he was a pioneer in an exclusively white theater environment. His plays, from production to the present, are nearly impossible to find. The civil rights movement, riots, and social unrest changed that. African American became the flavor of the moment. Black writers articulated our frustration.

In the 1960s, 1970s, and 1980s, black playwriting ascended from the plays of Lorraine Hansberry to the unprecedented contributions of August Wilson.

To get black plays to a wider audience, to expand boundaries, they must get productions or they must get published. The award-winning plays of the Theodore Ward Prize for African American Playwriting are now able to get both a production and published.

Veteran Leslie Lee's *Sundown Names and Night-Gone Things,* Pittsburgh's Mark Clayton Southers's *Ma Noah,* and Kim Euell's *The Diva Daughters DuPree* entered the Theodore Ward Contest for African American Playwriting, and for that, these plays will reach a wider audience through publication.

In 2007, when these award-winning plays reach publication—a time when the cost of everything from gas to housing to education is rising and a non-musical Broadway production hovers around $2 million, off-Broadway nearly $750,000, and regional theater upward of $150,000—where does a black playwright go? Especially since in the aforementioned venues, cost does not always equal quality.

When we look forward into the first decade of the twenty-first century, we see the problems within the black community being solved by the people within that community, within the families of these communities. Of course the diverse voices that distinguish each playwright propose diverse solutions.

Ultimately, no matter how difficult, these playwrights are saying we must attempt to solve our own problems. And that is what Theodore Ward did sixty years ago; what black theater did forty years ago; and what Chuck Smith and Columbia College Chicago began with the Theodore Ward Prize for African American Playwriting twenty years ago.

BEST BLACK PLAYS

SUNDOWN NAMES AND NIGHT-GONE THINGS

Leslie Lee

First-Place Winner

2002–2003

PLAYWRIGHT'S STATEMENT

I wrote *Sundown Names and Night-Gone Things* primarily because of the influences of Richard Wright on my life as a playwright. Wright, along with Lorraine Hansberry and James Baldwin, became my first literary hero and the impetus for pursuing a career in writing because of the scope, power, beauty, and imagery of his words. I voraciously read everything I could get my hands on, not only his novels and short stories but also about him personally. *Sundown Names and Night-Gone Things* is based on an actual incident in Richard Wright's life when, as a young man and part of the great migration of blacks, he fled north from Mississippi to Chicago in search of the promised land. Armed with few writing skills but great curiosity and the need to earn a living, Wright obtained a job as an agent in a black insurance company, which provided an indispensable service to blacks who generally lacked life insurance coverage by white companies. Still sowing his wild oats, Wright found himself involved in a scheme in which the agents, all older than he was, gave free insurance to impoverished female customers, married and unmarried, unable to pay the ten-cent weekly premium in exchange for sexual favors. They bartered and exchanged these desperate women when they tired of them or if "someone better" came along. Wright, still naive, a newcomer in terms of relationships, fell in love with an illiterate, eighteen-year-old single mother whose only means of survival were her wit and her sensuality. Obsessed, displaying frequent fits of jealousy because of her refusal to commit to a monogamous relationship, Wright was ultimately sent packing by the young siren. He recognized that what he and the others were doing was morally reprehensible, exploitative, and destructive to the fabric of the fragile black community in Chicago. He refused to participate any longer in a practice that was too deeply embedded, and he left the industry to seek his fortunes elsewhere.

The story interested me for a number of reasons. Authors are the sum totals of their experiences and environment. How an author evolves and becomes a literary and societal force is always fascinating. I was drawn to this moment in Wright's life because it exposed an error in judgment that he was able to rectify before it resulted in moral ruination. He is an example of how greatness allows flaws and how none of us, no matter how prominent or esteemed we are, is infallible.

Sundown Names and Night-Gone Things was produced at Columbia College Chicago and later by the Chicago Theater Company. Those are the only two productions to date. In addition, I retain the production rights to *Sundown Names and Night-Gone Things*, which was copyrighted in 2001.

PRODUCTION HISTORY

Sundown Names and Night-Gone Things, by Leslie Lee, was first presented by the Columbia College Chicago Theater Department at the New Studio Theater in February 2003. It was directed by Andrea J. Dymond, with set design by Brandon T. Lewis, costume design by Patricia Roeder, lighting design by Erik Steffensen, and sound design by David Sohl and Matthew Ulm. David Woolley was the fight choreographer, and Andrew Glasenhardt was the stage manager.

Boyd Henry	Mark James Heath
Cairo Biggs	Charles A. Jenkins
Travis McKinley	Michael Pogue
Mae Ann Morgan	Joi Sinigal
Arjay Thornton	Larry Towers
Ruby Meeks	Lauren Wells

The play was subsequently presented by the Chicago Theater Company at the Parkway Playhouse in September 2003. It was directed by Andrea J. Diamond, with set design by Peter Chatman, costume design by Karen Wells, lighting design by Eyde Jones, and sound design by Joe Plummer. Devon Love was the technical director, and Kimberly L. Smart was the stage manager.

Boyd Henry	James T. Alfred
Mae Ann Morgan	Inda Craig-Galvan
Arjay Thornton	J. J. McCormick
Cairo Biggs	Michael Pogue
Ruby Meeks	Natalie Slater
Travis McKinley	Byron Glenn Willis

Understudies: Tory O. Davis, Ray Baker, Sharyon A. Culberson, and Markietha Singleton

CHARACTERS

Ruby Meeks, black female, eighteen or nineteen
Cairo Biggs, black male, insurance agent, midtwenties
Travis McKinley, black male, insurance agent, forties or fifties
Mae Ann Morgan, black female, late twenties or early thirties
Boyd Henry, black male, insurance agent, forties or fifties
Arjay Thornton, black male, insurance agent, forties or fifties

STAGING

1938, Chicago. Staged realistically with no fourth wall. Onstage is an office area with four desks and a limbo space large enough to accommodate a bed and a dresser.

ACT 1

[*Night. A light rises in a small room across the stage. A bed dominates one corner of the space stage right. Nearby are a table with a radio on it and two chairs. A picture of a black Jesus on the wall hangs crookedly. Below the picture is a mirror. A kitchen sink, with cabinets above and below, is squeezed into another corner of the room. The door is upstage left. The song "Elevator Woman" by Sonny Boy Williamson is heard from the radio.* RUBY *stands in front of the mirror, singing and dancing suggestively to the music.*]

RUBY: "Elevate me, baby, five or six stories on down . . . Elevate me, baby, five or six stories on down . . ."

[*She continues, along with the music. The doorbell buzzes. She doesn't hear it at first, continuing to appraise her sexy body in the mirror. She's pleased with what she sees and accentuates her movements. The doorbell buzzes again. She hears it finally. She responds, without turning.*]

It's open.

[*The door opens slowly.* CAIRO *enters, carrying a book and a briefcase. He closes the door behind him. She knows who it is without looking. She turns, dances evocatively over, and rubs up against him, continuing to sing and dance, turning him on.*]

"Elevate me, baby, five or six stories down.
Elevate me, baby, five or six stories down.
And we gets down to the bottom
Let's elevate back up one mo', one mo' time . . ."

[*She kisses him.*]

Hi, Mr. Insurance Man. What'dja bring me?

[*She slides her hands evocatively over his chest, down to his waist, and then quickly to his crotch, clutching it and softly massaging it. He groans, dropping the book and briefcase to the floor.*]

I know you brung me this, but what else you got for me? I *know* you got somethin' else for me!

[*He kisses her passionately, trying to force her to the bed. She resists.*]

No, Cairo!

CAIRO [*as he continues to struggle with her*]: Don't tease me, will you!

RUBY: I said no, now stop it! [*Pause.*] I mean it, Cairo!

[*He lets go, groaning. She moves a step away and stands, a turn-on.*]

CAIRO: Always teasing me.

RUBY: You ain't brought me nothin' all week. *A whole week!* Now, that ain't right, specially for somebody fine as me.

[*She begins to dance to the music again, even more sensually. He fumbles in his pocket and quickly pulls out a gaudy piece of costume jewelry—a necklace—and dangles it in front of her. She stops.*]

Oooooo, look at that! *Look* at *that!* Now ain't you the sweetest thing!

[*She saunters over to him, a sex kitten.*]

This is for me?

CAIRO: Who else is it going to be for?

[*She takes it from him and appraises it.*]

RUBY: Oh, this is nice. I knew you had somethin' for me. You better had, you knew what's good for you.

[*She kisses him sensuously on the mouth.*]

Put it round my neck.

[*She hands it to him and then turns her back. He begins to clasp it. She rubs up against him. He fumbles, turned on. She laughs. He finally finishes. She goes to the mirror and looks at herself, pleased.*]

Oh, yeah, I like this. Oh, yeah!

[*She turns to him, sultry.*]

All right, you got somethin' else for me, baby? Bring it to me, will you?

[*He moves quickly to her. They embrace and go at each other, falling to the bed. The lights fade quickly to black.*]

[*Later. The lights fade in again in* RUBY's *apartment.* RUBY *and* CAIRO *lie on the bed, fully clothed and entangled.*]

RUBY: My premium's paid up this week now, right?

CAIRO: Uh-huh. How'd you like to get started on next week, and the week after that?

RUBY: I might do a whole year before I'm through with you tonight, man.

CAIRO: Think you can handle it?

RUBY: You best be careful, I'll wear you out, man.

CAIRO: Yeah, well, c'mon, start trying, then.

[*He kisses her and begins feeling her again. She pulls away, rises, and straightens her dress.*]

Where are you going?

RUBY: I didn't say right now. Besides, I'm like the Salvation Army: I serves the needy, not the greedy.

[*She laughs.*]

CAIRO: Come on, Ruby, don't let my fire go out.

RUBY: Don't worry; I'll light it up again when it's time.

[*She giggles. He slumps back to the bed, frustrated. She goes to the mirror and looks at herself, continuing to smooth her dress. She touches her face suddenly.*]

You need to shave better, Cairo. Your face's too rough. Got my face all scruffed up.

[*She waits for an answer that doesn't come.*]

Cairo?

CAIRO: I heard you.

RUBY: Couldn't even wait for me to get my dress off. All wrinkled up. Some folks don't have no manners at all. It's a pretty dress, ain't it? You haven't even said the first thing about it.

CAIRO: I didn't have a chance to.

RUBY: Well, you do now. You like it?

CAIRO: It's pretty, OK? [*Pause.*] Where'd you get it?

RUBY: Mr. John's Bargain Basement.

[*She is posing and primping now in front of the mirror. He watches her, turned on even more.*]

CAIRO: How much did it cost?

RUBY: Stop bein' so nosy. It's not polite.

CAIRO: I'm just asking, that's all.

RUBY: Well, none of your beeswax.

CAIRO: I thought you were supposed to be so short on cash.

RUBY: I am. Short as a doggone midget.

CAIRO: So, where'd you get the money?

RUBY: That's none of your beeswax neither.

CAIRO: How come it's not?

RUBY: I don't have to answer to nobody but me, Cairo. How come you can't keep that in your thick skull?

[*She throws him a fiery look and resumes primping.*]

This necklace goes real nice with my dress.

CAIRO: I told you I'd get it for you.

RUBY: Don't start with me, Cairo.

CAIRO: So, why didn't you let me?

RUBY: I can't help it if somebody else wants to buy me somethin'.

CAIRO: But, I *told* you I would, Ruby!

RUBY: You need to stop bein' so jealous, man.

CAIRO: I'm not being jealous. Who's being jealous?

RUBY: You are. Maybe you oughtta hear yourself. Other people can be nice to me, can't they? I'm supposed to say, "No, you can't be nice and buy me nothin', and take me out to the circus and stuff, 'cause Cairo Biggs don't want you to be nice to me, 'cause he thinks he owns me, and he's jealous?" That don't make the first bit o' sense. If you want to get me a dress so bad, get me another one. I'll take all the dresses I can get.

[*She laughs and then fiddles with the hem of the dress.*]

I might take this hem up a little. Make it a teeny bit shorter.

[*She pulls the hem up, revealing more of her legs. She looks at him.*]

What you think?

[*He looks at her legs, wanting her, but turns away.*]

Right here. Yeah, that's perfect. Bring me them safety pins from the table, will you, please, sugar?

[*He hesitates, unwilling.*]

C'mon, Cairo, I don't wanna lose my place.

[*He rises and goes to the table.*]

In that little brown box. You see it?

[*He doesn't answer, picks up the box, and hands it to her.*]

Now, hold the hem right here.

[*He does what he's told.*]

That's it. That's good.

[*She begins to pin the hem.*]

CAIRO: It's that's guy—Jim, isn't it?
RUBY: Don't let go, I ain't finished yet. Where's your mind?
CAIRO: He's the one who bought this stupid thing, isn't he?
RUBY: Stop dancin' with the devil, Cairo.
CAIRO: You may as well go ahead and say it. Go ahead! He did, didn't he?
RUBY: All right, since you're so crazy about messin' with TNT, it's him—all right? You feel better now, huh?

[*She pulls away and looks in the mirror again, checking the hemline, pleased.*]

CAIRO: You're always throwing him in my face.
RUBY: No, get it straight. You threw him in your own face. Kept naggin' me, wantin' to know, so I told you. I'm supposed to lie to you, just so you can feel better? I got lotsa friends, in case you don't know it.

[*She prances in front of the mirror.*]

CAIRO: Just don't go throwing him in my face, that's all.

[*He turns away. She goes back to the mirror for more primping.* CAIRO *goes to the bed and picks up the book.*]

RUBY: I do what you want me to do for you, and you do what you're supposed to for me. My personal business don't have nothin' to do with it, if I ain't mistaken. I'm not mistaken, am I?

[*She looks at him and then laughs.*]

Look at him over there, poutin', poor thing. C'mon, Cairo, we was doin' just fine, and you had to mess up.

[*She goes to the phonograph, winds it up, and plays a record. She dances wildly.*]

Let's you and me go over to the dance hall and cut a little rug, OK?

[*He doesn't answer.*]

Come on, Cairo, I got my dancin' shoes on tonight!

[*She dances about the floor, showing her moves.*]

Get it, Ruby! Go ahead, girl! [*Pause.*] Cairo, please?

CAIRO: I'm not in the mood to go dancing tonight.

RUBY: "I'm not in the mood to go dancing tonight." Sound like one of them high-dicty Negroes.

CAIRO: I don't sound anything like those people.

RUBY: Indeed you do. You and your big words. Life ain't about no big words, man, it's about havin' enough neckbones and cabbage and sausage cakes and bread and stewed prunes on your plate every day. All them big words ain't gonna get you nothin'.

CAIRO: The more words you know, the more white people can't fool you, Ruby.

RUBY: I don't care 'bout no white people right now. What do they have to do with anything? I just wanna tog up, go to a jive joint, get me a reefer, kick up my heels, and forget about all this damn Depression here on the South Side.

[*She stops dancing, eyeing him.*]

I ain't never seen nobody so stiff in all my life. Why don't you just let your hair down, man, and be yourself?

CAIRO: I am myself.

RUBY: Well, I sure wouldn't tell nobody. Are you gonna take me big-timin' or not?

CAIRO: You said you wanted me to teach you to read tonight.

RUBY: Well, I changed my mind, all right?

[*He opens the book.*]

CAIRO: Listen to this, Ruby.

RUBY: Cairo—

CAIRO: No, listen. It's a real good book, Ruby. It's by this guy, John Steinbeck, and it's called *The Grapes of Wrath*—

RUBY: I don't care about no junk about some grapes.

CAIRO: No, no, it's not "junk," Ruby. It's about these people who—

RUBY: Cairo, I'm nineteen years old, and I'm on relief. Readin' books ain't never gonna keep a roof over my head, put food in my daughter's belly, and have my premiums paid up. Ask anybody here on the South Side about readin' anything except a dream book, and they'll laugh you right off the block.

CAIRO: All right, forget the stupid book!

[*He throws the book across the room and sits on the bed, sulking. She hesitates, then picks up the book. She leafs through it, finally putting it down on the bed.*]

RUBY: I don't know what's in there, but whatever it is, it ain't me, Cairo.

[*She pauses and then walks slowly over and rubs against him. He tries to push her away, but she persists.*]

Come on, let's get low-down and go pitch us a little boogie-woogie. Sonny Boy Williamson's at the Blue Nile. Now, you *know* we got to be there! Maggie's with my mama, so you and me can have the whole night to ourselves.

[*He tries to push her away again. She won't let him.*]

We'll have us lotsa scotch, get us a little buzz goin', dance on the dime, and do a little grindin', too. You wanta grind with me, don't you, baby?

[*He doesn't answer, weakening.*]

Come on, you know you do.

[*She kisses his face and neck. He responds passionately, but she pulls away, leading him from the bed.*]

Then we'll come on back here and you can do it to me allllllll night long. And it's goin' to be good, too. OK? [*Pause.*] OK?

CAIRO: OK . . .

[*She gives him a wet kiss and then pulls away and starts for the bathroom door.*]

RUBY: I have'ta get myself cleaned up and look pretty for all the folks out there.

[*She stops at the door.*]

I like my necklace, Cairo. I'm gonna wear it tonight.

[*She opens the door and goes in. He stands, resigned. He sits on the bed and begins to read. The lights gradually fade, as* RUBY *can be heard, singing to herself. The lights fade out. Music is heard in the darkness, and voices. Cross-fade in on an insurance office. Morning. A small office cluttered with papers. Stacks of calendars and paper church fans sit in piles in a corner of the room. An old clock on the wall begins chiming suddenly, loudly, even though it's ten minutes before noon. It mingles with music, "Franklin D. Roosevelt Jones," from a battered radio on a shelf against one of the walls, which competes with a couple of noisy electric fans, struggling on a windowsill to stir the hot, humid air in the room. Upstage center is the entrance.* SOUTH SIDE BURIAL SOCIETY *is stenciled on the door in large black letters. Upstage left there is a bathroom door.* BOYD, CAIRO, *and* ARJAY *sit at their respective desks in spotlights, talking on telephones.* MAE ANN *sits in a chair at* TRAVIS*'s desk.*]

TRAVIS: You hit the nail right on the head, Mrs. Morgan. The one thing we colored people want for our dearly departed is a proper, befitting burial. Yes, ma'am. And just think, you can get all that for ten cents a week. You hear what I'm saying?

MAE ANN: Yes sir, ten cents a week.

TRAVIS: Now, you're not going to get a better bargain than that in heaven. Am I tellin' the truth?

MAE ANN: Yes, you are, Mr. Thornton.

TRAVIS: I know I am. This is whole-life insurance I'm talking about. And that means you're covered for as long as the Good Lord gives you breath. But, you have to keep up with your premiums now. Pay your rent, your light bill, and your premiums first. I tell that to all my clients. Now, how's all this sound, Mrs. Morgan?

MAE ANN: Oh, fine, just fine, sir.

TRAVIS: If you're satisfied, then sign right here on the dotted line.

[*He points to a sheet of paper on the desk and then hands her a pen. She hesitates, a little embarrassed.*]

MAE ANN: My reading's all right, but my writin's not so good.

TRAVIS: There's no need to rush. Take all the time you need.

[*She signs it slowly and poorly and then hands him the pen. He blows on the paper, drying the ink.*]

Good, your policy's in force. Now, read it carefully, and if there's something you don't understand, be sure and ask me when I come by Tuesday to pick up your next premium payment, all right?

MAE ANN: Yes, sir. I sure will. I really appreciate this, Mr. Thornton.

TRAVIS: That's what we're here for, Mrs. Morgan, to provide a service our community desperately needs. Because, we both know, the white insurance companies aren't about to touch us with a ten-foot pole.

MAE ANN: No, sir, they sure won't. All I can say is, God bless all colored insurance men, sir.

TRAVIS: Thank you, ma'am. We're just trying to do the best we can for our people.

MAE ANN: Well, I best be gettin' over by the lake. My madam will have her foot all over the back of my neck if I'm late.

TRAVIS: We sure can't have that white lady taking scraps off your table now, can we? No, indeed! All right, I'll see you next Tuesday.

MAE ANN: I'll be there. Thank you, Mr. Thornton.

TRAVIS: You're more than welcome, darlin'.

[MAE ANN *stands and walks toward the door.* TRAVIS *rises, accompanies her, and opens the door for her.*]

MAE ANN: Bye now.

TRAVIS: Bye-bye.

[*She smiles, obviously charmed by him. His smile is flirtatious. She leaves. He stares after her for a moment and then closes the door.*]

Lord, Jesus! That woman can crawl into my bed with *both* her shoes on, brother! Have mercy!

[*He turns toward* CAIRO.]

Hey, y'all, if you're going to Comiskey Park with me, we'd better be commencin'. I'm don't want to miss one pitch by Mr. Paige!

[*He assumes the pose of a pitcher on the mound.* ARJAY *gets up and assumes the role of a batter.*]

Satchel himself! You see me now! You see me!

[*The roar of the crowd is heard, building. He stares in at the imagined catcher, acknowledges the sign, winds up, and pauses.*]

Fastball, straight down the middle. I dare you to hit it. I dee double dare you! Come on, hit me. Come on! Whomp!

[*He throws an imaginary baseball.* ARJAY *swings his imaginary bat wildly and misses.*]

Strike one! All right, here I come again, straight down the middle. You won't even see it! Whomp!

[*He throws.* ARJAY *swings and misses by a foot, almost falling.* BOYD *and* CAIRO *are watching now, laughing.*]

BOYD: Get 'em, Satch! Stick it to 'im, baby!
TRAVIS: I got 'im. Moofoo is mine! Straight down the middle. Whomp!

[ARJAY *swings and falls flat on his face.*]

Strike three, yer out! Sit down, fool!

[*He laughs and pumps his fist in the air as* ARJAY, BOYD, *and* CAIRO *laugh. The road of a crowd is heard, drowning them out. Fade to black.*]

[*Fade in after a moment. The light rises on* CAIRO, *standing alone on the street in front of* RUBY's *apartment building, holding a bouquet of flowers. He rings the doorbell repeatedly. There is no answer. He paces, fretting, and rings the doorbell again. No answer. He stops and looks up at the window. There is no light coming from inside.*]

CAIRO: Ruby? Ruby? You in there? [*Pause.*] We're supposed to get together tonight after the game. You said you'd be here? Ruby? [*Pause.*] Ruby? You in there?
A MALE VOICE: Hey, pipe down, nigger! What's wrong with you? We're tryin' to get some sleep. I'll call the fuckin' cops! The bitch is out! She's always out!

[CAIRO *hesitates, frustrated, and then throws the flowers into an open garbage can nearby and strides angrily offstage. Cross-fade to the insurance office. It is morning, a few weeks later.* ARJAY, *a bib covering his shirt and tie, eats soul food, washing it down with iced tea, along with* TRAVIS *and* BOYD, *who sit at their own desks.* BOYD *has his face buried in a newspaper. The radio is on. Music is heard through the static: "I May Be Wrong," by Little Jimmy Rushing.*]

BOYD: I'll be darned! Did you all read about that little ruckus at the lake yesterday?
TRAVIS: Little ruckus, my ass. It was a damn near riot. Just because those colored kids got hot and sweaty, wanted to cool off and went swimming

over there. Now, since when is a piece of sand supposed be just for white folks? Somebody tell me.

ARJAY: You suppose it's in the Bible somewhere? Maybe I missed that sermon.

TRAVIS: You've missed a whole lot of sermons in your day, brother.

ARJAY: Yeah, well, I know one thing: I'm not the only backslider in here. I *know* that.

BOYD: Will you look at this. They arrested those kids for trespassing. Put them in jail and then had the nerve to fine them. Now, that's ridiculous.

ARJAY: It won't be ridiculous if it turns into a riot one of these days. You see, that's what's going to happen. Those kids'll be back there, because they know they have a right to the whole beach, not just part of it.

TRAVIS: And the worst part of it, too, there's more rocks and shit than sand on the colored part of the beach. They have all the damn good sand.

ARJAY: Segregated beaches. White folks drawing some line in the sand. Mark my words, something's going to happen, as sure as I'm born.

TRAVIS: Yeah, it's blowing in the wind.

BOYD: Oh, man, look at this! Little Persian in the fifth! I started to put a two-spot on it, but something told me to go with Vagabond Dreams, and the stupid rascal didn't even show. Little Persian was fifteen-to-one odds. Paid three forty! Why the world did I change my mind? I could have made a bundle. Put it on my mortgage and had some left over for a down payment on that sweet Cadillac in Wahlberg's showroom! Stupid!

[*He smacks himself on the forehead.*]

ARJAY: I keep telling you to follow your first instincts, nigger, but, no, Mr. Know-It-All over there.

BOYD: Man, I'm not studying you.

TRAVIS: Hey, those fans come in yet? I promised Reverend Cobbs I'd bring some over.

BOYD: Now, Reverend Cobbs, you see, he's different, as far as preachers go. He's no bullshitter. Wears the latest clothes, drives that flashy red Oldsmobile, cusses a little bit, but he's a good sport, though. Regular, you know?

ARJAY: Yeah, he's a cool cat all right. A bunch of us heard him on the radio a couple of Sundays ago. We pulled up to the radio, playing cards, drinking and listening. One cat was laid out drunk as a damn skunk. Another sister had already guzzled down three glasses of liquor, port and muscatel. Man, I'm telling you, we were all high as a kite by the time he came on the air.

You should've heard those folks sing, "Precious Lord, Take My Hand." Have mercy! And what's that other one? [*Pause.*] "He's a Rock."

[*He sings a little of it.*]

Yes indeed! And then, ol' Cobbs came on, preaching up a storm! Tearin' it up!

TRAVIS: What did he preach about?

ARJAY: Damned if I know. But it was a good sermon, though. You could tell the man was God-sent and that what he was saying was coming from inside. I mean, you could tell it!

BOYD: Yeah, I have to admit, Cobbs can cut loose now. "I want to walk down Hallelujah Avenue! Go down and meet ol' Abraham, talk with ol' Isaac, and see ol' Jacob!"

ARJAY AND TRAVIS: Preach it, Rev!

BOYD: "I want to go down by the great white throne and see my Jesus. I want to feel the nailprints in his hands and feet and put my hands in the spear hole in his side. Hallelujah, hallelujah, hallelujah!"

ARJAY AND TRAVIS: Praise his holy name! Praise him!

BOYD: "I wanta ask ol' Daniel about how God stopped the lion's mouth, that's what I want to ask him!"

ARJAY: Go on and ask him, Reverend!

BOYD: "I want to ask those Hebrew children how they felt in the fiery furnace."

TRAVIS: Ask 'em! Go ahead, ask 'em!

BOYD: "Yes, sir, children, I'm gonna have a *good* old time in heaven!"

[*They laugh.*]

TRAVIS: Being black sure is fun when ain't nobody lookin'!

ARJAY: Yeah, brother, that's one preacher who can fill up a collection basket! Nickels, dimes, quarters, and greenbacks now and then!

TRAVIS: Yeah, I have to give it to him, Cobbs is all right. The man's got balls. He's got colored folks awoke to getting into the unions, fighting for the rights of workers, and all that kinda stuff. He's not just about all that bullshit about getting your reward in heaven. Hell, no! It's about getting it down here, right now!

ARJAY: Yeah, my brother-in-law's a redcap. And before the unions come along, they had to depend on tips for their income. Most stations didn't even pay living wages. But now that the unions are on the scene, they've got recognition as bona fide employees, minimum wages, and bargaining rights. And Cobbs was right in there, helping to lead the charge.

TRAVIS: That's why I've got to get those fans to the church. It's like the fiery furnace over there on Sunday mornings. Congregation's too hot and bothered to get happy. Now, you *know* that's hot, brother! I wonder why they haven't been delivered yet.

BOYD: Nigger, are you blind?

TRAVIS: What do you mean, "blind"?

ARJAY: As in, "can't see for shit." All those fans sitting over there in the corner?

TRAVIS [*suddenly seeing them*]: How long've they been there?

BOYD: A week. In that same spot.

TRAVIS: No, they haven't.

BOYD: The same damn spot, man.

TRAVIS: I'd've seen 'em if they'd been there.

BOYD: Will you stop arguing about something that's a fact? A fact is a fact. You can't argue with it, because it's a fact. A tree is a tree, a rat likes cheese, and number two stinks. Those are facts. You need to save your breath for your deathbed, just in case you need to tell a whole lot of folks off. Am I right, Arjay?

ARJAY: Yeah, brother, I got me a big old list of folks I'm planning to blaspheme. Number one on the list is Old Man Joe Willis—

BOYD: I'm talking about those fans over there.

ARJAY: Yeah, like you said, going on a week now.

BOYD: Case closed. Next case!

[TRAVIS *goes to the corner, picks up one of the paper fans, and examines it.*]

TRAVIS: Why didn't somebody tell me?

ARJAY: Now you see, if the chicken stopped laying eggs, that Negro would blame the damn eggs.

TRAVIS: I'm just asking, that's all.

ARJAY: That's just like standing in back of a big-ass elephant and asking what just farted in your face.

[BOYD *and* ARJAY *laugh.*]

BOYD: What he needs to do is blame the woman, whoever she is, that has his nose wide open. That's why he can't see into that corner. Man, you're not supposed to get caught up with that doggone love bug.

[TRAVIS *puts the fan down. The radio fades out. He bangs on it. It comes back on. Jimmy Rushing is still singing.*]

TRAVIS: Hell, man, I ain't hardly in love with anybody but my old woman, my children, and myself, of course!

[*They laugh.* TRAVIS *sits down at his desk, reaches into his desk drawer, and pulls out a bottle of aftershave. He opens it and splashes it liberally on his face.*]

ARJAY: Oh, Lawd, there he goes!
BOYD: Smells just like some French whore!
TRAVIS: Nigger, you wouldn't know a French whore if she sat on your face.
BOYD: Go on, put her there, you'll find out. She will, too!

[*They laugh.*]

TRAVIS: Yeah, well, all I know is, the women *love* the way I smell. Always complimenting me. You two cats want to smell like some moldy drawers, that's your business.

[*He splashes on more and then puts the bottle away.* BOYD *fans the air.*]

BOYD: C'mon, Travis, ease up on that stuff! We can't breathe in here as it is. The last thing I need is to be walking around Chicago smelling like you!

[*The door opens and* CAIRO *drags in, wiped out, carrying a Styrofoam cup of coffee. The others turn and look at him.*]

Well, look what the cat dragged in!
CAIRO: It stinks in here.
ARJAY: Now, you see, Travis? You see? The boy walks in here and the first thing out his mouth is, "It stinks in here."
TRAVIS: He can go to hell with the both of you. Hey, did you get your beauty rest, Sweetie Pie?
ARJAY: Look at him! Whipped! One of those little heifers must've turned it loose on 'im last night!
TRAVIS: Yeah, probably that little Ruby Meeks child.

[CAIRO *sits at his desk.*]

ARJAY: Oh, she's a tender thing all right! What's she, eighteen or nineteen, Biggs?
BOYD: She's no more than seventeen, isn't she?

ARJAY: How many babies she have? Two, three? I know it's something like that.

[CAIRO *is uninterested. He opens the container of coffee.*]

BOYD: Whatever she is, she's no dummy. She's getting plenty of home relief for each one of those kids.

ARJAY: Yeah, well more power to her. She's survivin', brother. *Survivin'* in this unfriendly world! A heap see, but a few know!

[CAIRO *puts lots of sugar into the container and stirs it listlessly.*]

TRAVIS: That doggone sugar's going to reach up and slap you straight in the face, boy.

[CAIRO *shrugs, uninterested.*]

BOYD: Amen! Your pressure will be north of the border where mine is half the time.

TRAVIS: No wonder, nigger. All that salty, greasy stuff you're always shoveling into your mouth.

BOYD: And you're shoveling right along with me.

TRAVIS: I'm not the one who's got to worry about his pressure.

ARJAY: I made a deal with mine: if you don't bother me, I won't bother you.

TRAVIS: Now, that makes sense, too, doesn't it? Damn! Come on, Biggs, fess up. Which one of those honeys laid it on you last night?

CAIRO [*bothered*]: I was up late, reading.

TRAVIS: Boy, you come in here looking like that, it better be because some chippie's put some heavy sweat on your ass!

[*The others laugh.*]

CAIRO: Don't you guys have anything better to do?

BOYD: Not right now.

[CAIRO *takes a sip of coffee. It's too hot. He spits some of it back into the container, the rest on himself.*]

CAIRO: Dammit!

[*He wipes at his mouth and shirt.*]

BOYD: Gert's coffee's always too hot. Now, that's the kind of coffee you two heathens will be drinking down there in the fiery furnace, where you're headed.

TRAVIS: Yeah? And, you'll be down there sittin' at the same damn counter, too, brother. And Gert'll be behind it, brewing the shit!

BOYD: If that isn't hell, nothing is!

ARJAY: That's enough to make me repent right here on the spot.

[*They all laugh except* CAIRO, *who nurses a sore lip. The telephone rings on* BOYD'S *desk.* BOYD *answers it.*]

BOYD: South Side Burial Society, Mr. Henry speaking. [*Pause.*] What kind of insurance are you looking for, sir? [*Pause.*] Well, you have term insurance, cash value, whole-life, universal life, variable life—all kinds of choices. All right, let's make an appointment and I can run it all by you. Just a second [*picking up a pen*]. All right, let me have all your pertinents and particulars—name, address, telephone number, and all that.

[*He begins to write. As he does,* CAIRO *picks up his own phone, dials, and waits anxiously. There is no response. He hangs up a bit too hard. The others glance over at him curiously.*]

ARJAY: Yeah, man, speaking of "love," my daughter, here she is, all of twelve years old, and she's talking about she's "in love" with some little urchin down the block. I started to put my foot to her behind. In love, my ass! She doesn't know the half of it. I told her straight out, "You're not in love, so wipe it out your mind. Now that's the end of it, plain and simple." And if I catch that greasy, pointy-headed ruffian *anywhere* around you, the next thing his mama's going to be buying is a casket! I laugh and I joke, but I don't play!

BOYD: All right, sir, I'll see you on Tuesday. Nine o'clock sharp! Bye now.

[*He hangs up.*]

TRAVIS: I sure hope my daughter won't have "bad luck." So many of these girls are getting pregnant and having to get married.

BOYD: Yeah, well, if mine ever comes up with a baby, I don't want her to marry the little villain. I mean, not unless she really wants to.

TRAVIS: I hear you talking, brother.

ARJAY: I'm telling you, some days I'm tempted to send my kids back south and have my grandma raise 'em. I don't want any children of mine being like the ones I see on the street nowadays. Girls, fourteen and fifteen, toting babies when they ought to be carrying schoolbooks. People waste a whole lot of money trying to make something out of these little tramps.

BOYD: My brother's already sent his two girls back. Wicked little things drove him crazy. If he hadn't put them on that train, he'd be visiting them at that women's reform school in Geneva for sure. They are long gone!

TRAVIS: There you go.

ARJAY: Hey, Biggs, how many of them little ladies you've got running around knocked up out there?

TRAVIS: A half a dozen, I'll bet you. Right, Biggs?

CAIRO: None, all right?

ARJAY: Yeah, and my name's Franklin D. Roosevelt.

CAIRO: So don't believe me, OK?

ARJAY: I don't.

BOYD: Yeah, brother, don't talk about these boys out there. All they want to be are pimps and gangsters. Quitting school and buying clothes just to look sharp.

TRAVIS: And most of 'em don't have a thimbleful of brains!

BOYD: Before you know it, they're sitting in a cell at Joliet State Prison.

ARJAY: Yes, indeed, these children will put a switch in your hands and *calluses* on your knees! I have enough to worry about with the place I bought over on State Street.

TRAVIS: How's that going?

ARJAY: A big damn headache, costing me an arm and a leg. My wife's been nagging me to cut it up into kitchenettes.

BOYD: Oh, no, don't do it! I know you love your wife, but those kitchenettes'll just bring a lot of poor people folks into the neighborhood looking for cheap rent. I'm telling what I know.

TRAVIS: Amen, brother! Too many houses've been ruined by slicing 'em up. My block association, we formed a petition against it.

BOYD: Ours, too. Indeed we did.

ARJAY: I'm not about to cut anything up.

CAIRO: Where are they going to live, then?

BOYD: Try someplace else.

CAIRO: Where? It's hard enough finding a decent place as it is.

ARJAY: Biggs, the last thing I need is a lot of lower-class colored folks in my neighborhood.

CAIRO: But if you guys don't help out, then how are they going to survive?

TRAVIS: Biggs, that's not my problem. Let 'em do what I had to do—pull their asses up by their own bootstraps.

BOYD: Damn straight! I got a right to climb outta that barrel without all them crabs hanging on, trying to pull me back down to the bottom, don't I?

ARJAY: Indeed you do. Soon as you move to let 'em in, there goes the value of your property. Rock bottom!

TRAVIS: And there goes all your hard-earned sweat and tears. No, sir, I'm not goin' back, I'm going straight up and straight ahead.

BOYD: And I'll be right here with you, brother. I *know* I got a right to have some nice things.

CAIRO: I didn't say that. All I'm saying is—

BOYD: I heard what you said. And you better think twice about it before you go around trying to be some do-gooder and carry all these poor folks around on your back.

TRAVIS: That's right, a heap of folks see, but a few know!

[*"A Tisket a Tasket" by Ella Fitzgerald is heard on the radio.*]

Go 'head, Ella!

ARJAY: That sweet lady can set her tisket on my front porch any time. Her tasket, too, for that matter!

[*They laugh. The telephone rings again, this time on* CAIRO's *desk.* CAIRO *picks it up quickly, expectantly.*]

CAIRO: South Side Burial, Mr. Biggs speaking.

[*Pause. He is disappointed.*]

Yes, ma'am? [*Pause.*] No, ma'am, term insurance will offer you the largest insurance protection for your premium dollar. But it generally doesn't build up cash value. [*Pause.*] Yes, ma'am. [*Pause.*] All right, you think about it and get back to me. If I'm not here, leave a message. [*Pause.*] Thank you.

[*He hangs up, disappointed. He begins shuffling papers on his desk but then dials the phone and waits anxiously.*]

BOYD: Hey, Arjay, speaking of Eloise Hilton—

ARJAY: Eloise Hilton? Man, I haven't said the first thing about that woman.

BOYD: Well, let's say you did.

ARJAY: But I didn't.

BOYD: Hypothetically, I'm saying—if you did.

ARJAY: Nigger, you need to stop smoking them reefers.

[CAIRO *hangs up, again disappointed. He tries to do some work.*]

BOYD: If you *did*, is what I'm saying. If you did, would you be interested in trading her?

ARJAY: You can't be serious.

BOYD: As serious as Jonah was trying to get out of that whale.

ARJAY: Well, you sound like a fool. Watch it roll off my lip. A damn fooool!

BOYD: You've had that woman for six months now.

ARJAY: And I just might have her for six more months, if you don't mind.

BOYD: Now, you see, that's what I call being a glutton.

ARJAY: Look who's calling somebody a glutton. I wanted to trade you for Vera Woodson. You had her for a whole year, and you still didn't want to let go.

BOYD: I never said anything about getting rid of her. But you, every single day almost, swearing you're going to drop Eloise Hilton. Am I right, Travis?

TRAVIS: Doesn't miss a day.

ARJAY: The two of you ganging up on me doesn't prove camel shit. I'm not giving that little gal up. When I do, you'll be the first to know. Maybe.

[CAIRO *stops to listen, shaking his head in wonder.*]

BOYD: You see now, that's your problem. I *know* your problem.

ARJAY: You'd be better off knowing your own damn problem.

BOYD: He's not giving her up because she's light and has good hair.

ARJAY: Man, you're fulla shit.

BOYD: All your women—every single one of them. Light-skinned. The man's not looking for coal mines, he's looking for gold mines.

ARJAY: If you knew what the hell you were talking about, I might give you some damn credit. I don't have anything against dark-skinned women.

BOYD: You can tell all that to the marines, brother.

ARJAY: I'll tell you one thing, though, and I'm not blaspheming black girls, and you can say whatever the hell you want, but light girls are more affectionate, lovable, and understanding. And prettier and more intelligent, too.

CAIRO: Are you serious?

ARJAY: Damn right I'm serious!

BOYD: Baloney! *Ba-loney!* A friend of mine owns a restaurant, and he told me to my face, light women are harder to get along with than darker girls. That's just what he said. He said darker girls give the best service. If you ask them to help keep the place clean, they'll do it. Light girls just sit around and complain. And then, they'll take their spite out on the customers. They only serve the people they know who'll tip. He only hires black girls and he gives them a decent salary so they don't have to depend on tips.

ARJAY: So, good for him, all right?

CAIRO: Where do these people come up with all this stuff?

BOYD: Because it's true, Biggs. This shit isn't made up.

TRAVIS: Well, I like brown-skinned women myself. I'm not going to be like half of these supposed-to-be-educated colored men who'll go and marry some little light senseless, dumb chick. I started off in high school with a brown-skinned women, and I married her. And I'm still married to her. So, you can be against dark-skinned women if you want to.

BOYD: The blacker the berry, the sweeter the juice!

ARJAY: Now, how am I going to be against dark-skinned women, huh? I'm the darkest child in my family. My mother's dark and my father was very fair. My brothers and sisters used to call me "tar baby." That hurt me. But my mother would say, "Don't let 'em get to you. You've got more brains than they have." And sure enough, none of 'em went to school or made anything out of themselves except me.

BOYD: That's all well and good, but the proof is still in the pudding.

ARJAY: Oh, man, fuck you!

CAIRO: You guys are unbelievable!

[*The radio fades out again. The telephone on* ARJAY's *desk rings. He picks up the receiver. As he does,* CAIRO *dials his own phone and waits.*]

ARJAY: South Side Burial Society, Mr. Thornton speaking. [*Pause.*] Hi, Sugar. [*Pause.*] When? [*Pause.*] Did you call the plumber? [*Pause.*] What'd he say? [*Pause.*] There's no way in hell it's gonna cost that much. [*Pause.*] How fast is it coming out? [*Pause.*] Just a drip, huh? [*Pause.*] All right, throw a bucket under it. [*Pause.*] Tell him to drop dead. I'll find somebody else. [*Pause.*] I'll be home around seven. [*Pause.*] Cornmeal? [*Pause.*] That's all you need? [*Pause.*] Yeah, well, just keep it in the oven, Sugar, and I'll heat it up when I get there. [*Pause.*] All right, baby. [*Pause.*] Bye now.

[*He hangs up.*]

I'm gonna kill that goddamn plumber. Charging me an arm and a leg to fix those pipes. I know it's the Depression, but it ain't my fault.

TRAVIS: You're not wise to that shit yet?

ARJAY: I know what he's doing. Trying to be two-bit slick, pick my pocket and get me to pay for it twice, the no-count thief.

TRAVIS: You're not as dumb as I thought.

ARJAY: Thanks, I appreciate that.

[CAIRO *hangs up angrily, looking at his watch.*]

TRAVIS: My front door, the lock breaks, you see? I get this locksmith. I know the cat. He's a statistic, out of work, like a lot of folks. So, he changes the lock, right? And it works good. Two weeks later, it's busted again. Well, to cut a long story short, it's him.

BOYD: We shall see, said the blind man!

TRAVIS: That was bad enough, but I found out on the block that the mangy nigger had been going around bragging about how he'd put one over on me.

ARJAY: The Dee-pression! Hustlin', brother! Hustlin'!

TRAVIS: Yeah, well, I "hustled" my behind to the Blue Nile one night and caught him drinking cheap scotch at my expense. I walked over to him, put my nickel-plated .45 up against his big, nappy head and told him, "I will splatter your brains all over this got-damn bar if you didn't fix that lock." Then, I marched his black ass out the bar, down East Street, the gun still attached to his skull, straight to my house, and that lock was fixed before you could say "fatback and collard greens." Yeah, didn't I now?

BOYD: You do what you have to do. I keep telling my wife about things like that. I say, "Honey, you can't trust people like you do. Not here in the Windy City." And it just flies right over her head. I know what it is. And, I'm not blaspheming either. It's that church stuff she's got herself caught up in.

ARJAY: Uh-oh, look out, here comes that bolt of lightning.

BOYD: I just told you, I'm not blaspheming. It's all that "blessed are the meek" nonsense, and "it's better to give than to receive."

CAIRO: What are you, an atheist or something?

BOYD: Did you hear me say so? I mean, hey, it's nice to have religion and go to church, but you've got to look after yourself first. Most of our people have got their minds too deep on religion and they let everything else get away from them. If they'd stop so much religion and do a little more thinking, it'd be better for all of us. Half these preachers aren't right.

CAIRO: How about Reverend Cobbs, and all the stuff he's done? You can't lump everybody in the same boat, just because of a couple of preachers—

BOYD: I'm not talking about Cobbs. We already talked about Cobbs before you came limping in here. Cobbs is decent, but most of them do everything they're big enough to do, and expect *you* to live holy. And that's the trouble with my wife. That's why everybody's always taking advantage of her—the butcher, the baker, and every con man she runs into. Folks can give her a tale of woe, start bawling, and she's got her hands in her pocketbook, spreading joy with my hard-earned nickels and dimes.

TRAVIS: Yeah, well, this is Chicago, brother, where you are laughing and dying at the same time. It is a sho-nuff gamble.

[*Phones ring on* TRAVIS's *desk and then on* BOYD's. *Both men pick up the receivers.*]

TRAVIS AND BOYD: South Side Burial . . .

[*The radio comes on again, unexpectedly, with "Roll 'Em, Pete!" by Big Joe Turner. It's too loud.* TRAVIS, *still on the phone, motions to* ARJAY *to turn it down.* ARJAY *rises and turns it down as the phone rings on his desk. He answers it.*]

ARJAY: South Side Burial. Mr. Thornton speaking . . .

[*He continues to talk on the phone.* CAIRO *dials again and then waits.*]

CAIRO: Come on, will ya! Come on!

[*He's too loud again. The others look. He hangs up angrily.*]

   [*To himself*] Where the hell is she?

[ARJAY *hangs up.*]

ARJAY: Who are you beefin' at, Biggs?

[CAIRO *shrugs and pretends to work.* TRAVIS *hangs up.*]

TRAVIS: I keep telling that woman, you can borrow against a policy's cash value by taking a policy loan. If you don't pay back the loan and the interest on it, the amount you owe will be subtracted from the benefits when you die. That damn sure makes sense to me.

ARJAY: A heap of folks see, but a *few* know, brother.

[BOYD *hangs up, looking at his watch.*]

BOYD: I'd better go out and make some collections shortly.

ARJAY [*singing briefly to the music*]: "Roll 'em, Pete!" Damn, that reminds me: I have to get over to the wheel and place my number tonight.

BOYD: Yeah, me too. I think I'll put a dime on 56 in the Iowa book. If it falls, that's fifty cents more than I had.

TRAVIS: Hey, at least you're winning.

ARJAY: What's playing good?

TRAVIS: 9-9-29, Death Row. It saddled last night and again this morning. Nigger Baby Row, too—13-32-50.

ARJAY: That damn Death Row. I stopped playing it because it made me miss my mother's name once. My mother's passed over, and I dreamed about her. Now, instead of playing her name, I played Death Row and I missed out, because Mama's name fell out in the first sixes. Oh, man, I'm telling you, I'd be a rich nigger today!

BOYD: And instead, you're sitting here with us po' colored folks, right?

ARJAY: You've got that right, brother. My rusty dusty'd be *long gone!* I'd be in Paree right now. You hear me? *Rat now!* Sippin' on cognac, Josephine Baker on one knee and Lena Horne on the other.

[*The others crack up. Even* CAIRO *laughs.*]

TRAVIS: And both of those poor darlin's are over there right this minute, crying their eyes out because you aren't with 'em.

ARJAY: Hell, don't I wish it! Both those ladies can have my paycheck for the next six months. And you can throw in my house, my wife, my children, my dog, my cat, my pet chicken—

[*They laugh again, as the radio fades out.*]

Man, I *got to* find me a hot number. All those empties on LaSalle Street, you can get 'em for a snap.

BOYD: I know a guy who hit on the license plate of a car that almost ran him down. I mean, *big* money, too!

TRAVIS: Hell, that's one way. My luck, the car'd knock me senseless, and I wouldn't be able to remember the damn number.

BOYD: My cousin Ada hit on a hymn they announced at Lucy Smith's church. That woman goes to church *every* Sunday now—fifty-two Sundays a year. I didn't say fifty-one, fifty-two. Doesn't miss a one. And always hitting.

ARJAY: Damn, I need to get my black behind over there.

BOYD: Yeah, and a bolt of lightning will hit that building as soon as you put your number twelves in the door.

TRAVIS: I haven't been having much luck with Aunt Della's dream book, so I switched over to The Three Witches.

BOYD: Yeah, well I'm hanging onto the Japanese Fate for a little while longer. It tells you to stay on your numbers and don't change them too often.

And don't play too may different gigs. Put all your energy on one set and wait.

ARJAY: I like the Gypsy Witch. She says you're not going to have any success in your house if it's jinxed because of the evil of some of these relatives and so-called friends. It's not just about hitting the right number, it's about how you conduct your life.

TRAVIS: What about you, Biggs? You got anything hot?

CAIRO: I haven't played it in a while. It's nothing but a trap, getting people to spend money they don't have.

TRAVIS: And sometimes it's the *only* hope *folks* have to fulfill their dreams, such as they are.

ARJAY: Amen!

BOYD: You can say that again, brother.

CAIRO: Yeah, well . . .

[*He rises and goes into the bathroom, closing the door.*]

ARJAY: You know, that is one serious young man.

TRAVIS: That boy ain't serious, he is seeer-re-*us*, brother!

ARJAY: You don't know whether he's coming by land or by sea. The other day, all I asked him was how hot it was outside. Now all he had to say was, "Just like it is today, hot enough to make a camel commit suicide." But he starts telling me that the wind is blowing at forty knots, and the barometer's rising—some nonsense like that, like he was reading the weather report straight from the damn *Tribune*.

[*They laugh, as the telephone rings on one of the empty desks.* BOYD *answers it.*]

BOYD: South Side Burial Society. Johnny Mack's desk.

[*The bathroom door flies open and* CAIRO *sticks his head out expectantly.*]

Mr. Mack's not here right now.

[CAIRO *closes the door.*]

I can't tell you for sure. He had a heart attack a couple of weeks ago, and he's convalescing. [*Pause.*] This is in reference to the cancellation of your policy? [*Pause.*] Well, I'm sorry, you're going have to take that up with him. [*Pause.*] All right, I'll be sure to tell him you called. [*Pause.*] Bye now.

[*He hangs up, sits again, and resumes eating.*]

ARJAY: Yeah, man, I used to be like Biggs.

BOYD: No, sir, no way, not in this life.

ARJAY: I got witnesses.

TRAVIS: You can put a bandana, a dress, and stockings on it, and let it suck on a lollipop, it's still going to be a go-rilla.

[*They laugh.*]

ARJAY: I'm tellin' you, I'm serious. Just like him. Man, I remember at this party once, in this young lady's basement. And everybody's cuttin' a rug, cuttin' it up! And I *thought* I was, too. And all of a sudden, Perry Washington, this meddlin', frog-eyed, good-for-nothin' spade, looked over and yelled out at the top of his voice, "Bend your knees, Arjay Thornton! Bend your knees, brother!" And everybody heard him! The tubby little darkie had the loudest voice in creation. Always talked to folks like they were a mile and a half away, even though they were right in front of him. "Bend your knees, brother!"

[TRAVIS *and* BOYD *crack up.*]

Hell, I thought I was pickin' 'em up and layin' 'em, but instead I was dancing like some Quaker.

[*He demonstrates. Again,* TRAVIS *and* BOYD *laugh.* ARJAY *can't keep from laughing.*]

Man, I'm telling you, I thought seriously—I mean, *seriously*—about assassinating that ashy-looking nigger right on the spot. Anyway, that's what Biggs's got to do—bend his knees!

[*They laugh again.*]

TRAVIS: Being black is fun when ain't nobody lookin'!

[*The phone rings on* CAIRO'*s desk.* TRAVIS *answers it.*]

Mr. Henry speaking. [*Pause.*] He's here, but he's a little indisposed . . .

[*The door to the bathroom pops open.* CAIRO *stands eagerly.*]

Just a minute, he just got himself disposed. Biggs, for you.

CAIRO: Who is it?

TRAVIS: I don't know, some cat. C'mon.

[CAIRO *takes the phone.*]

CAIRO: Hello? [*Pause.*] You want to know if you can skip this week and pay double premiums next week? [*Pause.*] Just a minute, sir, let me get your records.

[*He sits, again disappointed, and gets out the records.*]

BOYD: Hey, Arjay, speaking of "bending your knees," I got a proposition for you. A double, two-for-one. I'll give you Maxine Walters and Bonnie Carter for Daisy Satterfield.
ARJAY: How come you want to insult my intelligence, huh? What I look like, just another bandana Negro with grease runnin' down his elbows?

[*He laughs, finishes eating, and dumps the remains into a wastebasket beside the desk. He goes to the radio and bangs on it. It comes on, playing Billie Holiday.*]

BOYD: You're not telling me you're turning that down, are you?

[ARJAY *scoffs and wipes his mouth and hands with the bib before throwing it away.*]

Maxine Walters and Bonnie Carter? They're all-stars, brother!
TRAVIS: Hell, I'll take it.
BOYD: I didn't ask you. Daisy Satterfield's the one I'm after.
TRAVIS: Damn, nigger, you act like that woman's the queen of Sheba.
BOYD: I don't want the queen of Sheba—she's long dead.

[CAIRO *hangs up. He pauses and then dials the phone, waiting anxiously.*]

TRAVIS: All right, tell you what, if he doesn't want 'em, I got an offer for you.
BOYD: Listen to this man! Last week, like the stingy colored man you are, you said you were holding tight to your "flock."
TRAVIS: That was last week. And, I didn't know you were going to offer Maxine Walters and Bonnie Carter then.
BOYD: Yeah, but I'm offering them to Arjay for Daisy Satterfield.
TRAVIS: And I'm saying is, I'll make you a trade. Two for two.
BOYD: If Daisy Satterfield isn't in it, forget it.
TRAVIS: Damn, just listen, will you? That's all I'm asking.
BOYD: All right, all right—who?
TRAVIS: Lottie Henry—
BOYD: Sorry, no speaka da English—

[CAIRO *slams down the receiver. The others look at him.*]

ARJAY: Got to be some chick. What she do, hurt your feelings, Biggs?

BOYD: Get used to it, son.

[CAIRO *scowls and then ignores him.*]

TRAVIS: All right, all right, I got a better offer. [*Pause.*] Yeah, Lottie Henry and . . . yeah, Minnie Green.

BOYD: You're saying Minnie Green? Minnie Green, huh?

TRAVIS: The one and only, brother.

BOYD: You're sure about that now, right?

TRAVIS: Minnie Green and Lottie Henry for Maxine Waters and Bonnie Carter, straight up, partner.

ARJAY: Hey, hold up!

BOYD: Why do you want to unload Minnie Green?

TRAVIS: She's a bona fide fox, brother.

BOYD: I know, and that's just why I'm asking. How come you want to get rid of her?

ARJAY: Wait a minute. Hold the fort here! How come you didn't mention Minnie Green before?

BOYD: Travis and I are negotiating, if you don't mind.

ARJAY: No, *we* were negotiating and you stuck your chops in it. [*To* TRAVIS] Man, how come you didn't say anything about the chick before?

BOYD: You blew it, Arjay. It's between me and *Travis* now.

ARJAY: Hey, who the hell do you think you are—King Farouk? Travis, can I get in on this or not?

TRAVIS: If you bring Daisy Satterfield along with you.

ARJAY: That's some lame shit, man!

TRAVIS: Nigger, I didn't promise you anything. It started with me and *Boyd* in the first damn place.

ARJAY: The hell it did! It started with you and me. Maxine Waters and Bonnie Carter for Daisy Satterfield! That's exactly what it was.

BOYD [*to* TRAVIS]: And I'm still asking: Why are you giving up Minnie Green?

TRAVIS: Because it's time.

BOYD: What's that mean? I smell a rat somewhere.

TRAVIS: What you smell is your damn upper lip, nigger.

CAIRO: You guys are too much!

BOYD: Stay out of this, Cairo, unless you want in.

CAIRO: No, thanks.

ARJAY: Her husband's probably found out, and your scruffy neck is in danger.

TRAVIS: Bullshit! He doesn't know squat.

ARJAY: Yeah, but is he sniffing the air? That's the question.

BOYD: You see what happened to Yancey, don't you?

TRAVIS: Man, everybody knows what happened to Yancey.

ARJAY: Except Yancey. That bullet from that woman's husband took his ass into hell before he knew it. He probably still thinks he's between her legs.

BOYD: Hey, that doesn't sound too bad.

TRAVIS: Yancey was a damn fool, always playing with fire. I'm no fire eater.

ARJAY: All right, then why you want to give up something fine like that? That woman can break wind in your face, make you grin and holler, "Do it again, Sugar Lump."

[*The radio, still playing Billie Holiday, fades out again.*]

TRAVIS: It's time to move on, that's all. Goddamn! You people are making this harder than it has to be.

ARJAY: All right, all right. I'll give you Daisy Satterfield for Minnie Green.

TRAVIS: You care to repeat that?

ARJAY: *Straight up!* Daisy Satterfield for Minnie Green. Now deal with that.

BOYD: Wait a minute, you and I are negotiating, Travis.

TRAVIS: No, we were talking.

BOYD: Oh, I see. I've got it. You're going to be an Indian giver now, right?

TRAVIS: Now the *hell* can I be some goddamn Indian giver, huh? The woman wasn't yours in the first damn place.

CAIRO: I don't believe you guys!

ARJAY: We have a deal then, right?

BOYD: Wait a minute. Pull over! I'll give you Maxine Waters and Bonnie Carter for Minnie Green and Lottie Henry. Now, turn it down. I dare you!

ARJAY: Damn! Are you serious? Hell, I might want in on that one myself.

TRAVIS: He's talking to me, stupid!

ARJAY: I got your "stupid" right over here, boy.

BOYD: Hey, hey, hey, there's no need to start acting like barking dogs in the back alley now. Every time we do this, we get to fussing and feuding, like the Hatfields and the McCoys.

CAIRO: Unbelievable! You guys ought to hear yourselves! I mean—

TRAVIS: Let's just forget the whole damn thing anyway. I'm not trading or giving up anything. Not to you cats.

ARJAY: Hey, that's fine with me. I'll keep my stable just the way it is.

CAIRO: Sounds like a bunch of horses.

TRAVIS: So, keep it. I don't want any of your yella women anyway.

ARJAY: That's your problem, brother.

BOYD: Yeah, well, I'm hanging onto mine, too. Being colored doesn't have to be as complicated as you two guys make it.

ARJAY: Hey, Biggs, how about trading me Ruby Meeks. I need some young stuff.

BOYD: Heck, you can't even handle the old stuff you already have.

TRAVIS: Brother, that young stuff'll kill you dead faster and deader than you know it.

ARJAY: Yeah? Well, at least I'll die with a smile on my face. And the undertaker won't be able to get the top to the casket down neither!

[*They laugh, except* CAIRO.]

BOYD: That's like the flea, lying on his back, floating down the river with a hard-on, yelling, "Open up the drawbridge, open up the drawbridge!"

[*All laugh, including* CAIRO.]

ARJAY: I'll tell you what, Biggs, I'll trade you Hattie Whitfield for that little girl.

TRAVIS: Shoot, I'll do you even better. I'll give you Sheila Dabney.

CAIRO: I already told you guys: I don't believe in that kind of stuff.

TRAVIS: You've crawled between the sheets with more than Ruby Meeks, haven't you?

CAIRO [*unnerved*]: Yeah, but . . .

ARJAY: Yeah, but, but, but what?

CAIRO: Not recently—not in a while.

BOYD: So, it's all right for you to crawl between the sheets with these broads, but it's wrong to trade 'em. That's what you're saying, right?

CAIRO: It doesn't matter, it's just not right, that's all.

TRAVIS: Then, stop doing it, nigger, if it's so wrong.

CAIRO: Yeah, and what do you call Ruby Meeks?

BOYD: She's called wanting your cake and eating it, too, Biggs.

ARJAY: Brother, we are *all* in the same kettle of boiling water, and the cannibals are making gravy for every single one of us.

CAIRO: We just shouldn't be doing it, doesn't matter who it is. Ruby or whoever.

ARJAY: Nigger, shut up and stop being so damned two-faced.

TRAVIS: Talking outta both sides of his face.

BOYD: These women get their insurance premiums paid, and all it costs 'em is a little nooky. It's minor, man.

CAIRO: You call that minor?

BOYD: Yeah, minor! All right?

ARJAY: Biggs, the one thing our people want is to be buried properly and with a little dignity. And that's what they get from us—no matter what else happens.

TRAVIS: Preach it.

CAIRO: All that trading stuff. Auctioning them off, like they're . . . cattle— a buncha slaves.

TRAVIS: Do y'all hear this man? The White Sox traded four players to the Philadelphia Athletics over the winter and got two back—nobody heard him complaining then.

BOYD: Yeah, went on and on about what a good trade it was. Didn't you, Biggs?

CAIRO: It's baseball, for Pete's sake!

ARJAY: But, it's the same principle.

CAIRO: No, you're talking about a game—sports!

TRAVIS: They're not trading baseballs, Biggs, they're trading people. It's as simple as that.

CAIRO: You're not trying to tell me baseball and slavery is the same thing?

ARJAY: Now you're being ridiculous.

CAIRO: But, that's what you're saying.

TRAVIS: Man, you need to clean all that wax from your ears.

BOYD: Biggs, if it wasn't for us, these women and their families wouldn't have the first bit of insurance.

CAIRO: I'm not talking about that. When I worked in North Carolina for Mr. Lawhorne—

ARJAY: Here we go again about Mr. Lawhorne.

BOYD: Biggs, let the man rest in peace—*please!*

CAIRO: Mr. Lawhorne treated people with respect.

TRAVIS: Excuse me. Excuse me, brother. I haven't disrespected a soul all these years I've been selling insurance.

BOYD: Me neither, brother.

ARJAY: You respect me, I'll respect you.

CAIRO: But, Mr. Lawhorne was *honest*. He didn't take advantage of folks, no matter how poor they were. And, that's what we do.

ARJAY: Biggs, you need to stop being so damn self-righteous and bend your knees. *Please* bend your knees, young man! Bend your knees!

[*He rises and demonstrates, bending his knees and then shaking his behind, as* TRAVIS *and* BOYD *laugh. He looks at his pocket watch.*]

I need to bend my knees right now and get outta here. I got a couple of appointments and a lodge meeting tonight. Yeah, and I have to get over to the Victory Theater and get me some tickets for Rochester and Hattie McDaniel. They're coming in, you know?

TRAVIS: I already got mine.

BOYD: Me, too. Last week. I wouldn't miss it.

[*He imitates Rochester. The others laugh.* ARJAY *picks up a briefcase, puts on a hat, and starts for the door.* BOYD *also gets up.*]

Wait a minute. I'll walk to the corner with you, then I'm getting on the dime jitney. Go over to Wahlberg's and sit in my Cadillac before I go home. Boy, that's a pretty car! "We shall see," said the blind man, "one of these days."

[ARJAY *waits, as* BOYD *picks up a tattered briefcase and his hat and starts out with him.*]

ARJAY: See you two chumps, later. Remember what I said, Biggs, "Bend your knees, boy!"

[MAE ANN *enters simultaneously and stands tentatively at the door, looking at* ARJAY *and* BOYD, *who ogle her, tip their hats, and then leave.*]

MAE ANN: Mr. McKinley, can I speak to you a minute?

TRAVIS: Certainly, Mrs. Morgan. Come in and have a seat.

MAE ANN: Thank you.

[MAE ANN *sits nervously in a chair beside* TRAVIS's *desk.*]

TRAVIS: I just need to finish a little business here. All right?

MAE ANN: Yes, sir. Take all the time you need.

[TRAVIS *begins writing, as* MAE ANN *fidgets.* CAIRO *riffles noisily through papers on his desk. He makes a phone call, casting frequent, uncomfortable glances at* MAE ANN *and* TRAVIS.]

CAIRO: Mr. Parsons, this is Mr. Biggs. How can I help you?

[*He listens and takes notes.* TRAVIS *turns to* MAE ANN *finally.*]

TRAVIS: All right, now what can I do for you, Mrs. Morgan?

[*She reaches into her purse and pulls out an envelope. She takes a letter from the envelope and gives it to him.*]

MAE ANN: My reading's not so good, but my niece told me what it says. You done canceled my insurance, haven't you?

[TRAVIS *reads the letter and lays it on the desk.*]

TRAVIS: I'm afraid so, Mrs. Morgan.
MAE ANN: How come? What'd I do? Cancelin' it just like that?
TRAVIS: Just a minute now. Let me see if I can get to the bottom of it. All right?
MAE ANN: I certainly hope so.

[TRAVIS *picks up a file and begins to read it.* CAIRO *hangs up, making more notes, glancing at* TRAVIS *and* MAE ANN.]

I don't see no reason why it had to be canceled, hard as me and my man work to keep a roof over our heads. We pays our bills!

[*On the verge of tears, she looks again at* CAIRO, *who smiles helplessly.*]

TRAVIS: Well, from what I see here, Mrs. Morgan, you're a payment late. And this coming Friday, unless you brought it with you, you're going to be two weeks behind.
MAE ANN: I know that, but—
TRAVIS: And you also know, because I explained it to you right from the start, if you miss one week, that's an infraction. That means your insurance can be canceled immediately. I told you that, didn't I? [*Pause.*] Come on, tell the truth now. I told you, didn't I?
MAE ANN [*weakly*]: Yes, sir, you did.
TRAVIS: All right, that's all I wanted to hear you say. Because I don't want you accusing me of treating you unfairly. The fact of the matter is, I was

more than fair-minded. You missed other weeks, but I let you catch up. I could've terminated your policy right then, Johnny-on-the-spot.

MAE ANN: Mr. McKinley, I appreciate it, I really do.

TRAVIS: Where are you residing now, Mrs. Morgan?

MAE ANN [*hesitantly*]: Decatur Street.

TRAVIS: Decatur? I thought you were still over on La Salle.

MAE ANN: We had to move. The woman that owns the building's from Biloxi. She had a lotta kinfolk comin' in, so she needed the rooms. So, my husband, me, and the children had to find someplace else.

TRAVIS: Now, you see, that's another reason. It says it right in your policy—

MAE ANN: Mr. McKinley—

TRAVIS: No, let me read it to you now. Let me read. It says, "Moving to another location means automatic discontinuance of said policy in question." That's exactly what it says, Mrs. Morgan. Right here.

[*He shows it to her; she doesn't look.*]

MAE ANN: I didn't have no choice, Mr. McKinley. She kicked us out. She didn't want nothin' but Mississippi folks in there.

TRAVIS: I hear what you're saying, but, it's here in the book, Mrs. Morgan. Isn't that right, Mr. Biggs? [*Pause.*] Biggs?

CAIRO [*reluctantly*]: Yeah, it's there.

MAE ANN: Mr. McKinley, folks is gettin' the influenza, the TB, and the pneumonia, and dyin' so fast. Lord knows, I needs my insurance.

[*She looks at* CAIRO *for sympathy. He turns away, picks up the phone, and dials.* TRAVIS *leans back in his chair, looking at her.*]

TRAVIS: All right, now what can we do about this, Mrs. Morgan? I certainly wouldn't like to see your insurance go down the drain.

MAE ANN: I don't wanna see it go down there neither.

[*She begins to cry.* CAIRO *hangs up the phone, annoyed at not getting an answer. He starts collecting papers from his desk and hurriedly stuffing them into his briefcase.*]

I hate it up here. This ain't no promised land! It's ain't fair to have to live this way.

TRAVIS: I was just doing my job. You understand that, don't you?

MAE ANN: I'm not blamin' you, Mr. McKinley.

TRAVIS: If I don't go by this book here, not only do I jeopardize my job and my reputation, but I'm out in the cold, too. And then none of us colored people will get a proper burial.

MAE ANN: Yes, sir, I hear you.

TRAVIS: But there is something I might be able to do. You had your lunch yet?

MAE ANN: I don't usually eat lunch, sir. Can't afford it. Most of the time now, I only work half days. I'm supposed to work for Mrs. Grimsby from one o'clock on. Her and her husband's got their own drugstore. I do all the laundry, which is considerable, *and* the cleanin', *and* the cookin'. And the thing is, she always waits till she gets home, tellin' me what she planned for dinner. And then she sends me to the store. Isn't that somethin'? She's so inconsiderate. Talk about bein' dead on my feet when I got home.

TRAVIS: All right, why don't we go somewhere and have a little repast and see what we can do? You have time? Or do you have to get back to your husband?

MAE ANN: No, sir. He's at work at the junkyard. My kids are at my grandma's. I got lots of time.

TRAVIS: Good. We're going to take this little mountain and turn it straight into a molehill. All right?

MAE ANN: I'd really appreciate it, Mr. McKinley.

TRAVIS: I know you do. You ready?

MAE ANN: Yes sir, whenever you are.

TRAVIS: Let's hit the road, then.

[TRAVIS *picks up his briefcase, takes* MAE ANN *gently by the arm, and urges her toward the door. She likes the attention.*]

See you tomorrow, Biggs.

CAIRO: Yeah . . .

[*They exit.* CAIRO *hesitates a moment and then picks up the phone, dials, and waits, as the lights fade out slowly on him. Cross-fade to outside* RUBY's *apartment house. It's late.* CAIRO *enters the area, hesitates, and begins to pace, looking anxiously around.* RUBY *appears finally, dressed skimpily, walking sexily, and singing to herself, imitating Memphis Minnie, singing "Bumble Bee Blues."*]

RUBY: "Bumble Bee, bumble bee, he ain't stung nobody but me . . ."

[*He moves to her and blocks her path, surprising her.*]

CAIRO: I've been calling you all day. Where've you been?

RUBY: Out.

CAIRO: Out? What do you mean, "out"?

RUBY: What's it sound like? *O-U-T.* Out!

SUNDOWN NAMES AND NIGHT-GONE THINGS ❈ 41

CAIRO: With who?

RUBY: That's none of your business, thank you.

CAIRO: Probably that guy Jim, wasn't it?

RUBY: I'm not tellin' you, so leave me alone, Cairo.

[*She starts to walk away. He blocks her path.*]

CAIRO: Wasn't it?

RUBY: Man, will you kindly move your big carcass!

[*She tries to barge past. He grabs her arm, stopping her.*]

CAIRO: You said you were going to be home.

RUBY: I changed my mind, all right?

CAIRO: Why didn't you tell me?

RUBY: You're not my daddy, I don't have to report to you.

[*She tries to wrench away.*]

Let go of me, Cairo. You're hurtin' my arm!

CAIRO: Why didn't you tell me?

RUBY: Stop it now!

[*She pulls away finally and rubs her arm.*]

What the hell's wrong with you? I oughtta call the cops. Have 'em throw your behind in jail, treatin' a woman that way. Look at what you did, bruisin' me!

CAIRO: I'm sorry.

RUBY: Yeah, well I'm sorry, too, you simple bastard! Just keep your damn hands to yourself!

CAIRO: Why don't you just admit it.

RUBY: I was out with my cousin and buncha other friends, OK?

CAIRO: You could've called. We were supposed to be together tonight.

RUBY: Things changed.

CAIRO: Well, what about now?

RUBY: I'm busy.

CAIRO: It's two o'clock in the morning.

RUBY: Good, I'm glad you can count.

[*She starts away. He tries to stop her.*]

Don't put your hands on me no more, I'm tellin' you, now!

[*She pulls away again and continues walking. He matches strides with her.*]

CAIRO: Busy doing what?

RUBY: Whatever it is, you ain't welcome, so go read your book about grapes.
Do somethin', just stop messin' with me!

[*He steps in front of her, blocking her path again.*]

CAIRO: I *know* what you're doing.

RUBY: Yeah, well, you better know I'm gonna start yellin' my fool head off if
you don't move yourself outta my way!

CAIRO: He's inside waiting on you, isn't he?

RUBY: It's none of your business, Cairo.

CAIRO: *He's in there, isn't he?!*

RUBY: *It's none of your business!*

CAIRO: *Isn't he?!*

RUBY: *Yeah! All right? Yeah!* You satisfied? You got what you want now?

[*He turns away, upset even further.*]

Yeah, that's exactly where he is. Waitin' to do me all night long.

CAIRO: I don't want to hear it!

RUBY: That's right—*all night long!*

CAIRO: *I don't want to hear it!*

RUBY: I'd rather be with him anyway. He knows how to make me feel like a
real woman. And he does it a lot better than you do, too—a *whole lot better,*
for that matter!

[*He lunges at her, grabbing and shaking her.*]

CAIRO: I oughtta kill you—break your damn neck!

RUBY: Go on, do it! Serve me right for messin' around with you in the first
place! Go on, go ahead if you're goin' to!

[*He shoves her away.*]

CAIRO: Get out of my face!

RUBY: Thank you, that's what I been tryin' to do.

[*She starts away, then stops.*]

You wanna be with me, you're gonna have to share me, Cairo. And not
just with Jim neither.

CAIRO: Go on, he's waiting for you. You're nothing but a tramp anyway!
RUBY: So now you know.

[*She begins exiting toward the door of the apartment. He stands, watching her.*]

CAIRO: You're nothing but a whore, that's all!

[*She doesn't turn, laughs, and resumes singing.*]

RUBY: "Bumble bee, bumble bee, ain't stung nobody but me . . ."
CAIRO: *Whore!* [*Pause.*] You *whore*, you! [*Pause.*] You *whore!*

[*She exits, continuing to sing. He sits on the pavement forlornly, holding his head in his hands.*]

[*To himself*] Nothing but a whore, that's all. A damn whore . . .

[*Lights fade to blackout.*]

ACT 2

[*Morning, the next day. At the insurance office. The room is empty. The radio suddenly comes on, playing a Lucky Millinder number. After a moment,* ARJAY *enters, wearing a hat and carrying a briefcase. He takes off his hat and sits down at his desk, heavily and wearily. He reaches into the briefcase and takes out some papers and then a pint bottle of scotch. He opens the bottle, takes a big gulp of scotch, and then closes the bottle and puts it back into the briefcase. He turns his attention to the papers and begins to work. The telephone on* CAIRO'*s desk rings.* ARJAY *rises, saunters over, and picks up the receiver.*]

ARJAY: South Side Burial Society, Mr. Thornton speaking. [*Pause.*] No, I'm sorry, he still hasn't come in yet. [*Pause.*] Yes, ma'am, I'll tell him you called. [*Pause.*] That's *Ruby*, right? [*Pause.*] All right.

[*He hangs up.*]

Have mercy! A heap see, but a few know! Yes, Jesus!

[*He resumes working but rises quickly after a moment and picks up a few calendars from the corner.*]

Lord's going to send a bolt of lightning down on me for sure if I don't get these over to Reverend Cobbs. People over there do *not* play! They pray *hard*, brother!

[*He puts them into his briefcase and sits. The telephone on his desk rings. He answers it.*]

Thornton speaking. [*Pause.*] He did what? [*Pause.*] Broke the glass in the back window. [*Pause.*] Doing what? [*Pause.*] I told that boy not to play ball against the back of the house. [*Pause.*] You tell him I'm going to tan his hide good when I get home. Tell him to have his britches down buck naked when I get there. Little hoodlum! [*Pause.*] All right, I'll stop at the hardware store on the way home. All right, see you later.

[*He hangs up.*]

Damn that child! I'll wring his neck!

[*The door opens.* CAIRO *enters, carrying his briefcase and a Styrofoam cup of coffee. He looks bedraggled and morose.* ARJAY *addresses him.*]

Hey, how you doing, Biggs?

[CAIRO *doesn't answer, sitting down hard on the chair behind his desk. He puts his briefcase on the floor beside the desk and his coffee container in front of him on the desk.*]

Let me try something else. "Good afternoon, Mr. Biggs, sir."

CAIRO: Good afternoon.

ARJAY: Damn, it worked! I'll have to write that one down.

[CAIRO *opens the container.*]

Boy, you look like somebody stole your mama's wig.

CAIRO: I have a headache, all right?

ARJAY: A headache and black coffee usually means a hangover.

[CAIRO *takes a sip of coffee and burns his lip again, almost spilling the coffee.*]

CAIRO: Dammit!

ARJAY: If a man does something enough times, you'd bet your *last* dollar he's going to learn something. How come you don't?

CAIRO: Because I'm stupid, all right?

ARJAY: Not unless you enjoy doing it.

CAIRO: I don't.

ARJAY: Then, stop doing it! That gal Ruby's been calling you all morning. Three, four times, in fact. Wants you to call her back.

[CAIRO *blows on the coffee, shrugging, not answering.*]

Tell you one thing: the way she sounds, I'd be calling her every five minutes. Voice just drippin' with honey! "Please tell him to call me. I really do need to talk to him." Mercy, mercy, mercy!

[*He laughs.* CAIRO *sips his coffee again. It's still hot.*]

Why aren't you calling her back? You're not through with her, are you?

[CAIRO *doesn't answer, shrugs.*]

If you are, what about the offer I made you a little while back for Hattie Whitfield? You wouldn't be interested in trading now, would you?

CAIRO: Maybe.

ARJAY: How come? You weren't the first bit interested in trading before. You got your jaws real tight about it.

CAIRO: I can change my mind, can't I?

ARJAY: Hey, fine with me. Hattie Whitfield is one lip-smackin' woman. Cutest little turd cutter you ever saw, brother. You want to shake on it?

[CAIRO *doesn't answer.*]

Biggs?
CAIRO: I'm still thinking.

[ARJAY *looks at him, baffled.*]

ARJAY: You know something, Biggs? Dealing with you is like doing a jigsaw puzzle. You've got the whole puzzle put together, except for this one last hole, right? And you only have one piece left. It's the same shape as the hole. But no matter how hard you try to squeeze it in there, the damn thing won't fit. That's you, Biggs.

[*The phone rings on* CAIRO's *desk. He hesitates but then picks it up.*]

CAIRO: South Side Burial Society. Biggs speaking. [*Pause.*] I'm sorry, wrong number.

[*He hangs up and then takes a big gulp of coffee.* ARJAY *reaches into his briefcase and pulls out the pint of scotch.*]

ARJAY: This is what you need, brother.

[*He opens the bottle, takes a big sip, and offers it to* CAIRO, *who hesitates, as the phone rings again. He ignores both the phone and the scotch.*]

Biggs, you have any idea what God is? Do you?
CAIRO: I don't feel like guessing.

[*The ringing stops; so does the radio.*]

ARJAY: Yeah, man, it took me a hell of a long time, but I figured it out. You know what God is? God's a prayer, a curse, a whistle, a song, a woman, a pill, and a bottle of Jack Daniels, as long as it gets you through to the next minute. Now, that's what God is, and that's how I live my life. And that's what you need to do: get yourself on to the next minute. And this bottle here is the way, not that nasty-ass coffee Gertie makes. That shit isn't going to chase anything away. Come on, drink this rotgut whiskey.

[CAIRO *hesitates.*]

Come on, come on.

[CAIRO *takes the bottle.*]

All right, now you're talkin'!

[CAIRO *takes a small sip and offers it back.* ARJAY *refuses.*]

That's not hardly going to do it. Come on, a big one. Let it burn down into your belly and make you feel good on its way back up to your head. Come on!

[CAIRO *takes a big sip.*]

Thataboy! Now you got the idea!

[CAIRO *hands the bottle back to him, coughing and grimacing.*]

You're no drinker, are you?
CAIRO: Not really.
ARJAY: We'll fix that.

[*He takes another sip.*]

It's not supposed to be that complicated with these women, Biggs. Damn, man, how come you're letting it? These chicks aren't for tomorrow. They're only for today—tonight, for a minute. They're nothing but sundown names and night-gone things, boy. You understand what I'm saying?

[*He shoves the bottle at* CAIRO, *who hesitates.*]

C'mon, c'mon! You're not through yet.

[CAIRO *grabs the bottle, takes a hearty gulp, and hands it back, coughing.*]

You'll get used to it.

[*He sips again.*]

No, brother, these aren't the kind of women you put in your scrapbook, bring home to your mama, or remember in your will. They're carrying too much baggage, man; too much misery and grief all by themselves.
CAIRO: I hate what I'm doing, Arjay. But . . . I can't stop myself!

[*He slams the desk with his fist. The radio comes on again, this time with Louis Jordan and "That Chick's Too Young to Fry."*]

ARJAY: That's right, keep on hitting that desk. At least you're feeling something and not doing all that goddamn thinking.

CAIRO: How do you stop it, Arjay?

ARJAY: Stop what?

CAIRO: Thinking.

ARJAY: By not trying to explain every goddamn thing. Keep it simple, Biggs. One and one is two, you hear what I'm saying? Ham hocks come from a pig, milk from a cow, and chitterlings smell bad but taste good, and that's the simple truth.

[*He takes another sip of whiskey and holds the bottle out to* CAIRO, *who hesitates.* ARJAY *waves it at him.* CAIRO *takes a quick sip and hands it back.*]

CAIRO: You know when it all started, Arjay? Back home, in Natchez.

ARJAY: When what started?

CAIRO: This stuff about sex.

ARJAY: Hell, you're not complaining about that, are you?

CAIRO: No, but it was something everybody hid in the closet, you know. You never talked about it.

ARJAY: Hell, I did. Shit!

CAIRO: It was, like, a crime. It was filthy and nasty. And every time I wanted to know something about it and asked my ma, she told my daddy, and he smacked me across the mouth and made me go to church on Sunday to listen to Reverend Wingate preach about how bad and sinful it was. And he had twelve children himself, the hypocrite.

ARJAY: Biggs, I know you love your mama and daddy—

CAIRO: I don't love my daddy.

ARJAY: Well, nothing says we have to, I guess.

CAIRO: He left us. Went off with some tent show.

ARJAY: You're not talking about the Rabbit Foot, Ma Rainey's group, are you?

CAIRO: No, but they did the same sorta thing—going out into the backwoods, singing and dancing. Daddy shoed horses for white folks for a living, but all he really cared about was entertaining. He could sing out of this world. People used to come to the church from miles just to listen to one of his solos.

ARJAY: That's some singing, brother!

CAIRO: Yeah. [*Pause.*] Then, one day, he went off with that troupe. He said he'd be gone just a couple of days, just like most times, but he never came back. He ran out on Mama, my little sister, and me. It's been five years now, and nobody's seen hide or hair of him. And Mama's still down there, thinking he's coming back. That's why she didn't come up north with me. She's never going to leave there. She's always going to be sitting on the front porch, peeling potatoes, snapping greens, shucking corn, and staring off across the field, hoping he'll come up over that hill one day.

ARJAY: A heap see, but a few know. You can never tell, Biggs. Stranger things have happened.

CAIRO: You don't leave your family to go off somewhere singing and dancing and never come back. I don't ever want to see that son of a—

[*He stops, unable to finish the words.*]

ARJAY: It's all right to call your old man a son of a bitch, if he deserves it. I can't tell you the times I've called mine that. He gambled and got drunk and didn't provide for our family, and had time to abuse my mother, too. Made her old before her time. Go ahead, call him a son of a bitch, if that's what he is.

[*The radio goes off.* CAIRO *pounds on it. Fats Waller's "Honeysuckle Rose" is heard.* CAIRO *sits again.* ARJAY *offers him the bottle. He takes it eagerly, a little high now, and drinks. He keeps the bottle.*]

CAIRO: I'd come home from church, Arjay, and lay in bed at night and listen to Mama and Daddy's bed creaking in the next room. And I'd hear her groaning and him telling her to be quiet so that we kids wouldn't know what they were doing.

ARJAY: I know those sounds, brother. Oh yeah!

CAIRO: But, it was too late, Arjay. It didn't matter how hard he put his hands over her mouth, the fire had already started in me.

[*He takes another sip and hands the bottle back to* ARJAY.]

ARJAY: Yeah, buddy, once that fire heats up, nothing's going to put it out, except dying. And to tell you the truth, I wouldn't be surprised if there isn't some nooky in heaven.

[*He laughs, sipping again.*]

CAIRO: I can't get enough of it, you know, Arjay?

ARJAY: Damn, Biggs, you're just being normal. Don't fight it, invite it!

CAIRO: No, I'm in this crazy place. I want her all the time.

ARJAY: Biggs, take my advice, all right? Get every bit of it you can. Don't waste a single drop. Get it all, brother, before you pass from this world.

CAIRO: But . . . I feel guilty.

ARJAY: Guilty? About what? Hell, you're not married and neither is she.

CAIRO: No, it's—it's like, I need another reason for going to bed with her.

ARJAY: You're losing me.

CAIRO: So I can get rid of this guilt I'm feeling.

ARJAY: Walk that by me again. Don't run it, walk it slow.

CAIRO: I want to teach her to read, but all she wants to do is dance and go to the circus.

ARJAY: Biggs, here, drink some more of this stuff. In fact, drink the whole damn bottle. You still haven't gotten on to the next minute.

[*He holds the bottle out to* CAIRO, *who refuses it. The radio is off again.*]

CAIRO: Don't you understand what I'm saying?

ARJAY: No. Hell, no! You might as well be speaking pig latin or Swahili.

CAIRO: If I teach her how to read, I won't feel so guilty, Arjay.

ARJAY: Nigger, will you kindly take this goddamn bottle! Please!

[CAIRO *takes it, gulps a little, and again holds the bottle. He's very high now.*]

That's it, that's it! Shit, drink it all!

CAIRO: Oh, man, Arjay, all I want to do is go to college one of these days and be a teacher, that's all. But getting there's so hard! That's why I came up north. I wanted to be like Mrs. Blocker, my teacher back home. She was really good. I was valedictorian in the ninth grade because of her.

[*The door opens, and* RUBY *stands.*]

RUBY: Can I talk to you, Cairo?

[*He doesn't answer.*]

Cairo? [*Pause. She continues, to* ARJAY] I'm sorry for intrudin'.

ARJAY: No, that's quite all right, young lady.

RUBY: Cairo, we need to talk.

CAIRO: Why don't you go talk to Jim, since he can do it so much better than me.

ARJAY: Uh-oh.

[ARJAY *rises quickly and heads for the bathroom, as* CAIRO *takes another sip.*]

You all excuse me, will you?

[*He enters the bathroom, closing the door.*]

RUBY: Come on, Cairo, let's go somewhere else. I don't wanna talk here.

CAIRO: Your premiums are all paid up, if that's what you're worried about.

RUBY: Don't be so simple, will you?

CAIRO: All right, I'll stop paying them.

RUBY: I'm not worried about that, Cairo.

[*She goes to him, taking his arm, and tries to urge him out of his seat.*]

Come on, let's go over to my place.

CAIRO [*pulling away*]: Leave me alone, will you? I'm doing fine, right here.

[*He takes a quick sip from the bottle.*]

RUBY: Cairo, please?

CAIRO [*mocking her*]: "Cairo, please?" You've got your boyfriend Jim for all that.

RUBY: He ain't my boyfriend.

CAIRO: I don't care what he is. I'm not going anywhere with you.

RUBY: Yes, you are.

[*She tries to take the bottle from his hand. He resists.*]

CAIRO: Come on, Ruby!

[*She pulls the bottle away, sets it on his desk, and begins to kiss his neck.*]

Stop your teasing! That's all you do—tease, tease, tease!

[*He tries to pull away and reach for the bottle, but she is relentless, continuing to kiss him on his neck.*]

Cut it out, will you!

RUBY: Make me. Go ahead, I dare you.

[*She kisses his face. He is weakening.*]

CAIRO: I'm telling you now, Ruby—

RUBY: Tellin' me what? What you tellin' me?

CAIRO: I hate your guts. All right?

RUBY: That's all right, that makes two of us.

[*She kisses him on the mouth passionately, at the same time urging him from his seat. She grinds against him.* ARJAY *starts out of the bathroom but stops, watching, the door slightly ajar.*]

CAIRO [*weaker*]: You're nothing but a . . .

RUBY: I know. A whore.

CAIRO: A tramp, too.

RUBY: Shhhhh! [*Pause.*] Don't say nothin'. Don't say nothin'.

[*She urges him toward the door.*]

CAIRO: My things.

RUBY: You ain't gonna need nothin' but me, baby.

[*She leads him to the door, opens it, and nudges him outside. She follows.* ARJAY *reenters, turned on. He sits, takes a big gulp of whiskey, and then quickly dials the phone.*]

ARJAY: Eloise? [*Pause.*] Hey, darlin', it's me. [*Pause.*] Your better half around? [*Pause.*] Working, huh? [*Pause.*] Good. How's about taking care of next week's premium? You up for that? I damn sure am. [*Pause.*] All right, twenty minutes, same place, the Sunshine Motel.

[*He hangs up and puts the bottle back into his briefcase.*]

Lawd, have mercy! A heap see, but a few know!

[*Lights fade out on him and then cross-fade in on* RUBY's *apartment, an hour later.* RUBY *sits on the bed watching, as* CAIRO *paces in front of her. An open suitcase is beside the bed on the floor.*]

CAIRO: You're not telling me it's mine, are you? You know doggone well I'm not the only one you've been going to bed with.

RUBY: I didn't say it was yours. I just said I'm pregnant. I don't know whose baby it is. It could be yours, it's could be Jim's, it could be—

CAIRO: Have you told him yet?

RUBY: I ain't had a chance.

CAIRO: Well, tell him, too, dammit. And everybody else. Just don't be telling me!

[*He pounds the wall with his fist. The picture of Jesus falls to the floor. He picks it up, carefully replaces it, and then sits, silent for a moment.*]

You're not planning to keep it, are you?

RUBY: I ain't gettin' poked with no coat hanger if that's what you got in mind.

CAIRO: How can you have another one? You can't hardly take care of the one you already have.

RUBY: I beg your pardon! Maggie ain't never gone without nothin'. I give to her before I give to myself, like a mother's supposed to. So don't be accusin' me, man. Home Relief'll help me anyway.

CAIRO: Yeah, and I guess next you'll want some more free insurance, won't you?

RUBY: I ain't askin' you for diddly-squat, Cairo. I haven't gotten nothin' free. Goin' to bed with you to keep my premiums up ain't hardly free, in case you're interested. I don't know what I'm gonna do, 'cept I ain't havin' nothin' stuck up inside me that ain't supposed to be stuck up there. I could've got rid of Maggie, too, but I didn't. And I'm glad, 'cause she's been a little blessin' to me.

[He sits on the bed, silent for a moment.]

CAIRO: Are you sure you're pregnant?

RUBY: I been through this before, Cairo.

CAIRO: Have you been to a doctor?

RUBY: Cairo, I ain't had my period! A woman knows when something different's happenin' to her. It ain't dyin' that's goin' on inside me, it's livin'.

[They are silent again.]

CAIRO: Oh, man! [Pause.] Oh, man!

[He gets up, pacing. He slams the wall. The picture of Jesus falls again. He replaces it almost apologetically.]

RUBY: Stop knockin' Jesus off the wall, will you? I ain't faultin' you or nobody else. I'll take the blame for it myself. I don't know what's goin' on no more.

[She rises, goes to a cabinet against the wall, and pulls out a bottle of scotch.]

Want some?

CAIRO: I had enough already.

[She pours herself a drink in a shot glass and downs it. She pours herself another, hesitates, then pours some in a shot glass for him. She goes to the bed, taking the bottle with her, and sits again, handing him the glass. They drink silently.]

RUBY: You did it good just now, Cairo. The best you ever did it.

CAIRO: But not as good as Jim, right?

RUBY: I don't wanta talk about that man—beatin' on me.

CAIRO: He beat on you? When?

RUBY: While you was gone.

CAIRO: Why did he do something like that?

RUBY: Because I'm the kind of girl men like to beat up on.

CAIRO: That's not true, Ruby.

RUBY: You said yourself—how you wanted to kill me.

CAIRO: I was just mad at you.

RUBY: So was he.

CAIRO: It was all talk, Ruby. I wasn't going to do it. You should've known that. Why'd he beat on you?

RUBY: He's got the cocaine habit—bad. Real bad. Spends every penny he's got on it. I didn't have no money to give him, so he flew off the handle.

CAIRO: Did he hurt you?

RUBY: He twisted my arm and puffed up my face a little, but I'm better now.

CAIRO: That . . . bastard!

[*He hits the wall. The picture of Jesus falls again.*]

RUBY: Stop knockin' Jesus off the wall, I told you!

[*He replaces the picture.*]

I might not tell 'im about this, Cairo. He don't deserve to know. Anyway, it don't matter. I'm thinkin' about goin' back home. My aunt Hallie's still down there. She's the only one had the good sense enough *not* to come up here to the "promised land." This ain't the real me you're seein', Cairo. You think I been this way my whole life? Yeah, I always been a little wild, but not like this: schemin', hustlin', and carryin' on like some tramp.

CAIRO: I was only shooting off at the mouth—

RUBY: I know what I am, Cairo. I ain't never been good at nothin', 'cept makin' a man crazy and hard over me. I didn't come up north for no other reason. There's a whole lot more men up here than in New Orleans. But if I don't get outta here soon, it's goin' to get me killed, or him, too.

CAIRO: Why don't you call the police?

RUBY: You know as well as I do, the po-lice don't care nothin' about us killin' each other.

CAIRO: Well, I'll say something to him.

RUBY: Stay out of it, Cairo, please. It's between me and him. Besides, you'd only lose.

CAIRO: The hell I would!

RUBY: You would—you really would! I'm not tryin' to hurt your feelin's, but Jim's nothin' but an animal. He don't know no fear, 'cause he don't think, he just feels. You're too gentle to live among us wolves.

CAIRO: That's bullshit!

RUBY: Stop swearin'. That's not you neither. And it's not goin' to help you whippin' him. There's no sense gettin' so upset nohow. It's all right to be better than somebody like Jim. I'm sorry I got mixed up with him in the first place. And to tell you the truth, it's not all on him neither. It's me, too, Cairo. I ain't no angel. I could put all the blame on him, but it's me, too. [*Pause.*] I was doin' the cocaine with him. Lots of times. [*Pause.*] I don't blame you for starin' at me like that. That's the same kinda disgusted look I get when I'm standin' in front of the mirror.

CAIRO: I wasn't judging you, Ruby—

RUBY: Listen to me a minute, OK? Just listen. [*Pause.*] Coupla weeks ago, I did some dust with him, and I was high as a kite when he left here. And little Maggie started cryin', 'cause I neglected her. And I couldn't stand her racket. She just wouldn't quit. "Come on, Maggie, shut up, will you! You're makin' my head burst open, girl! Shut up, will you, dammit!" And I shook her—harder and harder and harder. And all of a sudden, she stopped cryin'. She started shakin' and convulsin', and I panicked. And I ran outside with her, screamin' my fool head off. And this taxi stopped and drove me to the hospital. Little Maggie was all blue and havin' trouble breathin'. And I lied, Cairo. I lied. I told 'em she fell and hit her head on the floor. And they took her into the emergency room and made me stay outside. I couldn't hardly stand it, not knowin' whether I'd killed her or not. I ain't prayed since I was a little girl down on my knees at my bed with my mama, sayin', "Now I lay me down to sleep . . ." But I prayed sweat. I prayed bullets. It was pourin' down off me like a river. I prayed for the Lord to give me another chance with her. "Please, Lord, please, I'm beggin' you, gimme another chance, that's all I'm askin'. And finally, this doctor come out, and he told me she was gonna be all right. Oh, man, I bawled my eyes out! And you know what she did when I went into her room? You know what she did, Cairo? She said, "Mama, I love you." I nearly killed my baby girl, and she's telling me how much she loves me. Oh, man! That's why I'm goin' back home. I'm not goin' to hurt her no more with all my foolishness.

[*She begins to cry. He comforts her.*]

CAIRO: When are you leaving?

RUBY: Early in the mornin'.

[*She goes to the dresser, pulls out clothing, and begins to put garments in the suitcase.*]

CAIRO: You're serious, aren't you?

RUBY: Yes, I am.

CAIRO: Where are you going to be down there?

RUBY: You don't need to know.

CAIRO: What do you mean I don't need to know?

RUBY: I ain't never goin' to be the one for you, Cairo.

CAIRO: Ruby—

RUBY: No, the best thing for you is to get me out your mind quick as you can. You'll be a whole lot better off.

CAIRO: How am I going to know whether it's mine or not?

RUBY: You won't, and neither will I.

CAIRO: That's not fair, Ruby!

RUBY: How come you need to know?

CAIRO: He could be mine, dammit.

RUBY: And Jim's and whoever else's. You keep forgettin', I'm a tramp.

CAIRO: Stop saying that, will you!

RUBY: The truth hurts me more than it does you, Cairo. I'm sorry, but you don't need to be tied down by this child, I don't care whether it's yours or not.

CAIRO: And I don't have a say in this, huh?

RUBY: No, I'm sayin', you got brains, Cairo. Don't get mushy and stop usin' 'em. Go on and be a teacher, or whatever you're goin' to be, and just let this be a mistake, 'cause that's what it is. We'll just drag you down, and one day you'll be scornin' the both of us. I know you will, Cairo. I seen it happen.

CAIRO: Then, why'd you tell me, if you already made up your mind?

RUBY: I just wanted you to know the truth and why I was goin' back home. I didn't think you'd get so carried away. At first, you were talkin' about me gettin' rid of it.

CAIRO: It wouldn't be right, me running off. I'm not going to be like my daddy.

RUBY: I appreciate it, I really do. That means you're decent, Cairo. But, I don't deserve it right now.

[*He watches her as she packs.*]

CAIRO: Stay a little longer, Ruby? I'll help you, if that's what you're worried about.

RUBY: I'm not takin' money from you or nobody else, Cairo. That's been my whole problem.

CAIRO: All right . . . all right. [*Pause.*] Why don't you start sewing or something? That dress you made last year was really pretty. Better than some of the ones you see in the stores. You could sell them.

RUBY: Yeah, and who's gonna buy 'em? Colored people can't afford new clothes, unless they're hand-me-downs.

CAIRO: All right, I'll sell them for you, when I go to my customers.

RUBY: Material and stuff costs money, Cairo.

CAIRO: I have a little saved up.

RUBY: That's for your schoolin'—

CAIRO: It's my money; I can do what I want with it.

RUBY: Makin' dresses isn't goin' make me happy, Cairo. It's not the money, man. I have to leave here. I still got lots of demons knockin' around inside me. And if I don't get rid of 'em, I'm goin' to end up dead in the gutter like half my people. That's not what you want for me, is it?

CAIRO: You know better.

RUBY: Then there's nothin' else to talk about. Let's both of us do what we have to do to save ourselves right now, OK?

[*A church bell begins to peal.*]

I better hurry. I got to pack and go over to my grandma's for Maggie, else I'm gonna miss that train for sure!

[*She begins hurrying.*]

CAIRO: What about the baby?

RUBY: Leave it be, Cairo.

CAIRO: But suppose it's mine?

RUBY: And suppose it ain't? Cairo, what're you gonna do, run around the South Side braggin' about *maybe* it's your baby or *maybe* some other man's? Folks'll laugh you off the street. We're never goin' to know, Cairo. The doctors ain't goin' to know neither. It's always goin' to be a "maybe child," because that's the kinda woman I've been. So, just let it stay that way. I'll raise it and try to give it the best home I can. Just keep goin' on with your life and make somethin' of yourself. That's all you need to worry about right now.

[*She starts to close the suitcase. He stops her.*]

CAIRO: Take this, will you? I want you to have it.

[*He holds out the book.*]

RUBY: Don't you need it?

CAIRO: I can get another one. Besides, I've read it three times already. I know it almost by heart now.

RUBY: This the one about the grapes?

CAIRO [*nodding*]: Maybe somebody back home can teach you to read it, you know?

RUBY: My cousin Loretta went to the sixth grade. She might have some time.

[*She hesitates, takes the book from him, and reverently turns the pages.*]

All them words.

[*She kisses him lightly and then puts the book into the suitcase and closes it.*]

We better get a move on.

[*He takes the suitcase, and they go to the door. He stops her again.*]

CAIRO: Come back and find me when you get rid of them demons, OK, Ruby?

[*She stares fondly at him for a moment.*]

RUBY: I might. [*Pause.*] I just might.

[*They exit. Cross-fade to the office, the next day.* ARJAY *and* BOYD *sit at their respective desks.* ARJAY *is reading the newspaper;* BOYD *pores over the racing form. "The Drifting Blues" is heard from the radio, mingling with the noisy, whirring fan.* CAIRO's *briefcase is still by his desk.*]

BOYD: Hokie Pokie and Smart Alec in the sixth. Who do you like?

ARJAY: I'm not in it.

BOYD: Come on, man, give me a hunch.

ARJAY: I'm saving my hunches. Besides, if I'm wrong, I have to hear your mouth for days.

BOYD: All right, forget it. I'm sticking with Smart Alec anyway. He's been in the money the last three races.

ARJAY: So why'd you ask?

BOYD: I guess I just lost my head. Pray for me.

[*He picks up the phone, dials, and waits.*]

Hey, Onyx, it's me. [*Pause.*] Yes, give me Smart Alec in the sixth. [*Pause.*] Yeah, and Handsome Harry in the eighth. Two and two. [*Pause.*] No, that's it. [*Pause.*] I'll be over later. [*Pause.*] Good enough.

[*He hangs up.*]

I feel lucky! Yes I do, yes I do! First thing, I'll put some money away for my car in Wahlberg's, lay a nice payment down on the mortgage, and maybe take the wife on a cruise somewhere—the Islands, Hawaii, Tahiti—wherever! Smarty Alec and Handsome Harry, don't let me down, gentlemen!

ARJAY: Yeah, well, I wish I could "roll" a hot number. I haven't even come close for a month now. How's your cousin Ada doing?

BOYD: Still hitting.

ARJAY: I went over there to Lucy Smith's—

BOYD: You went to church?

ARJAY: Well, not exactly.

BOYD: What's that mean?

ARJAY: I didn't go in?

BOYD: Man, what the hell are you talking about?

ARJAY: I just stuck my head in the door and took down the numbers on the hymnal board.

BOYD: Now, you see, that's the reason why you're not hitting. My cousin Ada goes to church every Sunday. It's no accident. The Lord's not rewarding her for sticking her head in the door and stealing numbers. He's rewarding her for being in the pews fifty-two Sundays a year.

ARJAY: Well, I guess that takes care of that.

BOYD: Yeah, I guess you're not going to be visiting Lena and Josephine in Paris anytime too soon, are you?

ARJAY: Poor babies!

[*They laugh. The door opens.* TRAVIS *enters fanning himself, hot.*]

TRAVIS: I'm telling you, the huma-titty is *high* out there today, y'all!

BOYD: You're talkin' about the huum-tee, aren't you? That's what the old folks back in Mobile call it. "The huum-tee sho' is hot today!"

[*They laugh.*]

TRAVIS: Whatever it is, it's a bitch, brother!

BOYD: I've had two of my clients drop dead because of this heat. Now I can't be having that. I need my paycheck. Baby needs new shoes—bad!

TRAVIS: No more than mine, brother.

[*He sits heavily, wiping the sweat from his face. He reaches into the desk drawer, pulls out the bottle of aftershave, and splashes it on his face.*]

ARJAY: Come on with that stuff, nigger! Can't half breathe in here as it is. Rotgut, barbershop crap!

BOYD: Worse, if that's possible.

[TRAVIS *ignores them and puts the lotion away. He pulls a bottle of soda from his briefcase and begin to drink it. The radio fades out.*]

TRAVIS: Oh, brother! I just came through Washington Park. It is swarming over there! Folks laying around on the grass, splishing and splashing in the swimming pool, fishing and rowing in the pond, playing softball, and in all that damn heat!

BOYD: That's why they're dropping dead on us, the stupid bastards!

[TRAVIS *goes to the corner, gets one of the paper fans, sits, and fans himself vigorously.*]

TRAVIS: Man, this heat! I'm telling you, Massa would've had to kill me before I'd slave on a day like this, brother!

ARJAY: And Massa would've, too.

TRAVIS: Hey, I told you two knuckleheads to come over to Luella Bagwell's rent party last night, didn't I?

ARJAY: How was it?

TRAVIS: Man, I've been to a hundred rent parties, and none of 'em came close! Fit for a king, Jack! All the food you wanted: ham hocks, hog maws, collards, ribs, butter beans, fried chicken, potato salad, turnip greens—

BOYD: My goodness!

ARJAY: Turn out the lights and call the law!

TRAVIS: I have *never* seen so much liquor in one place in all my born days. The word is, Miss Luella's got something goin' on with this I-talian rack-eteer. But, whatever she's doing with him, it's working, brother!

ARJAY: She didn't water the liquor down, did she?

TRAVIS: Top-shelf, brother. None of that gutbucket, bottom-of-the-barrel shit you niggers serve at your parties.

BOYD: Hey, I've been to yours. Include yourself in it, too, brother.

ARJAY: Damn, man, sounds like the bee's knees!

TRAVIS: The bee's knees, hips, elbows, and toes. I didn't want to go home. I left there about two in the morning, as it was, and the joint was still jumpin'. I'm tellin' you, being black is fun when ain't nobody lookin'!

ARJAY: Hell, I'd've been there if I hadn't been messing with Minnie Green the other night. I ran out of excuses with the missus.

BOYD: I was running on empty with my wife, too.

TRAVIS: Yeah, well, you missed it. There were a whole flock of white folks on the scene, too! I'm not talking about hillbillies, either. These folks had shiny, black limousines waiting outside for 'em.

BOYD: I am impressed!

ARJAY: How'd she do it?

TRAVIS: Woman hustled her ass off. Put ads in the *Defender,* the *Pittsburgh Courier,* the *Chicago Bee.* Sent out flyers. The woman was determined to make some bread. And guess who else was there? Bertie Suggs herself!

ARJAY: You're lying!

TRAVIS: If I am, I'm a cripple and I got ringworms. In the flesh, brother! Now, eat your heart out, both of you!

BOYD: God bless America!

TRAVIS: And the woman sang her drawers off. Y'all hear me?

ARJAY: Bertie Suggs can make the ground tremble, yes, she can now!

TRAVIS: Well, she had the floor shakin' last night. The whole building was swaying. She had some sissy playing the piano for her, but I give him credit, the sweet little nigger could tickle them ivories! Folks were plunking nickels, dimes, quarters, half-dollars, and dollar bills into that rent bucket. That pail was making all kinds of pretty noises. I'll tell you one thing: Miss Luella made enough money last night to pay her rent the rest of the year.

BOYD: More power to her. I know there were a lot of women there.

TRAVIS: Yeah, and not an ugly one among 'em. I'm serious. And a whole slew of yella gals. The kind you like, Arjay.

ARJAY: Man, come off that, will you?

TRAVIS: Some of 'em were so light you could hardly tell, until they opened their mouths.

BOYD: That's *exactly* how you know.

TRAVIS: And then you wish to hell they hadn't.

[*They laugh.*]

ARJAY: A heap see, but a few know!

TRAVIS: I picked up some customers with deep pockets, too.

[CAIRO *enters, somber, carrying a Styrofoam cup of coffee.*]

BOYD: There he is! On time, as usual!

ARJAY: So nice of you to honor us with your presence this morning, Mr. Biggs.

TRAVIS: Yes, good of you to drop in and pay us a little visit, Your Majesty.

[CAIRO *shrugs them off. He sits down at his desk, pulls insurance papers from the briefcase, and opens the container of coffee. He takes a sip of hot coffee, burning his lip again.*]

CAIRO: Ouch!

ARJAY: Every single time, doesn't miss a one! Just like clockwork.

TRAVIS: It must mean something.

CAIRO: It means I'm stupid, OK?

BOYD: No, you're stupid if you don't trade me Ruby Meeks.

CAIRO: I'm not trading anybody, so stop bugging me about it!

[*He pounds his fist on the desk, spilling the coffee onto his lap. The radio comes on suddenly, playing Bessie Smith. He jumps to his feet, holding his crotch.*]

Ouch, ouch, ouch!

[*He hurries toward the bathroom. The door to the office opens and* MAE ANN *stands, as* CAIRO *stumbles into the bathroom, slamming the door shut.* TRAVIS *is surprised.*]

TRAVIS: Hello, Mrs. Morgan, nice to see you.

MAE ANN: Mr. McKinley, we need to talk—it's really important.

TRAVIS: That's what I'm here for. Come in and have a seat.

[*He rises and goes to her and gently nudges her toward the desk.*]

MAE ANN: Take your hands off me, please.

[*She pulls away.* TRAVIS *and the others are taken aback.*]

TRAVIS: I'm sorry, I certainly didn't mean to offend you.

MAE ANN: I'm not goin' to bed with you no more, Mr. McKinley. I never intended things to be this way.

TRAVIS: Sister Morgan, why don't we go somewhere private and chat?

MAE ANN: So you can trick me some more? I know what you done to me. It's not right, and you know it!

TRAVIS: Now, look, I can't have this kind of commotion in here. This is a respectable office. Come on, now.

[*He tries to urge her out the door. She pulls away again.*]

MAE ANN: Don't touch me, man!

TRAVIS: Mrs. Morgan, I was only trying to help you out.

MAE ANN: No, you wasn't. You took advantage of me, and I let you do it.

[CAIRO *reenters from the bathroom, trying to cover the wet spot on his pants. He goes to his desk and sits down behind it.*]

TRAVIS: Well, if that's the way you feel, ma'am—

MAE ANN: Yeah, that's exactly how I feel—exactly. I guess I don't have no more insurance now, do I?

TRAVIS: If you want to know the truth, no, you don't.

MAE ANN: And all because I don't want to degrade myself and cheat on my husband no more? That's true, too, isn't it?

TRAVIS: Mrs. Morgan, stop acting like it's some great big surprise. You knew the program right from the start. Now, if you got ten cents a week, you can keep your insurance. And, that's the long and short of it.

MAE ANN: You're a real no-account . . . *heathen*, ain't you?

TRAVIS: Hey, wait a minute—wait just a minute! There's no need for name-calling. Now, if you're going to insist on causing a rumpus, I'm going to have to call the cops. But, if you want to use some common sense, we'll go somewhere and talk this thing out like two grown people.

MAE ANN: I'm not goin' no place with you and let you sweet-talk me! You pretty men think you can get a woman anytime you want—

TRAVIS: All right, then, take yourself out of here!

MAE ANN: Oh, man! [*Pause.*] Oh, man!

[*She hesitates, frustrated, highly agitated, and then begins to pace.*]

You and all your sweet-smellin' perfume. He smelled you on me!— my husband. Started askin' me questions, this awful look in his eyes, suspectin' me—scared of the truth. And I lied. And he believed the lie I was tellin'. And it tore my heart out! I never felt so low in all my life! Damn you, man! Damn you!

[*She reaches into her purse, snatches out a gun, and points it at him. He is frozen.* ARJAY *and* BOYD *duck down behind their desks.*]

ARJAY: Holy shit!
BOYD: Oh, my God!

[CAIRO *sits, stunned.*]

ARJAY: Get down, Biggs!

[CAIRO *is also frozen, staring at* MAE ANN.]

MAE ANN: See what you done, pretty man? You done this. I can't even look
    my husband and chil'ren in the eye no more. Can't even walk down the
    street or sit in my church without feelin' guilty and scared and wonderin'
    when God's gonna strike me down.
TRAVIS: Come on, use your head now, sister.
BOYD: Yeah, calm down—just calm down, all right?
ARJAY: It's not worth all that, ma'am.
MAE ANN: Nobody's talkin' to either one of you. I oughtta be. All of you
    probably doin' the same thing, I betcha.

[*She points the gun at* BOYD.]

Ain't you?

[*He cowers. She turns, training it on* ARJAY.]

Ain't you?

[*He can't speak, tongue-tied.*]

Yeah, that's right, guilty as sin, that's why.

[*She looks at* CAIRO *without training the gun on him.*]

They got you doin' it, too, don't they? [*Pauses a beat.*] Yeah, I can see it in
    your eyes. It's a damn shame, because you got such a pretty-lookin' face,
    but that's the way the devil works. Get yourself out of this place, boy, and
    save your damn self. What the hell are you doin' here anyway, huh?

[*She trains the gun on* TRAVIS *again.*]

Look at me, Mr. McKinley—a supposed-to-be Christian woman, stand-
    in' here with a gun, ready to blow your brains out. Somethin's *not right*!
    I oughtta be helpin' those women out there organize a domestics union,
    but you see, that's what happens when you get yourself so desperate! We're
    desperate around here, man. Don't you know that?

[*She turns away, distraught, and leans wearily against the door, choking back tears.*]

TRAVIS: Mrs. Morgan, I sincerely apologize if I wronged you.

MAE ANN: Oh, shut up! I don't believe anything you say anymore.

[*She begins to pace in front of the door.*]

Reverend Cobbs's right: "We're livin' in the time of the end. This old world can't last much longer. Even now, the Four Horsemen of the Apocalypse are ridin', ridin' hard! Gettin' closer. The end is near. You better get your days in order and be ready." That's what he preached the last Sunday I had the nerve to show my face in church. And he was lookin' dead at me. He knew. Oh, yeah, he knew!

[*She moves to* TRAVIS, *shoving the gun closer to him.*]

How am I goin' to get to heaven now, messin' with you, huh? How I'm goin' to get there, pretty man?!

TRAVIS: Mrs. Morgan, all this isn't necessary.

BOYD: Yes, let's all sit down and reason together.

ARJAY: Yes, please, ma'am.

CAIRO: Ma'am, look—

MAE ANN: Just be quiet, all of you! Lord Jesus, I feel so low-down! It's like there's these big scars on my heart. I know I ain't no angel. I know I put some of 'em there myself, but you just kept pilin' on more and more of 'em. How come you did that? You're a *black man,* and I'm a *black woman.* We're not supposed to do that to one another. My sweet mama left this world, thinkin' I was somethin' I wasn't: the decent, Christian woman she brought me up to be. But here I am, just another outlaw. Why did you do this to me, nigger!

[*She points the gun at him and starts to pull the trigger. Her hand shakes.* TRAVIS *leaps out of his seat and grabs the gun. They wrestle for control. She screams.*]

TRAVIS: Unhand the damn thing, woman!

[BOYD, ARJAY, *and* CAIRO *rush over and struggle with* MAE ANN, *who continues to scream.*]

ARJAY: Let go of it!

BOYD: Come on, ma'am!

CAIRO: Don't hurt her!

[*The gun goes off.* TRAVIS *cries out in pain, clutches his shoulder, and slumps to the floor.* BOYD *wrests the gun away from* MAE ANN.]

TRAVIS: Oh, man, I'm hit!
ARJAY: Shit! *Shit!*

[ARJAY *and* CAIRO *kneel beside him, as* MAE ANN *runs out of the room.*]

BOYD: Crazy bitch!
ARJAY: Gimme some help over here!
TRAVIS: Oh, man, my chest, it's killin' me!

[*He groans in pain again, as* BOYD *hurries over.*]

ARJAY: Biggs, call the ambulance—hurry up!

[CAIRO *runs to the phone and dials. The lights black out. A siren is heard in the darkness, mingling with the static of the radio. Music is heard: "Sonny Boy's Jump." The lights rise to full again.* BOYD, CAIRO, *and* ARJAY *enter, shaken. They sit, drained.*]

ARJAY: These dogs are talkin'—conversatin', brother!
BOYD: Yeah, I know what you mean.

[ARJAY *takes off his shoes and massages his feet, groaning.*]

ARJAY: Lawdy, Lawdy, Miss Clawdy! A heap see, but a few know!

[*They are briefly silent.* CAIRO *is the most visibly shaken.*]

BOYD: I sure could use a drink.
ARJAY: Yeah, tell me about it. Getting him to the hospital, dealing with the cops, missing all my collections.
BOYD: He's lucky that bullet didn't kill him.
ARJAY: Came close. Busting his collarbone. That'll put him out of circulation for a long while.
BOYD: That woman's going to be in the slammer for a long while, too.
CAIRO: Why? She gave herself up right after she left here.
BOYD: So what the hell's that mean?
CAIRO: She wasn't trying to run away—she didn't shoot him on purpose.
BOYD: What are you talking about, Biggs? The woman had the gun right in his face and was about to blow him away.
CAIRO: But if he hadn't gone for her, maybe she wouldn't have.

BOYD: Biggs, shut the hell up and trust what your eyes were seeing, instead of making up a bunch of maybes!

ARJAY: Yeah, well, she sure did blab down at the police station about what's going on in here.

CAIRO: Somebody needs to.

BOYD: Say what?

CAIRO: Somebody needs to, that's what I said.

BOYD: I don't give a good damn what she told them. The police can't do anything about it. I already talked to a client of mine—a lawyer—and he told me, as a defense against attempted murder, it's irrelevant. Doesn't have a goddamn thing to do with anything. So, just shut your trap and don't worry about it.

CAIRO: Yeah, and suppose her husband comes busting in here?

BOYD: That man's not going to do shit. I wasn't the one sleeping with his old woman, and neither were you and Arjay. Travis was the one, and she took care of him. And besides, he knows doggone well what'll happen if he makes too much fuss over it. Folks on the South Side will laugh his behind off the block and question his manhood. "What's the matter, man, you done lost your balls? You mean to tell me some other nigger's got to do your job between the sheets? What the hell kind of man are you?" And whatever beef he's got with Travis, he ought to have enough sense to know he needs the rest of us, too. Somebody colored has to bury his ass, and we're it.

CAIRO: That's bullshit!

BOYD: No, brother, it's on the dime. It's honest-to-god-1938-Chicago truth.

ARJAY: Wait a minute, hold up, I know *just* what the young man needs.

[*He goes to* TRAVIS's *briefcase, reaches in, and finally pulls out a bottle of scotch and holds it aloft.*]

I knew it was in there! John Walker Red!

BOYD: Welcome to the party!

[ARJAY *opens the bottle, takes a big gulp, then hands the bottle to* BOYD, *who also drinks.*]

My, my, my!

[*He holds the bottle out to* CAIRO.]

Come on, son, grab some of this.

CAIRO: I don't want it.

BOYD: You may not want it, but you damn sure need it, all the shit you're talking. Now take a swig of this and do yourself a favor.

CAIRO: I don't want any!

BOYD: Fine with me, brother.

[*He takes another gulp and hands it to* ARJAY, *who guzzles.*]

That crazy-ass woman almost had us on the obituary page, and I am *not* ready!

ARJAY: Hell, she pointed that thing at me, and I swear to God, I saw my life flash by right in front of me! Zip, zip, zap! Didn't miss a minute of it from the day I was born.

BOYD: Mine flew by two or three times. I saw colored people I didn't care if I *ever* saw again!

ARJAY: Yeah, well, I saw my wife and children on the bread line, beggin'.

BOYD: I saw your wife, too—at your funeral, throwing stones at your casket.

ARJAY: Yeah, and I saw yours at your funeral, too. Throwing *rocks! Big ones!* And your kids were heaving 'em right along with her. Using slingshots.

BOYD: Oh, shut up. You see, the thing is, Biggs, Travis wasn't paying attention. He lost his judgment. It's just simple. You can't let that nooky get too good to you. You hear what I'm saying, because it will make you forget your grandmama's name! Am I right, Arjay?

ARJAY: Oh yeah, it'll mess with your brain all right.

[*He motions for the bottle.* BOYD *hands it to him. He takes a gulp.* CAIRO *rises abruptly.*]

CAIRO: I have to get out of this place.

ARJAY: Yeah, we've all been through a lot today. We ought to take the rest of the day off.

CAIRO: No, out of here—out! I'm leaving—I quit!

ARJAY: Aw, come on now, Biggs.

BOYD: Son, don't let that woman send you to the poorhouse, because if you walk out of here, that's exactly where you're headed.

CAIRO: Maybe she should've shot us all.

BOYD: Now, wait a minute! I *know* you're not talking about me.

CAIRO: That's right—you, me, and everybody in here.

BOYD: Give the young man the bottle, Arjay.

[ARJAY *offers the bottle again.*]

CAIRO: Get that crap away from me.

BOYD: Son, take that liquor and stop talking like some goddamn sissy.

CAIRO: I don't want it, dammit!

BOYD: Forget him. Give it here! Shit!

[ARJAY *hands the bottle to* BOYD, *who quickly gulps and hands it back.*]

You're as irrational as that woman is, Biggs. She and all these women ought to be down on their scruffy knees, sweatin' bullets, thanking us—

CAIRO: For what? What the hell've we ever done for them?

BOYD: If you don't know the answer to that one, then you're dumber than I thought.

[ARJAY *holds the bottle out to* CAIRO.]

ARJAY: C'mon, Biggs—c'mon, c'mon! I'm beggin' you!

[CAIRO *shoves* ARJAY'*s hand away.*]

I know you're upset, so am I. Nobody wants someone snap like that, but—

CAIRO: Why the hell do you think she snapped, huh? Because all we do is . . . fuck them up.

BOYD: Biggs, if these women are messed up, it happened long before they got to us, so take your got-damn pity someplace else.

CAIRO: You don't get it, do you?

BOYD: Oh, and you do, huh? Shit, the boy can't even bend his knees, and *he* "gets it."

CAIRO: Yeah, go ahead, laugh. I don't care whether you want to admit it or not, we look down on people like her.

BOYD: Son, will you *please* put this bottle in your mouth and shut your trap and let me enjoy my Johnny Walker!

CAIRO: Stick it up your ass, all right?

BOYD: Keep talking like that and see what happens.

CAIRO: Go ahead, try me.

ARJAY: All right, everybody just calm down now. We've had enough turmoil today already.

CAIRO: These women, we treat them like scum. They're the bottom of the barrel. We blame them for their own misery. Just because they're down-and-out, they're "lazy and ignorant and—"

ARJAY: You're taking this *way* too seriously, Biggs.

CAIRO: Do you really think that woman wants to live the way she does? Do you really think she wouldn't get a better job than scrubbing white people's floors, if she could, huh? I mean, Jesus! That's not something she brought on herself, for crying out loud!

ARJAY: Biggs, it's time to get on to the next minute.

[*He grabs the bottle from* BOYD.]

Here, take it and move on!

[*He shoves the bottle out at* CAIRO, *who pushes it away again.*]

CAIRO: No, *you* move on! These women don't mean a cotton-pickin' thing to us. They don't mean anything to the guys who beat up on 'em, they don't mean anything to white people, they don't mean anything to anybody, dammit!

BOYD: Oh, bullshit! *Bullshit,* nigger! My accountability is to provide these people with a service so they can have a proper burial for themselves and their families. And I do a damn good job of it, I don't care how many women I crawl between the sheets with. They know exactly—*exactly* what they're getting into. And that crazy, lunatic woman's no different. So stop trying to put a halo over the head of the devil, because the light's not going to come on. Weep all by your lonesome.

[CAIRO *jumps to his feet.*]

CAIRO: Oh, forget it! I don't give a damn whether you guys want to admit it or not, we're all crabs in the same barrel, and if they're riffraff, so are we.

ARJAY: Bend your knees, man. C'mon, do like I tell you!

[CAIRO *starts for the door and stops.*]

CAIRO: Yeah, I'll bend 'em—right out this damn door. We're all wallowing in the same shit and you can't smell it, you freaking hypocrites!

[*He leaves, slamming the door.*]

ARJAY: I bet I know what it is. That Meeks gal must've burned his ass. I'll betcha.

BOYD: A young fool's as bad as an old one. Let him stay out there for a while. He gets tired of those crabs in that barrel dragging him down to the bottom, he'll be begging to get back to that desk. Because, let me tell you something, brother, all those dark, dusty roads out there lead straight back here to paradise. That's right.

ARJAY: Yeah, but I've got to give the boy credit, though. At least he left here with a little fire in his belly. He bent his knees a little bit, I'll give him that.

BOYD: That's on you.

[*He takes a swig of liquor, then holds bottle out to* ARJAY.]

You want the last corner?

ARJAY: I'm done with it.

[BOYD *guzzles and then drops the bottle into the wastebasket. He rises and puts papers into his briefcase.*]

BOYD: I have got to get home. I'm putting down new flooring in the den. One of my wife's favorite aunts is arriving from South Carolina, and the last thing I need is for her to get splinters in her feet. I won't hear the end of it. You coming?

[ARJAY *also stands and collects his belongings.*]

ARJAY: Yeah, I have to run by and get some tickets to the circus. That's all my kids've been talking about. I like it myself, to tell you the truth.

[BOYD *goes to the door.*]

BOYD: Yeah, "We shall see," said the blind man.

ARJAY: "A heap of folks see, but a few know."

[BOYD *laughs and exits.* ARJAY *hesitates and then picks something up from the floor—a bracelet.* MAE ANN's. *He stares lengthily at it for a moment and then hesitates again. He starts to put it into his pocket but stops. He goes to his desk, opens a drawer, puts the bracelet into it, closes the drawer, and exits. The radio crackles after a moment and then comes on. Muddy Waters is heard singing "Baby, Please Don't Go." The lights fade out slowly in the room and fade in in the office. A few weeks later.* ARJAY *sits at his desk, working. Big Bill Broonzy is heard on the radio.* ARJAY *stops suddenly and then opens the desk drawer and pulls out the bracelet. He stares at it. The door opens.* CAIRO *stands, tentative. The two men match stares. The radio crackles to a halt.* CAIRO *goes to his desk and begins to put various items into his briefcase. He finishes and stands, looking at* ARJAY, *who sits stoically, staring straight ahead.* ARJAY *laughs suddenly and then reaches into his briefcase and pulls out a pint of scotch. He uncaps it and offers it to* CAIRO, *who shakes his head, refusing.* ARJAY *takes a gulp and then hesitates, holding onto the bottle.*]

Sit down a minute, Biggs.

[CAIRO *hesitates.*]

C'mon, sit down. I'm not gonna bite.

[CAIRO *finally sits at his desk.*]

You dream much, Biggs?
CAIRO: Yeah . . .
ARJAY: What do you dream about?
CAIRO: Green snakes mostly.
ARJAY [*laughing*]: Green snakes means you got sex on your mind. I was your age, I dreamed about green snakes, too. All the damn time.

[CAIRO *shrugs, not answering.*]

I never thought much of dreams, Biggs, unless it had to do with the numbers, until last week. You know who I dreamed about? Old Man Joe Willis. I hadn't thought about that man for years. A big drunk, a real nasty son of a bitch. I don't know how many folks he sent to the hospital, knocking 'em down, stompin' on 'em. Nigger was so mean he walked like he was kicking folks out of the way. But for some funny reason, he liked me. Probably because I was fool enough to date his daughter, Carlotta. All the other guys in the neighborhood stayed five hundred feet away from her, but I was willing to go through the fiery furnace to get to her. I loved that pretty little girl. She was my queen; but, brother, I paid a price for it. Yeah, buddy, I'd walk in the front door, and I belonged to him first. He'd sit me down on the couch and wear me out with his crazy-ass inventions: bullets that went around corners, chasing down crooks, automobiles that flew—ridiculous shit.

[*He laughs and takes another gulp of scotch.*]

One day, Biggs, he said to me, "Son, I know the odds are against me, but all I wanna do is get *one* foot in the door of heaven and just *oooooooooze* the rest of the way in." He was counting on the fact that he loved the ladies! I don't mean just for nooky either. He loved 'em; said they was God's greatest creation. To hell with Adam. It was Eve who was the one, brother. I swear to God, there wasn't a woman he didn't love—old, young, short, tall, fat, skinny, yella, brown, dark, black, and damn black. You should've seen him, tipping his hat, bowing and smiling—the politest, most charming man you'd ever seen. They knew that he was a rascal, but they ate it up, because he really meant it. And I'll tell you, if Old Man

Willis ever caught you disrespecting a woman, he'd go upside your head, right on the spot. He died one night, on his knees, drunk, praying, trying to *ooooooooooze* his way into heaven. That's some story, isn't it?

CAIRO: Yeah, it really is.

[ARJAY *takes another sip of scotch and then hands the bottle to* CAIRO, *who hesitates.*]

ARJAY: C'mon, c'mon, this ain't no ambush. C'mon.

[CAIRO *finally takes a swig and hands it back.*]

Anyway, Willis came to me in this dream last week. He was just standing there, looking dead at me. And you know what he did? He gave me a number.

CAIRO: You're kidding!

ARJAY: So help me God. 15-45-80. Death Row. I played it, Biggs. And as God is my witness, I hit on it.

CAIRO: You're kidding!

ARJAY: So help me. Last week. I hit on it. Made me some cash! I'm talkin' about a bundle! I plunked some of it down on my Cadillac. Won't be long, brother, before I'll be driving in style, because of Ol' Man Joe Willis! But you know what he did after he gave me the number? Know what he did? He took his big, black finger, pointed it at me, and started shaking it, mad as a hornet, started yelling at me, the veins popping out on his neck. "You forgot what I told you, didn't you, you stupid, black motherfucker? I should've never let you see my daughter. Don't you know, once you lose respect for a woman, you lose respect for yourself! You ought to know that, you big black dummy! Keep it up, you hear? Just keep it up. I got in, boy. I *ooooozed* my way. I am here, brother! And I got permission from the Lord to knock you down if I have to. Now try me, all right? A heap see, but a few know!" I got that from him. He's the one that used to say it all the time. And then, you know what he did? The nigger slapped me.

CAIRO: He did what?

ARJAY: Slapped me. Wham, wallop!—right across the chops. I woke up, and my face was stinging, man.

CAIRO: Come on!

ARJAY: I'm serious as flies on watermelon. Slapped me! I can still feel it, and that was last week. I'm half afraid to go to sleep, afraid he's gonna whip my ass again. I mean, I thought it might've been my old woman, you know, me blabbing out the names of one of these women, but she swore on her dead great grandmama's grave she didn't have anything to do with it. So, I have to take her at her word. Had to be Joe Willis, Biggs. You ever hear anything like that, Biggs?

CAIRO: No . . . I can't say I have.

[ARJAY *hands the bottle to* CAIRO, *who takes a sip and hands it back.*]

ARJAY: Yeah, man, Ol' Man Willis loved the womenfolk. By the way, how's that little Meeks girl?

CAIRO: She . . . went back home.

ARJAY: Oh, yeah? Well, I'm not surprised. It's a spiteful world up here, Biggs.

CAIRO: I might've made her pregnant, Arjay.

ARJAY: Yeah? Well, I figured you were heading that way.

CAIRO: What do you mean?

ARJAY: The chick had your nose wide open, Biggs. Wide enough to drive a bootlegger's truck through at full speed. And that's when shit like that happens, sooner or later, when you keep thinking with your dick.

CAIRO: Why the hell didn't you say something?

ARJAY: You found out, didn't you? I've been there, Biggs. Travis and Boyd, too; all of us, got some chick pregnant at one time or the other.

CAIRO: So what did you do about it?

ARJAY: Me? I married her. I better had. Her daddy is one of these crazy-ass West Indians, who knows *exactly* where he keeps his .45; and her brother, Buster, stands six foot five and goes two hundred an' fifty. But, I'm glad I did. She's a good old woman.

[CAIRO *reaches for the bottle.* ARJAY *hands it to him. He takes a gulp, not a sip.* ARJAY *is pleased.*]

CAIRO: She says it could be somebody else's. Maybe a couple of guys.

ARJAY: All the better.

CAIRO: But it could be mine.

ARJAY: Yeah? So?

CAIRO: I could be its father, Arjay, and she doesn't want me to have anything to do with it.

ARJAY: What are you, Biggs, a glutton for punishment? Shit, you still thinking with your dick, man. Why you think you've got that big noggin between your shoulders? All that romantic bullshit. You need to thank your lucky stars and jump for joy, she let you off the damn hook. Hell, nigger, you got plenty of time to be some crumb snatcher's daddy. Little niggers'll wear you out before your time. Now, may a word to the wise be sufficient.

[ARJAY *picks up the bracelet.*]

This is hers. Was on the floor. Looks like it cost a couple of pennies. Maybe a family heirloom or something. Anyway, I'm sure she'd like to have it back.

[*He holds it out to* CAIRO, *who takes and appraises it.*]

CAIRO: It's nice.

[*He hands it back to* ARJAY.]

ARJAY: I haven't been getting much sleep lately, Biggs, between Joe Willis and this stuff happening here. I'm like a zombie, man. I'm going to take this down to the jailhouse and give it to her. Maybe help her out a little bit. She oughtn't be down there taking the blame all by herself.

CAIRO: That's right, she shouldn't.

ARJAY: Like you were trying to say: who knows who pulled the trigger? We were all scufflin' over it. You, me, and everybody. Even though I know she fully intended to shoot that nigger. Come on, fess up to it. She was going to, right? C'mon, admit it.

CAIRO: Yeah, she might've.

ARJAY: Damn right she "might've," crazy as she was acting. Anyway, I know a couple of the boys down there at the precinct, clients of mine. I give 'em good deals—discounts. I'll put a good word in for her. I still have a little bit left from my numbers hit. Maybe it's enough to get her out of there.

CAIRO: I have a little bit saved up I can throw into the pot.

ARJAY: All right, come on down with me, then.

CAIRO: Yeah, sure. [*Pause.*] Arjay, the stuff we were doing with these women, it was wrong, wasn't it?

ARJAY: So Joe Willis told me.

CAIRO: But it was wrong, right? I wasn't just being some obnoxious idealist, was I?

ARJAY: Yeah, you were pretty damn obnoxious, Biggs.

CAIRO: But what we were doing is wrong, right? I shouldn't have even been messing with Ruby Meeks. I was wrong, too, right? Come on, Arjay. You want Joe Willis to slap you again?

ARJAY: Hell, no!

CAIRO: It's not right, is it? [*Pause.*] Right? [*Pause.*] Come on, Arjay!

[ARJAY *takes a quick sip of scotch, caps the bottle, and puts the bottle back into his briefcase.*]

ARJAY: No, Biggs, it's not. Never was, never will be, all right? It doesn't mean you don't keep doing it, because as time goes on, you find all these ways to justify it. In fact, it gets easier and easier because you've got the power to do it. But it's wrong as fried tomatoes without gravy and biscuits without butter. And, brother, that's wrong!

[*The telephone on* ARJAY*'s desk rings. He stops and picks up the receiver.*]

South Side Burial, Thornton speaking. [*Pause.*] Well, if it isn't Eloise Hilton herself. How are you doing, young lady? [*Pause.*] Yeah, it has been a while, hasn't it? [*Pause.*] It's good to hear your voice, too, Sugar. [*Pause.*] Well, we'll have to see about that, won't we?

[*He reaches for his face suddenly, as though it's been hit. He hesitates, rubbing his cheek, looking at* CAIRO, *and then hesitates.*]

Yeah, I'm here. [*Pause.*] Next week? [*Pause.*] Look, darlin', I don't mean to throw you a curve, but I'm gonna have to put an end to this thing. [*Pause.*] No, no, baby, it's nothin' you've done, you've been right on time. It's me. And what I've been doing is wrong. [*Pause.*] No, no, you don't have to worry about your premiums paid up, that's the least of your worries. We'll work that out. [*Pause.*] No, you're a good lady, Eloise. [*Pause.*] Yes, you are, I'm serious. Don't go low-rating yourself. And I apologize for the predicament I put you in. [*Pause.*] Yes, I really do. [*Pause.*] We'll talk and straighten things up, all right? [*Pause.*] I know, I know. [*Pause.*] Everything's going to be all right, OK? [*Pause.*] I'll talk to you tomorrow, OK? All right, good-bye now. [*Pause.*] Bye.

[*He hangs up, unnerved, rubbing at his cheek.*]

He got me again, Biggs.

CAIRO: He did? Willis?

ARJAY: Yeah, nigger just hauled off on me. If I'm lyin', I'm flyin'. [*Pause.*] It's still stinging. That old son of a bitch. Damn! [*Pause.*] And she—Eloise—started bawling, crying her eyes out, like I had lifted this heavy burden from her. I mean, sobbing, man—water gushing out of a faucet. Damn! Here I am now, feeling guilty and good at the same damn time; like the same burden's been lifted from my shoulders, too. And you know what, it feels kind of nice, you know? Like, I've got wings on my back.

CAIRO: That's great. That's great.

ARJAY: Hey, let's you and me bend our knees, get ourselves on to the next minute, and see that woman at the jailhouse, while I still got wings. You ready?

CAIRO: Yeah, I'm ready.

ARJAY: All right, let's do it.

[*They start for the door.* ARJAY *feels his face again and then looks up toward the ceiling.*]

You're really up there, aren't you? You *ooooooooozed* your way on in, didn't you? Well, I guess that means there's hope for me, too. But, ease up on the slappin' part, all right? I mean, I got the message.

[*He and* CAIRO *laugh. He opens the door.* CAIRO *starts to follow him out.*]

Hey, what about your stuff?

[CAIRO *hesitates, looking.*]

CAIRO: Let it stay for a while. I mean, you know?

ARJAY: That's the ticket.

[*He laughs and then exits.* CAIRO *follows, turning out the light to black.*]

MA NOAH

Mark Clayton Southers

First-Place Winner

2003–2004

For all of the mothers who struggle for an answer

PLAYWRIGHT'S STATEMENT

I personally think it is first and foremost the duty of the African American playwright to inform—and to inform everyone, which will undoubtedly educate in the process.

My introduction into theater came in the form of Kuntu Repertory Theatre in Pittsburgh, run by Dr. Vernell A. Lillie. The resident playwright was none other than the iconic Rob Penny, whose plays taught me at the ripe old age of thirty much more about African history and African American history than the school systems ever could.

Currently the issue of urban, often called "chitlin' circuit," plays versus real socially conscious dramas has been a hot topic among theater folks. These plays certainly place entertainment above cultural awareness. I personally believe we have several distinct audiences; some may say it relates to several levels of class in our community, with the middle class drifting toward higher or lower levels at will.

Ma Noah was my attempt to write a play that would speak to all classes of African Americans. Some may find some of the language offensive, but not only is it dealt with within the script, it is necessary to give these characters and this play a sense of realism, which I hope will assist the audience in understanding just who these individuals are, why they make the choices that they do, and, most important, what they are up against in this tough world in which we all live.

I've always contended that white American theatergoers flocking to see the works of August Wilson reached deeper than the fact that he has written a great canon of work; I believe that in doing so, he has created an opportunity for white America to take a closer look at black America in the safety of a regional theater. In other words, August has cracked the door open and allowed them to stand right outside the perimeter of black life and witness all of its joys and triumphs and its pains and sorrows. *Ma Noah* is my attempt to unite the distinct worlds of black theater audiences and touch whomever else may want to listen and feel.

Ma Noah is the tale of a family whose household is governed by the mother, Rebecca. She has four adult children, three of whom live with her. The older daughter is single and pregnant. The younger daughter struggles with her identity, her sexual being, and her perceived loss of her father. The younger son has been caught up in the drug trade. The older son, who lives away from the rest of the family, has wound up at the other end of that spectrum. Rebecca must use all of her strength along with a little ingenuity to break the destructive cycle that has plagued her family and to maintain a sense of peace in her household. From a distance, this family may appear to be dysfunctional, but its members are merely making their way through life.

I would like to thank everyone involved with the Theodore Ward Prize and especially Chuck Smith for helping me hone this play and make it stageworthy. Thank you, Chuck!

PRODUCTION HISTORY

Ma Noah, by Mark Clayton Southers, was first presented by the Columbia College Chicago Theater Department at the New Studio Theater in February 2004. It was directed by Chuck Smith, with set design by Jacqueline Penrod, costume design by Frances Maggio, and lighting design by Mike May. David Woolley was the fight choreographer. Shina Fujito and Mai E. Thompson were the stage managers.

Larry	Mark James Heath
Francine	Krystal Mosley
Ham (Pig)	Larry Towers
Rebecca	Regina Whitehead-Mays
Mary	Amber Whitted

The play was subsequently presented by the New Horizon Theater in Pittsburgh, Pennsylvania, in October 2004. It was directed by Mark Clayton Southers, with costume design by Heddie Thomas, lighting and sound design by Eric Smith, and set design by Mark Clayton Southers. Kirsten Stanton was the stage manager.

Rebecca	Brenda Marks Dukes
Larry	Mark James Heath
Ham (Pig)	Nathan James and K. L. Brewer
Francine	Tonya Marie Milbourne
Mary	Monique Pappas

CHARACTERS

Mary, older daughter
Rebecca, mother
Francine, younger daughter
Larry, younger son
Pig (Ham), older son

STAGING

The play is set in the present in the Philadelphia, Pennsylvania, home of Rebecca Pratt. The set consists of a living room stage left and a much smaller kitchen stage right. There is a regular-size sofa in the center of the living room. Stage right of it is an easy chair. Stage left of it is another chair, and downstage center is a television set. Upstage, stage left of the door, is an entertainment stand with a stereo, books, and other assorted items. Stage left of the living room is another hallway, which leads to Rebecca's bedroom. Stage right is the kitchen, which has an entrance from the living room and from the narrow hall, which leads to several bedrooms and a bathroom offstage.

ACT 1

SCENE 1

[*The lights come up on the living room. It's not particularly fancy but does offer the necessities for comfort. The front door opens and* MARY *enters. She is nearing a full-term pregnancy and is patiently waiting for that day. She places her key back into her purse and looks around the room.*]

MARY: Mother! [*Pause.*] Mother!

[REBECCA *enters from her bedroom. She is a woman in constant motion.*]

REBECCA: Mary?

[*Puts her eyes on* MARY *and her tummy.*]

Mary, is that you?

MARY: Yes, it's me.

REBECCA: Hmph, hmph, hmph. That's something I'm going to have to get used to.

[*They embrace.*]

Never thought I'd see the day. Humph. What a sight.

MARY [*laughs*]: Where is everybody?

REBECCA: No one tells me a thing, they just come and go. Where's your bags?

MARY: In the hall.

[REBECCA *exits out the door and comes back in with two small suitcases.*]

REBECCA: You carried these all the way from the station?

MARY: Most of the way. Some guy gave me a hand for about the first four blocks. He seemed very nice. I invited him to service this Sunday.

REBECCA: Yeah, and that's probably right around the time he set these down and disappeared. [*Pause.*] Well, where's Roy?

MARY: He's still down there.

REBECCA: You all haven't ironed things out yet?

MARY: There's nothing to iron out.

REBECCA: You want me to call and have a little talk with him?

MARY: *No!* [*Pause.*] There's nothing to talk about.

REBECCA [*pausing*]: Look, you should have called. I'da had Larry come down to meet you. [*Pause.*] Well, come on and sit down.

[*She walks into the kitchen, opens the refrigerator door, takes out a carton of juice, and pours a glass.*]

When you due? I know you told me already but . . .

MARY: A little less than six weeks now.

REBECCA: What's the date?

MARY: Well, Mama, just count.

REBECCA: What . . . is . . . the . . . date? I'm tryin' to write it down on the calendar in here.

MARY: June fifteenth.

REBECCA [*writing*]: I gotta go through all that for your due date?

MARY: No, sorry.

[REBECCA *brings* MARY *the glass of juice.*]

REBECCA: Here.

MARY: Thanks.

REBECCA: I had you all set to stay in Ham's old room, but they went and made it into their little getaway place.

MARY: Getaway?

REBECCA: It's where they take their company. They've got their video games and a couch. They even have a little fridge in there. The couch opens up into a bed. As soon as I got it straightened up, Larry decided now he wanna stay in there. So, I guess you just gonna hafta to just stay in his room.

MARY: That's fine, I'm not hard to please.

REBECCA: All right, well, look. I hafta go on across town in a little bit, to see about some things.

MARY: You want me to go with you?

REBECCA: Noooo, you stay put. Somebody will be popping in here soon enough, you're not gonna be by yourself for too long. I'll be back around eight or nine. You catch Francine when she comes in and tell her I said to make sure she gets dinner ready. Oh, and tomorrow, you know we have our family meeting?

MARY: You all still doing that?

REBECCA: Yes, we are. Why wouldn't we? We're gonna start right at seven.

MARY: Pig gonna be here, too?

REBECCA: Of course. He's part of this family. Isn't he?

MARY [*dismayed*]: Great. What a homecoming.

REBECCA: Now see, that's what I don't understand. You Miss Church Lady. You, more than anyone else, suppose to be able to forgive and forget. Now he still your brother, and I want you to give him a chance. He's been going to his meetings. He's working and he's staying out of trouble. [*Pause.*] He's clean, Mary.

MARY: Working where?

REBECCA: Some nightclub.

MARY: Oh, great, that's just the place for him.

REBECCA: Actually, it is. He has a little setup in the bathroom there. After the people wash their hands, he gives them a paper towel and they tip him. He's got cologne, mints, gum—all kind of stuff in there for them.

MARY: How could he stand to do something like that?

REBECCA: He says it doesn't bother him none. I guess standing up in there all night, he gets to see up close what drinkin' and doin' drugs does to a person.

MARY: And you think that's good for him?

REBECCA: Yes, I do. It seems to be working. You'll see. Just give him a chance. We don't want him relapsing, so try to support what he's doing. OK?

MARY: All right.

REBECCA: Besides, he gets great tips. Sometimes. Over a hundred dollars a night.

MARY: That much?

REBECCA: Yeah. Now, you be nice to him. Try to have a clean slate about him in your mind.

MARY [*sighs*]: I'll try.

REBECCA: Good. Now, Mary, our meetings are s'til necessary, plus it'll give you a chance to see what everyone has been up to and for everybody to hear about what you been up to. [*Laughs.*] Well, we can see what you been up to. But if you don't feel like talking about you and Roy, I can understand that. But, honey. We family. It might do you some good to get some of that frustration off your chest.

[FRANCINE *enters wearing a Taco Bell uniform and carrying a knotted white plastic shopping bag.*]

MARY: Francine? Look at you, girl, getting all grown.

FRANCINE: Look at you . . . [*amazed at her size*] I don't ever wanna be pregnant.

REBECCA: That's how you got here.

FRANCINE [*hugging* MARY]: I thought you weren't comin' 'til next week?

MARY: Change of plans.

REBECCA: All right, look, I have to leave.

FRANCINE: Well, here, here's the stuff you ask me to get.

REBECCA: Oh, yeah, OK. Just put them away in the kitchen.

FRANCINE: Where you off to?

REBECCA: I have an appointment. I'll be back a little later on. I need you to take care of dinner tonight. All right?

FRANCINE [*sighs*]: Oh, Mom, I'm s'pose to be goin' oooout!

REBECCA: Well, you can still go. Soon as you're finished.

FRANCINE: Well, what time you comin' back?

REBECCA: I don't exactly know, just . . . put something together. There's plenty of things in there.

[*She hugs* FRANCINE *and* MARY.]

I'll be back, as soon as they let me . . . As soon as I'm done.

[REBECCA *exits out the front door.*]

FRANCINE: What kind of appointment she got? Every Saturday afternoon she runnin' off somewhere. She always got somethin' goin' on.

MARY: That's a good thing. [*Pause.*] Isn't it?

FRANCINE: Yeah, I guess so.

MARY: So, you working south of the border now?

FRANCINE: What?

MARY [*motioning at* FRANCINE's *uniform*]: Your gig?

FRANCINE [*drab*]: Oh . . . yeah. I've been there for about five months.

MARY: You like it?

FRANCINE: Are you serious? I can't stand it.

MARY: Then why are you there?

FRANCINE: It's close. I can walk to it. Don't ever have to worry about bein' late. I ain't really planned on bein' there this long though. [*Pause.*] When you due?

MARY: About a month and a half.

FRANCINE: Maaaan. You know what you havin' yet?

MARY: No. I want it to be a surprise.

FRANCINE: Mary! You called your baby a "it"!

MARY: What?

FRANCINE: You just said "it."

MARY: I did?

FRANCINE: Yes! And that's the reason why you should wanna know what you havin'. You pick out any names yet?

MARY: No.

FRANCINE: Come on, I know you thought of some.

MARY: Well, all right. I was thinking if it, if she—if . . . my . . . baby . . . is a girl, I was thinking about maybe calling her Samantha.

FRANCINE: Samantha? Oh, please. That's a witch name.

MARY: What?

FRANCINE: That's the chick that be wigglin' her nose name.

MARY: What?

FRANCINE: Darren's woman. The witch! The one that be on that show on TV land.

MARY: Oh, come on.

FRANCINE: No, for real.

[*She walks over to the kitchen table.*]

Come on. Let's sit down and think of some names. There's plenty of great names out there. I hate mine, especially when people wanna call me Fran.

MARY: I like your name.

FRANCINE: Shoot! You can have it. [*Pause.*] Seem like Mommy put the Bible down when me and Lawrence came along. Hey, what about Sateira?

MARY: No! That sounds too devilish.

FRANCINE: Hey, there's this girl that works with me named Precious. Isn't that a pretty name?

MARY [*pulling out a notebook*]: Yeah, it's cute. I like it.

[*She writes in her notebook.*]

I was thinking about maybe Isaiah if—

[LARRY *enters quickly through the front door, carrying a small bag.*]

LARRY: Where everybody at? Hey, hey, hey, Big Sistah!

MARY [*rising*]: Hey, Larry.

LARRY: Whoa, look at you, mama. Damn! You need to be sittin' out in front of the hospital. When you s'pose to be spittin' him out?

MARY: Not for a while.

LARRY: Shoot! That's what you think. Sit on down there. You better keep still, real still. Hey, where's Mom at?

FRANCINE: Why, you broke?

LARRY: Twenty-four seven.

MARY: Mama went to go see about something.

LARRY: I thought she was workin' steady night shift?

FRANCINE: You need to start payin' attention to what's goin' on around here.

LARRY: What you talkin' 'bout? I pay attention.

FRANCINE: Yeah? Well if you did, you would have known she got herself a half a day job now.

LARRY: Doin' what?

FRANCINE: Probably cleanin'.

MARY: Fran . . . Francine, you don't know if that's what she's doing for real.

FRANCINE: Well, what else she gonna be doin' for half a day?

MARY: Maybe she got herself a man. [*Pause.*] Sorry, I shouldn't have said tha . . .

FRANCINE: That's all right, ain't nobody thinkin' about nothin' like that. Don't nobody expect her to wait on him anyway. She be sixty years old time he get out.

LARRY: Sixty-seven.

FRANCINE: Same thing.

MARY: How's he doin'?

[*Pause.*]

LARRY: Got a 'brella. You need one?

FRANCINE: What color?

LARRY: Blue . . . navy.

FRANCINE: That's all right. I need a tan one.

LARRY: Tan? It's to keep the rain off of you! Rain don't care what color it fall on.

FRANCINE: I want it to match.

LARRY: Match what? You don't even go out the house. 'Cept for work.

FRANCINE: Then why you tryin' to sell me a umbrella?

LARRY: I'd sell it to you, Mary, but your belly still would get wet.

[*He laughs.* MARY *smiles. Pause.*]

What y'all doin'?

MARY: Writing some names down for the baby.

LARRY: What you come up with so far?

MARY: Well, if my baby is a boy, I'm thinking maybe Isaiah.

[*Excited,* LARRY *sits down at the table.*]

LARRY: What, you havin' a little neph for me?

FRANCINE: She doesn't know yet.

LARRY: What? How come you just don't go ahead and find out what you havin' first?

FRANCINE: That's what I tried to tell her.

MARY: It's bad luck.

LARRY: No, it ain't either. Mama said she knew what I was up front 'cause they x-rayed her stomach.

MARY: It's called a sonogram.

LARRY: Whatever! They did it, and she knew it was me in there. I seeent the picture. I was in there like this.

[*He strikes a cool fetal pose, flashing a gang sign with both arms crossed.*]

MARY: Like I said, it's bad luck.

LARRY: What I got to do with bad luck? Huh? Ain't nothin' wrong with my name. Well, what Roy think you should name the baby?

MARY: It doesn't matter what Roy thinks.

LARRY: Aw, that ain't right, Mary.

MARY: There's a lot of things in this world that aren't right. [*Pause.*] Roy's one of 'em.

LARRY: You shouldn't be freezin' the brother out like that.

MARY: Freezing him out? Wait a minute. First you and Pig bring him up in here to meet me. Then when he brings me home late, y'all wanna kick his butt!

LARRY: Oh, it was late, all right! It was three o'clock the next day! In the P-M! All right, forget Roy. What if it's a girl?

MARY: "It"? My baby isn't a "it"!

[FRANCINE *giggles.*]

LARRY: Aw, Mary, you know what I mean.

MARY: If my baby is a girl, then [*looking at* FRANCINE] we're thinking about maybe naming her Precious.

LARRY: Precious? Oh, hellllll no! She'll be spoiled rotten. When she get older, 'stead of guys callin' her baby, they'll be sayin', "Come here, Precious baby." Naw, naw, naw, that's a ho name.

MARY: Shut up! It is not.

[*She closes her notebook.*]

You done went and messed it all up. I'm not telling you nothing else!

LARRY: Where Mama cleanin' at?

FRANCINE: I don't know, and what it matter to you anyway?

LARRY: I can't see Mama cleanin' for no white folks.

MARY: Why she got to be workin' for white folks?

LARRY: Come on now, Mary.

[*He rises.*]

Who you know black, got somebody black cleanin' for 'em? And Geoffrey on the *Fresh Prince* don't count. He fictional.

MARY: Listen. Dirt is dirt. As long as she's getting paid, it shouldn't matter.

FRANCINE: That's right! Besides, you don't seem to have no problem cleanin' for white folks.

LARRY: Naw, see, I work for an authority. Which is a group of people.

[*He crosses into the living room.*]

And there's a few brothers and sisters in that group, some lawyers and shit.

[FRANCINE *gets up and follows him into the living room.*]

FRANCINE: You cleanin' up after baseball and football games for some white man sittin' up in some office somewhere. You can try and fool yourself all you want.

LARRY: I know who I work for. An' I ain't got no problem with it. I'm just sayin if . . . [*sighs*]. Forget it. I'm hungry. What time she s'pose to be back, anyway?

MARY: Francine's preparing dinner tonight.

LARRY: What? [*Sighs.*] Looks like it's gonna be another 'tucky fried night!

FRANCINE: You ain't gotta eat here. You can go to work early and scrape you a super dog up off the ground!

[LARRY *crosses back into the kitchen.*]

LARRY: I don't eat that stuff. It's a common rule you don't eat before you go in there. Mary, I'm tellin' you. People is nasty. You got wet stinky cigarette butts, beer-soaked peanut shells, leftover sandwiches, liquor, pop, piss! All mixed together! It's the worst smell I ever smelled in my whole life. I got a hoodie over there that I wear when I'm cleanin'. It stink all the b-damn! I hang it up when I get done, outside our little locker room. Ain't never got to worry about nobody stealin' it. 'Cause it stink! That smell done got up in it and it ain't never comin out. The new people, [*sighs*] they don't even last that long. They come in there thinkin' they gonna find themselves a wallet, a watch, or a ring or somethin'. As soon as that smell get a grip on 'em, whew! Seem like they heave up everything they then ever ate in their entire life, and it just adds to the stench. [*Pause.*] Naw, I'ma settle for whatever we got goin' on up in here.

FRANCINE: There's a bag with some tuna and stuff in there. You can make your own meal.

LARRY [*trying to open the bag*]: Damn. 'Cine, you put all these knots in this bag?

FRANCINE: No, the lady at the store did that.

LARRY: They at it again.

MARY: What are you complaining about now?

LARRY: The Y-Ts! Look at this.

[*He holds up the bag.*]

You can't even get your shit back outta here!

FRANCINE: Mrs. Shaw be doin' that. She do it to everybody.

LARRY: Yeah, and everybody that go in her store is black!

[*He tears open the white plastic bag, revealing a brown paper bag.*]

And look at this!

FRANCINE: What?

LARRY: I bet you ain't even notice this.

[*He shows her the brown bag.*]

See? [*Pause.*] They got to always be tryin' to show their superiority. How come they can't make brown plastic bags and have them on the outside?

MARY: What? What's that suppose to mean?

LARRY: It means . . . that they think they got to always be around us on the outside, controllin' things.

MARY: What?

FRANCINE: Then what about the Oreo cookie? The white stuff is on the inside.

LARRY: That's different. That's about taste. And the white stuff do taste the best. That's why they got it on the inside. But on the for real for real. The cookie part nasty as hell! If they had it the other way around people would just eat the outside and throw the rest away. But naw, they got to eat that nasty-ass cookie just to get to the good stuff.

MARY: What?

LARRY: It's just like a boiled egg. You ever have one and you sprinkle a little salt on it and start eatin' it? Time you get to that hard-ass little green alien eyeball-lookin' shit in the middle, you don't want to eat that, and mess up that good taste that's already in your mouth.

FRANCINE: Larry, really? All this over a damn bag? It ain't nothin' but a bag. Nobody in this world looks at things the way you do.

LARRY: That's the problem. That's what we need to start doin'! They kill me when they be doin' this sneaky shit.

MARY: They've got brown plastic bags out there. I've seen them.

LARRY: You know what? You're right. At the liquor store. See, it ain't no problem there. That's 'cause they wanna keep us down. Shoot, they put your bottle in a brown paper bag and then top it off by puttin' it in a brown plastic one. That's 'cause they wanna keep us comfortable. Wanna keep us comin' back. Tryin' to get us to where they got the Indians.

FRANCINE: Would you please quit trippin'? Ain't nobody tryin' to put us on no reservation.

LARRY: What you think the projects is? Huh? It's the truth, y'all just don't wanna recognize it.

MARY: There are plenty of white folks living in the projects, too.

FRANCINE: And on welfare.

LARRY: That's because the problem is bigger than it was way back when they was dealin' with the red man. See, they can't control us and their poor folks. They knew some of their own was gonna slip through the cracks. Them is the ones that's in the projects and the trailer parks. They call 'em white trash. We ain't never called them that. They just white folks to us. But to the white man, they white niggers, but they ain't never gonna call 'em that. They don't wanna mess up that whole nigger thing. Yeah, they got a good one there. Cracker, redneck, honky. None of them even comes close to nigger. We get so mad, we gotta add something extra to it. *Cracker motherfucker!* And it still don't catch up with nigger. [*Pauses a beat.*] Yeah. [*Pause.*] Nigger. [*Pause.*] That's a mean-ass word there. And we be tryin' to mutate it. Even call ourselves it. Spell it and even say it a little different.

"Niggah." Try to break it down. Try to take away a little of its harshness. [*Pause of several beats. To* MARY] What's your social security number?

MARY: Why?

LARRY: I'm tryin' to show you somethin'. [*Pauses a beat.*] All right, jus' tell me what the middle two numbers are.

MARY: Five-eight.

LARRY: OK, and 'Cine, yours is?

FRANCINE: Two-oh-three, six—

LARRY: Naw, jus' the middle two.

FRANCINE: Six-two.

LARRY: Mine is six-two, too.

FRANCINE: You said just the middle two.

LARRY: What?

FRANCINE: You just said yours was six-two-two.

LARRY: No. *No!* Six-two also. Same as yours. See, that's how they know, when they look at a job application or somethin', whether you white or black.

FRANCINE: What is you talkin' about?

LARRY: Our middle two numbers is always even. White people's is odd.

FRANCINE: You're crazy.

LARRY: Well then, go ask somebody! Ask your boss at work.

FRANCINE: My boss is black.

LARRY: Well, ask him, I bet you his is even, too.

FRANCINE: My boss is a woman, thank you very much.

LARRY: *Well, then ask her ass!* I'll guarantee you it's even. [*Pauses a beat.*] I hate when they do that sneaky shit! All I want is a fair shot from the door. It's that little hidden shit like that, that pisses me off!

MARY: Subliminal.

LARRY: What?

MARY: Subliminal, that's what it's called.

LARRY: Whatever. It's some fucked-up shit!

MARY: Larry! Would you mind all the cussing?

LARRY: My bad.

MARY: I don't appreciate that kind of language.

LARRY: All right, I said my fault! What, you ain't never cuss befo'?

MARY: Not like you. [*Pause.*] It's ridiculous.

LARRY: That's just the way it is. That's how I roll. [*Pause.*] But I'll try to ease up around you.

MARY: I would appreciate it. How are you ever going to hold down a real job talking like that?

LARRY: Fuck a real job! Real is what you make it!

MARY: Why are you so angry?

LARRY: 'Cause we ain't shit to nobody . . . even ourselves. Don't nobody trust nobody. Don't nobody wanna give nobody no respect. And ain't nobody got no real love for nobody no more.

MARY: Now, how can you say that? I love you, Francine and Mama love you, and so does—

LARRY: *I ain't talkin' 'bout round here, Mary!* I'm talkin' 'bout out there! Out in the real world. Shoot, we ain't got no reason to hate each other. I mean, we got different daddies and all, but we s'til family. I'm talkin' 'bout them niggahs out there that will stab yo'll ass in the back and stomp on yo'll neck to keep you down.

FRANCINE: Crabs in a barrel.

LARRY: It's gettin' to the point where we can't even be mad at the white man no mo', 'cause we keep fuckin' up our own shit! Excuse me.

[*He pauses two beats.*]

You know I went and saw my daddy the week before last. I sat there with him for two hours. The whole two hours, he ain't have nuttin' new to say. Just kept talkin' 'bout the same ol' shit he talked about the last time I was there. No signs of hope. Musta talked about these new honey barbecue chips they got for over a half an hour. What kind of shit is that, huh? The man sittin' there.

[*He pauses several beats.*]

I mean, come on. How the hell can you get that unfocused on life. Honey barbecue chips?

[*He sighs.*]

Them motherfuckers sure must taste good.

MARY: Your father's not all that bad.

LARRY: Oh, he's a damn fool.

FRANCINE: Don't nobody know what really happened.

LARRY: He know, and he know his ass is a fool, too!

MARY: You shouldn't say that.

LARRY: He ain't never once said, "I ain't do that shit!" All right?

FRANCINE: Did you ask him?

LARRY [*indignant*]: *Did you ask him?*

FRANCINE: I don't wanna know.

LARRY [*slowly*]: Well, I know! And he know. *Hell!* Everybody know! 'Cept for you, and it's about time you know.

FRANCINE: *I said I ain't wanna know!*

[*She gets up and marches off, stage right, toward her offstage bedroom.*]

LARRY: You can hide from the truth all you want. He did that shit and he know it. He guilty as hell and his ass is in jail! And it wasn't like it was some kinda pride thing, either.

[*Offstage,* FRANCINE *slams her door.*]

He just said fuck you and me and Mama, too! All of us! Shit, I wish Noah would have been my daddy! At least I'd have a little more sense in my head, be able to fill in my own blanks about life, . . . not hafta look at this niggah sittin' up in there talkin' 'bout some damn potato chips!

MARY: Larry, relax.

LARRY [*pacing*]: Naw, I ain't relaxin'. That's what they want us to do. Relax. That's the first thing the cops say to you. [*Mimicking*] "Relax, buddy . . . pal." Just to give them enough time to put the cuffs on your ass . . . so they can beat the shit out of you. Relax. [*Pause.*] That's what Martin was doin' when he went out on that balcony. [*Pause.*] Relaxin'. Out there thinkin' about his next speech. [*Pause.*] That's what they want the black man to do . . . relax.

[*Lights fade.*]

SCENE 2

[*Lights come up on the living room. It's Saturday evening, family meeting night.* MARY *sits on the couch writing in her notebook.* FRANCINE *enters from her offstage bedroom stage right wearing a warm-up suit and carrying a duffel bag. She makes a beeline toward the door.*]

MARY: Where you going?

FRANCINE: Out.

MARY: Oh, no, no, no. It's Saturday night.

FRANCINE: And?

MARY: Sit your fast butt down.

[FRANCINE *marches to the couch and plops down.*]

FRANCINE: This ain't nothin' but a waste of time. I don't even know why
   Mommy even bother doin' this. It's the same old thing every week. Pig's
   clean and he's makin' money now, Larry ain't got no money. And Mama,
   she off scrubbin' floors somewhere. The only thing that's changin' around
   here is the size of your belly.

MARY: And what about you?

FRANCINE: What about me?

MARY: What kind of changes are you making?

FRANCINE: Why, who cares?

MARY: I care. What's the problem? Why are you and Larry always so
   angry?

FRANCINE: I ain't angry.

MARY: OK . . . I guess you just forgot how to smile then.

FRANCINE [*smiles*]: I'm not mad. I just don't see the sense of havin' these mini
   family reunions. Don't nothin' change.

MARY: We have them so if one of us needs some sort of help, then we can all
   get together and support them.

FRANCINE: That don't even make no sense. Why do I have to wait 'til Saturday night to ask for some help?

MARY: You're missing the whole point.

FRANCINE: You're right, I don't get it. If I need some help, I'ma ask for it
   when I need it. Not wait 'til the end of the week.

MARY: So what are you mad about?

FRANCINE: If I tell you now, can I skip the meeting?

MARY: What's in the bag?

FRANCINE: Nothin'.

MARY: What's in the bag?

FRANCINE: Why? Why you so concerned about me all of a sudden?

MARY: 'Cause you're slippin' in and out of here and nobody knows where
   you're going.

FRANCINE: You been here two days, what you know about me slippin' in and
   out? Huh?

MARY: What, you got you a boyfriend now?

FRANCINE: No, Mary, I don't have a boyfriend. Do you?

MARY: No!

FRANCINE: Well, what's with up Roy? Ain't that his baby?

[*Pause of several beats.*]

MARY: Of course it is.

[*She gets up.*]

Come on and show me that dance you all do.

FRANCINE: No, not right now.

MARY [*moving toward the stereo*]: Aw, come on. Just a little bit?

FRANCINE: Nooo, Mary! I don't feel like it. And you don't need to be dancin' anyway, 'sides, I gotta roll. I ain't got time to be dancin'.

[*She gets up.*]

Bump this meeting. S'pose to be a family meeting and ain't even nobody here.

MARY: We're here.

[*She turns on some music and starts to bop around.*]

Come on. I need some exercise. I've been doing nothing but sitting on my butt for the last three months.

FRANCINE: Well, you can wait one more, can't you?

MARY: Oh, come on, nothing's going to happen.

FRANCINE [*sighing as she gets up*]: All right.

[*She walks toward the stereo.*]

But this ain't gonna get it.

[*She plays a different CD and starts to move from side to side.*]

See, you gotta have that type of rhythm there. See, watch what I do. Step like this [*stepping*], uh-huh. Come on.

[FRANCINE *holds* MARY's *hand.* FRANCINE *laughs.* MARY *covers her mouth.*]

OK, start again. Step to left [*stepping*], step to the ri—

[PIG *enters. He's a sturdy man who carries himself as if he's the head of the household, but without the inherent responsibilities.*]

PIG: Ladies. How are yah?

[MARY *turns the music off.*]

MARY: Pig.

[PIG *hands out a few dollar bills each to* MARY *and* FRANCINE.]

PIG: Here you go. Compliments of them partying fools. They just be throwin' the money at me.

[MARY *walks back to her chair and sits.*]

MARY: I don't see how you do that.

PIG: I don't see you sendin' them dollars back my way, so I guess it ain't all that much of a problem. Now is it?

FRANCINE: What's a "valley," anyway?

PIG: It's "valet." [*Pause.*] I provide a special-needs service for the alcohol-impaired.

MARY: He's a twenty-first-century slave.

PIG: Well, it's good to see you, too. [*Pause.*] Mary, why you got to look at it like that?

MARY: 'Cause that's the way it is.

PIG: They got black people comin' in there, too.

MARY: So what's that supposed to mean?

PIG: It means it ain't all white people in there.

MARY: How you know they black?

PIG: Now how you sound?

[*He laughs.*]

You hear her?

MARY: How you know they ain't white?

PIG: 'Cause they black, Mary. I can look at 'em and see that they black.

MARY: That don't mean nothin'.

PIG: The hell it don't! Shoot, everywhere we go, it means something. Especially the black man. But now you wouldn't know nothin' 'bout that. But see now, Francine, I might be able to save you.

FRANCINE: From what?

PIG: From that evil void you 'bout to slip into. See, most black women channel themselves right down into it.

FRANCINE: Into what?

PIG: The void. It's like they in a zombie zone, where in their mind, the black man ain't shit and never will be. Yep, no respect for the black man. No matter what he do! Actin' like a bunch of damn zombies!

FRANCINE: Why we gotta be zombies?

PIG: We? Naw, naw, naw, naw, naw . . . You, you, you ain't there yet. See, I'ma save you.

FRANCINE: I'ma woman and I ain't lost!

PIG: Yeah, but you 'bout to be. Long as you keep listenin' to the ones that are [*looking in* MARY's *direction*].

FRANCINE: Pig, you talkin' a bunch of trash. I hear enough of that at work.

PIG: Naw, naw look here. I'ma hep you to what I know. You ever watch any of them old spooky movies where all the dead folks be walkin' around, climbin' up out of their graves?

FRANCINE: You mean like on "Thriller"?

PIG: Right, right. Their faces be all white. You ever notice how they just keep on 'bout their business no matter what a livin' person is sayin' to 'em? A man be standin' there with a double-barrel shotgun [*demonstrating in pantomime*] aimed right at their head tellin' them to stop.

[*He imitates a zombie walking.*]

But naw, they got tah keep on steppin', draggin' their leg, arm all bent up and shit. Bam, off go their head. Come another one. Bringin' up the rear. [*Pause.*] *Uuuuhhhhh!* See? That's how our black women are gettin'. Gettin' to the point don't matter what the black man say to 'em. Got their mind made up and don't even know what it's made up about. Always walkin' around frownin' all the damn time. A brother try to speak to one of y'all, and y'all act like a damn mute!

FRANCINE: That's 'cause y'all always tryin' to get into somebody's pants!

MARY: That's right!

PIG: Yah damn right it's right! Who else pants we s'pose to be gettin' into? Huh? Y'all need to lighten up with all that evil shit! Ain't nothin' but a bunch of damn zombies! I'm tired of bein' disrespected! You might as well paint your faces white and blend in! And you gonna sit here and talk to me about whether somebody black or not!

MARY: If they was real black men, they wouldn't be up in that white club looking for some snow bunnies!

PIG [*staring at her*]: I'm talkin' 'bout the people that come into that club.

[*He walks over and snatches the dollars back from her.*]

Not some two-bit niggah that left you for some white woman!

[MARY *gets up and crosses into the kitchen as* LARRY *enters through the front door.*]

FRANCINE: Why you always messin' with her?

PIG: Mess with her? I ain't messin' with her.

LARRY: Who's messin' with who?

[PIG *sighs and walks toward the kitchen.*]

PIG: Mary. Tell me somethin'? Why you always mixin' in your problems in a conversation?

LARRY: Ut-oh! Y'all on Mary.

PIG: I'm up in here tellin' them about the loot I'm makin', and she wanna make some type of jungle fever shit out of it.

LARRY: What, you pimpin' a white girl?

[MARY *returns to the living room with a bowl of ice cream.*]

MARY: Naw, he's pimpin' himself.

PIG: Is that right? All right, you know what? [*Pause.*] I ain't talkin' to you about nothin' else!

MARY: Good. Don't!

LARRY: How you pimp yourself, man?

PIG: She don't know what the hell she talkin' about.

FRANCINE: Mommy need to come on. I got somewhere to go.

LARRY [*to* FRANCINE]: Hey, let me hold a few dollars, I'm tryin' to get me a pass before the deadline.

FRANCINE: I don't have no money, Larry.

LARRY: You do so.

FRANCINE: Whatever. Ask Pig. He's the one handin' out dollar bills.

MARY: Why you wait 'til the last minute? How come you can't never plan ahead?

[LARRY *quickly looks down at her stomach and back up at her.*]

LARRY: Mary, don't even talk to me about no plannin' ahead.

PIG: How much you need?

LARRY: Ten.

[PIG *reaches in his pocket and removes a wad of bills.*]

PIG: Here. Here go five. You gonna have to get the rest somewhere else.

FRANCINE: Get it from your job!

LARRY: You don't wanna talk about no job.

FRANCINE: I got a job, thank you very much.

LARRY: You got two jobs.

FRANCINE: Shut up!

LARRY: Yeah, you don't wanna talk about that, do you?

[*He holds his hand out to* FRANCINE *as if asking to be paid off.*]

MARY: What?

FRANCINE: Nothin', he just actin' silly.

MARY: What are you talking about, Larry?

FRANCINE [*reaching into her bag*]: Here! Here go the other five, and you better pay me back!

MARY: What's going on with y'all?

LARRY [*looking at* FRANCINE *as he puts the money into his pocket*]: Nothin'.

PIG: All right, I got to go to work, we gonna have to start without her.

[*He sits down on the couch next to* LARRY.]

OK, who wants to go first?

MARY: We suppose to pray first.

PIG: Yeah, we can do that when Mama get here. Go ahead, Francine, what's goin on with you?

LARRY [*singing*]: "She's rockin' to the go-go beat!"

FRANCINE: Shut up, Larry! I ain't doin' too much. Just goin' to work every day.

PIG: That's it?

FRANCINE: Yeah, that's all.

PIG: Nothin' new goin' on at your gig?

FRANCINE: Like what?

PIG: I don't know, I'm askin' you.

FRANCINE [*sighs*]: Ah, let me see. Oh, people keep bringin' their Sprite back 'cause it don't taste right. They say it taste like Alka-Seltzer.

PIG: All right, Mary, what's goin' on with you?

MARY: We suppose to pray first!

PIG: Now why you got to go get all religious all the time? Huh? When the last time you been to church?

MARY: I go to church!

PIG: I ain't ask you did you go, I said when? And weddings don't count.

MARY: Look, Mama say we suppose to pray first. Why is that such a big problem?

PIG: You wanna pray? Then go ahead and pray.

MARY: You pray when Mama's here. What's wrong? What? You can't pray when she's not here?

PIG: I pray in her presence out of respect for her. All right?

MARY: You suppose to be prayin' to God. Not be doin' it for Mama's benefit.

PIG: You wanna pray? Then go ahead and pray. Ain't nobody stoppin' you.

[MARY *holds her hands out.* LARRY *and* FRANCINE *join hands with her and form a circle. They leave an opening for* PIG. *He reluctantly joins in.*]

MARY: Dear Lord. Thank you for letting us come together again as a family. Thank you for giving us the strength to carry on in our lives on a daily basis and still manage to keep a smile on our faces. Lord, please help us continue to try our best to do right and set a good example for others. In your precious name we ask of you, Lord, these things. Amen. [*Pause.*] All right, we may continue.

PIG: You know you just lied to God.

MARY: What are you talking about?

PIG: You just sat there and told the man 'bout some smile you s'pose to be havin' on your face.

FRANCINE: Why God got to be a man?

MARY: Can we continue?

PIG: It's on you . . . Sistah.

MARY: Well, I really don't have anything new to talk about since last week. Oh! I felt the baby kicking some more the other day. Just a little bit, though.

[FRANCINE *moves over near her and feels her stomach.*]

FRANCINE: Where?

LARRY: Ease up! It was the other day.

FRANCINE: Shut up! It ain't like she can't do it again.

LARRY: It ain't no she!

FRANCINE: She ain't no it!

LARRY: You gonna have a boy. Ain't that right, Mary?

MARY: I don't know.

PIG: All right. Anythin' else, Mary?

MARY: No, that's about it.

PIG: OK, brother man. You got the floor.

LARRY: Nuttin', nuttin' chillin', chillin', you know, tryin' to do my thing. I
think I'm gonna break up out of this mode I'm in, though.

PIG: Oh, yeah.

LARRY: Yeah, see I'm 'bout to embark into some new shit.

MARY: You wouldn't be cussin' if Mama was here.

PIG: Like what?

LARRY: Aight, check it out. You know how all these white boys be rollin' up
in the hood fixin' people's shit . . . stuff?

PIG: Yeah, contractors.

LARRY: Right, right, them Bob Villa type motherfuc—

[*He looks at* MARY.]

Anyway, check it out. I'ma roll up on 'em and be like, "Hey, my man,
check it out. I'ma be the eyes in the back of your head for you for a small
fee, so your ass don't get robbed while you up in here workin'."

MARY: How you gonna do that?

FRANCINE: Yeah, you can't be everywhere.

LARRY: Don't need to be; ain't no different than bein' a parkin' lot attendant.
'Sides, ain't nobody up tryin' to steal nothin' in the mornin'.

FRANCINE: You talkin' a bunch of nonsense! I got to go. Pig, can we finish?

LARRY: Forget y'all, then. Ain't y'all never watch *The Godfather*? Huh? The
Kennedys. How you think they all got started? People always think you
got to go to college and shit to get over.

PIG: All right man, you done?

LARRY: Yeah, I'm finish. Forget y'all. Jus' 'cause y'all brains is limited! I'ma do
what I got to do. Aight?

PIG: Well . . .

[REBECCA *enters through the door carrying a cloth bag.*]

REBECCA: Sorry I'm late.

FRANCINE: Mama, where you been?

REBECCA: What, you all started already?

PIG: Yeah, Ma, it's Saturday night. We got things to do.

MARY: You want us to start over?

PIG: Come on now, Mary! We ain't got time for all of that. Just 'cause you
ain't got nowhere to go. You can give her an overview or somethin' when
we done.

REBECCA: That won't be necessary. You all go ahead and finish. Who's up?

MARY: Hamster.

PIG: All right. I was just goin' to say that everything is goin' well with myself. I'm comin' up on two years now. God is good!

MARY: Oh, please.

PIG: Uh, and my little gig I got is workin' out real good.

REBECCA: What are you doing?

PIG: Whatcha mean?

REBECCA: What kinda gig are you doing?

PIG [*staring at his mother*]: Mama, you know what I'm doin'.

REBECCA: You mean that bathroom thing?

PIG: Yes, Mama, I'm still doin' the bathroom thing.

REBECCA: All right, I'm just asking. I didn't know whether you were still in there or not.

PIG: Anyway, everything's cool on that end. Some guy keep comin' up to me askin' me to come work at some new joint he openin' up in a couple of weeks.

LARRY: You gonna go?

PIG: I don't know. I'm makin' some good loot where I'm at. But I can hook you up. You wanna check it out?

LARRY: Naw, man, you ain't gonna have me up in there doin' that . . . stuff.

PIG: You can get paid!

LARRY: Man, I ain't tryin to get paid like that.

PIG: I'm talkin' 'bout four or five hundred a week.

LARRY: Man, what I look like standin' up in a bathroom smellin' people's farts and shit?

MARY: Larry!

LARRY: Well, that's what it is! I'm sorry, Mama, but ain't no other way to say it.

PIG: All right, whatever. Just don't be lookin' my way when you need some more funds.

FRANCINE: Where's this new club gonna be?

PIG: I ain't even ask him, he was all highed up anyway.

REBECCA: Does that bother you?

PIG: No.

LARRY: Shoot! You a better man than me. That be some hard stuff to handle.

PIG: I look at it like a big mirror. I see them fools, and I see how I once was.

Only difference, they got money to burn and more bank to bail 'em out. Goin' to rehab for them is like me goin' down to visit Grandma every summer.

LARRY: You a bad man, you a bad man.

PIG: All right, Mama, go ahead. Your turn.

REBECCA: Well.

LARRY: Come on, Mama, tell us about your new job.

MARY: You all are just breaking all the rules.

LARRY [*sighs*]: Aw, Mary, chill. We got a whole new regime goin' on up in here.

FRANCINE: Come on, Mom. 'Cause I got to get outta here.

REBECCA: Why are you in such a hurry? You don't work tonight? Do you?

LARRY: "Dancin, dancin', dancin'. She's a dancin' machine . . . all baby . . ."

FRANCINE: *Shut up!* I got somewhere to go, that's all.

REBECCA: All right, well I want to say that I'm glad that Mary's home and I'm looking forward to having a grandbaby, although I don't think I'm gonna like the idea of being called Grandma, but I'm sure I'll get use to it.

PIG: Mama, you already a grandma.

REBECCA: I haven't put my eyes on your boy since he was two. Now that was four years ago.

PIG: What you sayin? He don't count?

REBECCA: I'm saying you need to go and work things out so that we can all see him. Now that's all I'm gonna say about that.

LARRY: Daaaamn! Mama turnin' up the heat in the family meetin'!

PIG: *Shut up!*

REBECCA: All right, you all settle down.

FRANCINE: Are we done?

REBECCA: Yes.

[FRANCINE *gets up and grabs her bag.*]

FRANCINE: Good, it's about time.

[*She heads toward the door.*]

MARY: Wait a minute! We suppose to close with a prayer.

LARRY: Mary, we done changed all that up.

MARY: Well, we need to change it back!

FRANCINE: Pray for me. I gotta go.

[*She exits out the door.*]

LARRY: Me too. Later.

[*He exits out the door.*]

MARY: Mother?

REBECCA: Mary, it hasn't been easy since you've been gone.

[MARY *looks at her mother and then at* PIG *and quickly exits into her room.*]

PIG [*sarcastically*]: Mother Teresa has returned.

REBECCA: She means well.

PIG: Yeah, look, Ma. I'ma hafta roll, too.

REBECCA: I wish you would talk to Larry again about that job.

PIG: It ain't the right kinda thing for him.

REBECCA: Why not? You do it.

PIG: Mama, the boy ghetto. He ain't gonna last one day in there 'round all them white folks, drunk ones at that.

REBECCA: He's not "ghetto."

PIG: Mama, he from round here. All right? [*Pause.*] It's ghetto in a good way. I ain't puttin' him down. I'm jus' sayin' is, he ain't gonna be able to . . . you know . . .

REBECCA: What? Adapt?

PIG: Well, yeah. You know, he got to be able to know what he there for. That's all. Which is to make money and nothin' else. He get up in there and see the way they be actin' and listenin' to the music they be playin' and to some of the stuff they be sayin'. Shoooot, he gonna wind up beatin' somebody's ass! He ain't too far off from bein' his daddy's roommate, you know.

REBECCA: Well if it's that bad, then maybe you shouldn't be in there either.

PIG: Naw, I got my emotions under control. I'm there for the loot and the loot only. I don't care how they act or what they say. Just as long as don't nobody touch me.

REBECCA: You stayin' for dinner?

PIG: Naw, I got a meetin' tonight. But maybe I'll come back through later on after work. Save me sometin'.

REBECCA: What happens in those meetings?

PIG: Nothin' too much. They just wanna make sure you stayin' clean, that's all.

REBECCA: But what do you all talk about?

PIG: All they just talk about whatever's goin' on in their world.

REBECCA: You mean like our family meetings?

PIG: Sort of, but half these cats, [*sighs*] they s'til gettin' high. They just goin' through the motions, that's all.

REBECCA: Don't you all get tested?

PIG: Not there. It's just like a roll call, that's all.

REBECCA: Well, you hang in there. You do your best.

PIG: Like they say, Mama. You take it one day at a time. I know I made some mistakes, and I know I'ma always have this in me. I ain't never gonna really be totally cured of it.

REBECCA: How you know?

PIG: What?

REBECCA: How do you know?

PIG: 'Cause . . .

REBECCA: What? Because that's what they're telling you in those meetings?

PIG: Yeah, it's part of the process.

REBECCA: Well they wrong! You hear me? [*Pause.*] You hear? They wrong!

[*Pause a beat.*]

Come here.

[*She hugs him.*]

You can overcome anything you see fit. But it's got to come from you. Deep inside you there's a strength that can't nobody gauge. You use that strength. You make fools out of all those so-called specialists. You're special. You hear?

PIG: I hear you, Mama.

[*Lights fade.*]

SCENE 3

[*Several weeks later. The lights come up in the living room. Rap music is playing on the radio.* LARRY *is asleep on the sofa. After several moments, the phone rings. After the fourth ring,* MARY *emerges from the hall, stage left. She has a towel wrapped around her head and is wearing a housecoat. She doesn't notice* LARRY *as she turns the radio off and answers the phone.*]

MARY: Hello? [*Pause.*] Pig? [*Pause.*] What? [*Pause.*] No, I haven't seen him. [*Pause.*] All right. [*Pause.*] Yes, if I see him. [*Pause.*] OK. [*Pause.*] Bye.

[*She hangs up and walks over to the chair and sits. As she picks up the remote, she notices* LARRY.]

Larry. *Larry!*
LARRY [*startled*]: What?
MARY: Pig just called for you.
LARRY: Oh, yeah, what he want?
MARY: He said you're suppose to be working tonight.
LARRY: Aw, damn!

[*He sits up.*]

What time is it?
MARY: It's almost eleven.
LARRY: Shoot!

[*He gets up.*]

MARY: What time were you suppose to be there?
LARRY: It don't matter, I'm late.

[*Pauses a beat.*]

What Pig say?
MARY: He just said they were looking for you. You still going?
LARRY [*cranky*]: Yeeeahh, I'm s'til goin'! They just wanna get me in there early so they can have me clean up from the night before. They think they slick. They tryin' to get me to do janitor duty too. And I know this little white boy . . . this, this bar back s'pose to be doin' it. The first couple of nights he was in there sweepin' his ass off. Soon as I rolled up on the scene, he kinda eased up a little. They don't start tippin' 'til after they get a few drinks up in 'em anyway. Round about midnight they just be goin' hog wild. Shoot, I made a buck and a quarter last night. Now I see what Pig was talkin' 'bout. Cats come in there wanna get their high on in the back stall, they just slide me a fin and I ain't seen nothin'. Security guard roll in, I just bump into the light switch . . . by accident.

[*He laughs.*]

Shoot . . . hum, I don't see how that don't affect Pig. If he call again, tell him to tell them I'm on my way.

[*He gives her a hug.*]

Later.

MARY: You be careful.

LARRY [*exiting out the door*]: For sure.

[MARY *turns on the TV with the remote. After channel surfing for several minutes, she turns off the TV. She then gets up and turns on the radio. After a few seconds she puts a CD in the player and listens to the same song that she and* FRANCINE *listened to before. She goes behind the couch and attempts to try the dance that* FRANCINE *was teaching her.*]

MARY [*stepping to the beat of the music*]: Step to the right . . . Step to the left . . . Jump back! Jump back! Spin, spin, y'all!

[*The movement starts to get good to her.*]

Aw, yeah now!

[*She claps as she continues to dance.*]

I still got it! Step . . . Step . . .

[*She continues to go through the motions. She starts to get a little dizzy as she inches closer and closer to the door.*]

Jump back! Jump ba—

[FRANCINE *bursts through the door, almost knocking* MARY *down. She doesn't notice* MARY. *She slams her bag down and walks about furiously.*]

[*Turning the music off*]: Whoa! Whoa! Whoa! Settle down. What has gotten in to you?

FRANCINE: I can't believe it!

MARY: What?

FRANCINE: Mama. She, she . . .

MARY: What's wrong with Mama?

FRANCINE: She's crazy!

MARY: What are you talking about?

FRANCINE: She embarrassed me.

[MARY *sits down into her chair.*]

MARY: Well, what did she do?

FRANCINE: She comes down to my job.

MARY: Come on now, she doesn't even like fast food.

FRANCINE: Noooo! To the Poodle.

MARY: The who?

FRANCINE: The Pink Poodle. [*Pause.*] My other job.

MARY: What, are you groomin' dogs now?

FRANCINE: Somethin' like that.

MARY: Well, what happened?

[FRANCINE *plops down onto the couch.*]

FRANCINE: She ruined my job. I can't ever go back there again!

MARY: I'm sure it will be OK; she was probably just checking up on you, that's all.

FRANCINE: I'm ruined. She chased all of my clients away.

MARY: She never did like dogs.

FRANCINE: She ain't seem to have no problem with these ones.

MARY: Where is she?

[*We hear* REBECCA *singing outside the door. She enters, singing, wearing a black trench coat.*]

REBECCA [*singing*]: "Baby, baby, baby . . . Hey, hey, hey
    You can,
    Rub me baby

[*She reaches into her pocket and pulls out a wad of bills.*]

    "But you, you better pay your way
    You can
    fall in love with me baby

    "But you better,
    you better pay your way!

    "Baby, baby, baby . . . Hey, hey . . ."

MARY: Mama, what are you doing?

REBECCA: Coming from work. I got myself a new job.

MARY: I heard. At the doggy place?

REBECCA: Yeah, Francine told you, huh? It's an exciting place. They've got plenty of good music. Here, look! Check out my uniform.

[*She opens her coat to reveal a tight-fitting pink-and-white kitty cat outfit.*]

MARY: Mama! You shouldn't have went in there dressed like that! No wonder you chased all those little doggies away.

[REBECCA *takes off her coat, places it on a chair, and removes money from its pockets.*]

REBECCA: Actually, they came runnin' toward me. Had dollar bills in their mouths and was tryin' to stick 'em everywhere.

[FRANCINE *rises.*]

FRANCINE: You know somethin'? You're crazy! *I hate what you did tonight!*

[*She storms offstage right to her bedroom.*]

REBECCA: Fran—

[*She starts to go after* FRANCINE *but stops herself.*]

MARY: Why is she so upset? [*Pause.*] What did you do down there at her new job?

REBECCA: Baby, your sister's barely eighteen years old, and she's over there on Delaware Avenue in some dark hole in the wall, dancing on bar tops and sliding up and down poles.

MARY: Get out of here! Are you serious? Little Francine? I don't believe that.

REBECCA: Believe it.

MARY: And that's . . . where you were at?

REBECCA [*pulling her tail off*]: Uh-huh.

MARY [*slowly comprehending the big revelation*]: Oooohhhhhh.

[*She exhales forcefully.*]

And you . . .

REBECCA: Yes.

MARY: Mama, no, you didn't!

REBECCA: I sure did, look!

[*She takes all of the money out of her pockets and her bra.*]

I made more money in one night than I make cleaning for a week.

MARY [*growing more and more uncomfortable*]: Mama, what are you trying to prove?

REBECCA: I run out of ways of trying to get through to her.

[*She takes off her cat ears.*]

I knew what she was up to. So I had to. I had to do what I had to do.

MARY: Yeah. [*Pause.*] I guess you're right. It seemed to work. [*Pause.*] Mother, look, I didn't want to come all the way back here and tie up the house and everything, but . . .

REBECCA: It's OK, baby. You know you're always welcomed here. Everything's gonna be OK. As soon as the baby comes, you'll see. Roy will show up and everything will be back to normal for you all.

[MARY *slowly rocks back and forth, silently crying.*]

Oh, baby, it's not that bad. Roy seems to be a nice man. I know what you say happened and all. But you might have to put all that behind you for the time bein'. At least for this child's sake. He'll show up, you'll see. And when he does, then maybe, maybe you ought to give him another chance. Men, even the good ones, need a second chance at some point in their life. And a good man always takes care of his children.

MARY [*shaking her head, in a whisper*]: Mama, you don't understand. [*Pause.*] I don't think . . .

REBECCA: He will! You'll see. One day you'll look around—

MARY: No! You don't understand.

REBECCA: What? What's wrong?

[*Pause of several beats.*]

MARY: I don't think this is his baby.

REBECCA: What?

MARY: Oh, Mama! I made a big mistake. A really big mistake.

REBECCA: Honey, what are you talking about? What did you do?

MARY: I know. I know he was messin' around on me.

REBECCA: I know, baby, you told me. But . . .

MARY: No! I mean I know I told you, but I thought, I really thought he was.

REBECCA: You mean you never really saw him like you told me.

MARY: No, it just seemed like he really was. I seen them out together. Havin' drinks.

REBECCA: What did you do, Mary? Whose baby is it?

[MARY *stares at her mother, unable to speak.*]

Mary. [*Pause.*] Mary, what did you do?

MARY: *Uhhh!*

REBECCA: Baby?

MARY [*holding her stomach*]: Ohhhh!

REBECCA [*comforting her*]: Hold on, Baby. *Francine!* Hold on, I'ma take you to the hospital. You think you can walk down the steps?

MARY: I, I, I don't know. Ahhhh!

REBECCA: *Francine!*

[FRANCINE *emerges from the hall stage right with earphones around her neck.*]

FRANCINE: What? Is the baby comin'?

REBECCA: I think so. Get her coat!

[FRANCINE *gets* MARY's *coat.* REBECCA *helps* MARY *to her feet. They all exit.* REBECCA *quickly returns and puts her overcoat back on and then exits out the door again. Lights fade.*]

SCENE 4

[*Lights come up in the living room.* FRANCINE *sits in the chair stage right listening to music on her headphones. There is some commotion out in the hallway.*]

LARRY [*offstage from behind the front door*]: Come on, man, watch, *come on, man, come on! Watch what you doin'!*

[*The door swings open and* PIG *enters, walking backward and carrying one end of a large box containing a color TV, followed by* LARRY *carrying the other end of the box.*]

Come on, man! I paid top dollar for this. Watch how you be bumpin' it.

PIG: Look! We already in here, all right. You better ease up with all that roughneck shit. I ain't none of your damn mule.

LARRY: All right, sit it down right over there next to the other one. 'Cine. *Francine!*

[FRANCINE *takes off her headphones.*]

FRANCINE: What?

LARRY: Move all that shit off the top of the TV and unplug it.

[FRANCINE *gets up and does so.*]

Yeah, wait 'til Mommy see this shit up in here. What time she gonna be back?

FRANCINE: I don't know. She's down at the hospital checkin' on Mary.

PIG: How much you pay for this?

LARRY: Big loot, baby, big loot.

PIG: How much?

LARRY [*moving the old TV from its stand*]: Six hunerd and forty-nine dollars.

PIG: Damn.

LARRY: And, I got the extended warranty.

[*He stops and sets the old TV down on the couch and reaches in his pocket and pulls out some papers.*]

'Cine, here, fill this out and mail it back in for me. Here, man, take that and put it back in Mommy's room. I'ma hook it up in there for her later.

[PIG *exits with the old TV stage left.*]

FRANCINE [*looking down at the box*]: What, it got the VCR already in it?

LARRY: Hell, yeah! Built right in.

[*He opens the box.*]

This is some new shit here. They even had the ones with the DVDs in 'em, but all Mama got is a bunch of tapes. Plus it was like another hunerd dollars.

PIG [*returning*]: You cleanin' up in that new joint, huh?

LARRY: Oh yeeeeeah.

[*He extends his hand for some dap.**]

Thanks for the hookup. Come on, help me pull this outta here.

[*They remove the new TV and place it on the stand.*]

A lot of cats be comin' in there tellin' me they know you.

PIG: Yeah, everybody wanna check out the new spot. [*Pause.*] Business at our joint done slowed down a bit.

LARRY: We packed! [*He laughs.*] They be turnin' folks away at the door. Cats be in there four or five deep waitin' to piss. Even be women tryin' to sneak up in there.

---

*"Dap" refers to touching fists together.

PIG: Yeah, they try that. You got to watch that.

LARRY [*hooking up the TV*]: Man, it ain't nuttin' but some liquid goin' down a hole. I don't care whose it is.

PIG: Naw, naw, you got to watch them comin' in there. I'm tellin' you. They could shut the place down.

LARRY: Man, ain't nobody shuttin' nuttin' down. They gettin' paid. We gettin' paid! Everybody! Cops too. Shoot, they talk about how we be actin' up. Man, them folks is a damn trip. They be doin' shit like twistin' each other's nipples.

[*They laugh.*]

'Cine, I'm talkin' 'bout two guys. They just walk up to each other and—

[*He reaches out and attempts to show* PIG. PIG *steps back.*]

PIG: I know, I seen them too.

LARRY: One guy gave me five dollars . . . for a breath mint.

[*He laughs as he continues.*]

Five motherfuckin' dollars for one tiny-ass little breath mint.

FRANCINE: Damn!

PIG: All right, y'all, I'm gone. I'll see you in a minute.

LARRY: Thanks, man.

PIG: No problem. You let Mama know I helped you bring that in here.

LARRY: All right, all right, all right.

[PIG *exits.* LARRY *mimics* PIG *as he turns toward the new TV.*]

You hear him? "Let Mama know I was involved."

[*He turns back and looks at the TV.*]

That's bad as hell, ain't it?

FRANCINE: Yeah, it's nice.

LARRY [*hooking up the cable box*]: You want me to try to hook you up as a backup in the ladies' room? The girl they got ain't even show up Thursday. That's our slowest night. I don't even wanna go in, but it all adds up. You want me to say somethin' to 'em?

FRANCINE: No. Thanks to you, I don't work for tips no more. Matter of fact, I don't work, period!

LARRY: What? I ain't said shit to nobody 'bout you. Why you grittin' on me?

FRANCINE: Why you try to be all funny all the time?

LARRY: What?

FRANCINE: You know what I'm talkin' about. Messin' with me about what I do in front of everybody.

LARRY [*laughing*]: Aw, I ain't say nuttin'.

FRANCINE: You the one that told Mommy, ain't you?

LARRY: I . . .

FRANCINE: You want me to tell her you be sellin' weed?

LARRY: If you want to, go ahead. [*Pause.*] I don't sell it nomore anyway. What'n no money in it. You wanna make some real loot, you gotta sell some other shit. It's one thing for somebody to roll up on you for some herb, but them crackhead clients jus' . . . They just fucked up. They embarrass a brother. Naw, I ain't about to go to jail. If I end up in there, it's gonna be for some real shit. [*Pause.*] Hey, when you gonna break down and go see Daddy?

FRANCINE: I'll see him when he gets out.

LARRY: Why you gotta be so damn cold? That's your old man sittin' down there.

FRANCINE: He's stupid!

LARRY: All right, look, I ain't gonna argue with that. He did some dumb shit, but you shouldn't leave him hangin' like that.

FRANCINE: He the one that left us hangin'! You know how much shit I had to go through in school? I had to listen to that jailbird stuff all the time. Couldn't look forward to him bein' there for nothin'. And look at what he did to Mommy. She ain't been nowhere since he's been gone. All she do is go to work and come home and go back to work. Yeah, we survivin' without him, but at what cost? Huh?

LARRY: All right, look. I feel you. I know exactly what you talkin' about. But this is just the way things is with us. We can't change none of the shit that happened with him. But it ain't gonna hurt none to go down there and see him. You ain't got to worry about him talkin' about what happened. He ain't gonna say nothin' about it unless you ask him. Now, I'ma go back in a few weeks. I want you to go with me. [*Pause.*] Francine, look, he ask me to bring you.

FRANCINE: He did?

LARRY: Yes!

FRANCINE: You lyin'!

LARRY: No, I ain't either, he did. He say he miss you and he wanna see you.

FRANCINE [*sighs*]: Well, then why ain't you tell me that before?

LARRY: 'Cause we jus now talkin' 'bout it! I mean what difference do it make anyway? Either you gonna go or you ain't.

FRANCINE: I ain't goin'.

LARRY: Fine, if that's the way you wanna be. Your loss.

FRANCINE: I already got use to that.

LARRY: So that how it's gonna be. You just gonna keep on bein' mad at him? [*Pause.*] Go on, then! Go on and keep it inside you. I guess that's the kind of mind you got to have to be up there allowin' them greasy niggahs to look at your body anyway. Tell me somethin', what you be thinkin' when you up there doin' that shit, huh?

FRANCINE: I don't be thinkin' 'bout nothin'!

LARRY: Oh, you thinkin' about somthin'. You ain't no airhead.

FRANCINE: You really wanna know what I think? I'm thinkin' "Why the hell is this world so fucked up?" That's what I'm thinkin'. Twenty-four seven. I'm thinkin' "Why I got to be doin' this shit?" "Why is shit so hard for us? Why ain't we got a nice big house with a yard and a garden? A dog, and not no fuckin' pit bull either! A regular dog. Huh? Why ain't we college-bound? How come there ain't no college money saved up and set aside for us? Why ain't we got a role model in our own family to look up to? Huh? And why? Why does everything always got to be a damn dream for us?" That's what the hell I'm thinkin'!

LARRY: Damn. Ask a simple question.

FRANCINE: Ain't nothin' simple 'bout my life. Ain't no fairy tales goin' on round here.

[*She pauses a beat.*]

You right. I wish Noah woulda been our father; at least Pig and Mary can have good thoughts about him and how things use to be. The trips they use to all go on. They would just jump in the car and go. They use to go out to the country and have outings and stuff. Mary say they just use to stay out there all day. She go out and gather a bunch of flowers and Pig would go fishin'.

[*He laughs.*]

She told me one time she came back from a long walk in the woods and she saw Mama and Noah layin' on the blanket . . . kissin' . . . We ain't never done or seen nothin' like that.

LARRY: 'Cine, we city folks. I mean, I been fishin' before. And shoot, if you wanna go get some flowers, [*pointing*] Mrs. Giles right there over on Clayborne got a whole bunch in her backyard.

FRANCINE [*sighs*]: That ain't what I'm talkin' about. They had a family. A real . . . live . . . family. Noah made it that way.

LARRY: Yeah, but he dead now. All they got is memories.

FRANCINE: Well, as far as I'm concerned, Lloyd is dead too.

LARRY: You need to quit sayin' that type of shit!

FRANCINE: Well, he might as well be. He ain't never gittin' out! He can't do nothin' for us in there.

LARRY: Then maybe it's our turn to do somethin' for him.

FRANCINE: What can we possibly do for him?

LARRY: If he was sick and in the hospital, wouldn't you go see him?

FRANCINE: Yeah, I guess.

LARRY: Well, then, what's the difference?

FRANCINE: The difference? He ain't sick, and he ain't in no hospital! He in jail.

LARRY: You're right. He's not in the hospital, but he had to be sick to do what he did in the first place. Now I know you don't wanna know nothin' about it, but he needs you right now, 'Cine. He really do. [*Pause.*] So you think about maybe goin' with me next time. All right?

FRANCINE: All right, I'll think about it.

LARRY: Good. It would mean a whole lot to him. Make you feel better, too. I felt the same way at first. But I ain't had no regrets since. Look, I'll be back later on. If Mama get home before me, don't say nothin' to her about the TV. Let her see it on her own.

FRANCINE: All right.

LARRY: Later.

[LARRY *exits out the door.* FRANCINE *turns on the TV and plops back down into the chair. After channel surfing for a bit, she turns it off and resumes listening to her music. After several more moments,* REBECCA *enters through the door.*]

REBECCA: Where was Larry running off to?

[FRANCINE *does not hear or see her.*]

Francine!

[FRANCINE *takes off her headphones.*]

FRANCINE: Yes?

REBECCA: I was wondering what Larry was up to. I just saw him heading down Eldridge.

FRANCINE: I don't know.

REBECCA: Was he just here?

FRANCINE: I don't know . . . I guess so.

REBECCA: You guess?

[*She laughs.*]

You sure are deep into that music.

[REBECCA *goes into the kitchen.*]

I stopped by and checked on Mary.

FRANCINE: Yeah. I talked to her on the phone today.

REBECCA: Well, she looks fine. They gonna check her fluid tomorrow, see if the baby's lungs are ready. If everything's OK, then they're thinking about maybe going ahead and inducing labor on Monday.

FRANCINE: Yeah, she told me already. She said she didn't want to do that.

REBECCA: Oh, so you did talk to her. You need to go on down there and spend some time with her. She could use the company.

FRANCINE: You know you didn't have to come down there and do what you did. When you found out, you shoulda just said somethin' to me. Not come down there like that.

REBECCA: Well . . .

FRANCINE: I can't do nothin'. I don't even wanna go out the house no more. Everybody knows! People was even comin' through the drive-through talkin' 'bout "How's your Mama doin'?"

[REBECCA *sits at the kitchen table.*]

REBECCA: Is that why you quit?

[FRANCINE *gets up and storms into the kitchen.*]

FRANCINE: *Yes*, it's why I quit! Ain't nothin' right with this family! Them meetings we have, they ain't nothin' but a joke.

REBECCA: How would you like things to be?

FRANCINE: I wish things was normal. I wish we were normal.

REBECCA: Well, what is normal to you?

[FRANCINE sits *down at the kitchen table with her arms crossed.*]

FRANCINE: I don't even know. [*Pause.*] I mean, either people at school was lyin' about the stuff they do at home, or we jus', we just messed up. That was the only thing I could talk about. Our meetings. But I had to always add stuff to it. Talk about things that never really took place. But everybody know about Daddy, and everybody know about Pig, and Larry, and Mary, and . . . Look, Mom, I'm just tired of it. Our family is screwed up! I was down there doin' that 'cause . . . because . . .

REBECCA: Because you wanted to feel special?

FRANCINE: *Yes!* I was special. People came in there just to see me.

REBECCA: Is that what you want to do for the rest of your life?

FRANCINE: Do you plan on cleanin' for the rest of your life?

REBECCA: No, Francine, I don't! But you're not raising any kids, and you didn't nurse a dying man or have one taken away from you. I'm cleaning because at the time that was all I could handle. That was all I was prepared to do. You don't have to be down there shaking your stuff. You're special to me, and if I have to hand you dollar bills every time I tell you, then so be it.

[*Pause of several beats.*]

FRANCINE: What happen with Daddy?

REBECCA: What?

FRANCINE: What did he do?

REBECCA: Why are you all of a sudden interested in that?

FRANCINE: I wanna know.

REBECCA [*sighs*]: Well, it's a long story. How much of it do you already know?

FRANCINE: Somebody said he shot a police officer while he was robbin' a bank. Aunt Alicia say he climbed the Essex building butt naked, and then Pig come tell me he stole a police car and rode down Fifth Avenue through some kind of a parade with the lights flashin'.

REBECCA [*matter-of-factly*]: It was all of that.

FRANCINE: What? You jokin'?

REBECCA: 'Cept for the shootin' the cop bit. Don't nobody really know for sure what happened with that. Your daddy and a friend of his, Lester Smalls, they had themselves a little ritual that they did every year on Veterans Day, where they stayed up all night drinking and getting high in remembrance of their friends that they lost in Vietnam. Well, in the morning, they decided to take their little party downtown. Figured that America still owed them something. Lester knew a woman that worked at the Great American Federal Bank. Well, somehow he convinced her to give him extra money whenever he got in her line. Well, this day the security guard took notice to him and told the manager and he stood back there and watched this girl like a hawk. When she didn't give Lester what he wanted, he flipped out, pulled out a gun, and aimed it at the security guard.

FRANCINE: Well, what was Daddy doin'?

REBECCA: He was standin' by the front door. Anyway, the manager stuffed two bags full of money and opened the door and threw them out on the floor. He musta pushed the alarm button 'cause they could hear police sirens. Lester grabbed the money, and the two of them went out the back door. The police showed up and drove around the back. Now ain't nobody see what really happened back there, but one of the policemen got killed, and so did Lester. The other police, he got shot. He said that Lloyd shot him and his partner. They never found no gun. But they pinned everything on Lloyd. The people in the bank even say it was Lester that had the gun.

FRANCINE: What about this naked stuff?

REBECCA [*laughs*]: Well, you know they got them dye packs they put in there with the money?

MARY: Yeah.

REBECCA: Well, according to your father, he never had no gun. Lester shot the one police and killed him and the other one shot Lester, and Lester shot him back. Then he said Lester crawled over and started choking him and died right there on top of him. Your daddy thought they were both dead. That's when he got into the police car and took off. With all the confusion, he couldn't figure out how to turn off the lights, so he just drove off, lights flashing and everything. Now being that it had rained the day before, they had moved the Veterans Day parade back a day and it was going on at that very moment. People was busy getting out of his way 'cause they think either it's a police emergency or he's part of the parade. He rode by all of those vets standing there with their medals on, and he started crying. He said he couldn't stop crying. He thought that if he gave the money to these vets, then everything would be all right. So he stopped the car and opened one of the bags and reached into it and grabbed a handful of money and threw it out at them. He reached in again and threw out some more, and just when he went to grab another handful, one of those dye packs they put in there exploded all over him. Now he don't know what to do. People started to crowd around him, he slammed the door shut and took off. He gets to the end of the street and gets out and runs into the Essex building with the other bag of money and takes the elevator up to the top floor. All along the way he's busy taking off his clothes on account of they got all this red dye on 'em. When he gets to the roof, he runs out to the ledge and he gets up on it, and by this time he ain't got no clothes on at all. He opened up that last bag and dumped all that money down to them vets below.

FRANCINE: Daaaag!

REBECCA: Yeah, he was a trip.

FRANCINE [*sighs*]: We don't know if that's really what happened.

REBECCA: He's the one that told me.

[*Pause of several beats.* REBECCA *gets up and walks into the living room and notices the new television.*]

Where this TV come from?

[FRANCINE *gets up and stands in the doorway between the kitchen and the living room.*]

FRANCINE: It's a gift from Larry. He and Pig just brought it in here.

REBECCA: Where'd he get it from?

FRANCINE: He said he bought it.

REBECCA: He did? You seen a receipt?

FRANCINE [*walking back to the chair where she laid it down*]: Actually, yeah, here.

[REBECCA *looks over the receipt.*]

He wanted me to send in this registration card too.

REBECCA [*sighs*]: Where he get that much money from?

FRANCINE: From his new job, I guess.

REBECCA: I don't like this.

FRANCINE: What's wrong? It's nice. It's a gift. Look, it even has a built in VCR.

REBECCA: I'm talking about your brother. I'm worried about him.

FRANCINE: Why? He's workin', makin' honest money. That's what you wanted him to do.

REBECCA: Yeah, but he scares me when he does things like this.

[REBECCA *turns toward* FRANCINE.]

    I wanna ask you something.
FRANCINE: What is it, Mama?
REBECCA: Is your brother still selling?

[FRANCINE *takes a deep breath.*]

FRANCINE: Why would you ask me that?
REBECCA: 'Cause if he is, you would know.
FRANCINE: I don't smoke none of that stuff!
REBECCA: What stuff?
FRANCINE: Reefer, herb.
REBECCA: Is that all he sells?
FRANCINE: Look, Mama, he said he don't mess with that stuff no more.
REBECCA: "Mess with" it? What, was he using it, too?
FRANCINE: No, Mama! Look, I don't think so. I mean, he was just sellin' it to make some extra money. But he say he don't do it no more.
REBECCA: I see.
FRANCINE: You gonna say something to him?
REBECCA: Why? You don't want me to?
FRANCINE: I don't want you sayin' nothin' about me, 'cause I ain't volunteer nothin' to you 'bout him, you ask me.
REBECCA: Is that what really worries you? Who told who? Huh? What about "Let's keep him out of jail." If I had that opportunity, I'd choose it a thousand times over whether I snitched on somebody or, or hurt their little feelings. Especially my own brother. Child, you need to wake up! I done lost too many men in this family! And I'll be damned if I'ma lose another one over some little secret! Your sister down there right now won't let them do what they need to, 'bout to lose her mind and possibly her child over some nonsense. Now you tell me what you know 'bout Larry right now and where the *hell he got the money for this damn TV*!

[*Lights fade.*]

ACT 2

SCENE 1

[The lights come up on MARY. *She stands looking out of her hospital window. She gently rubs her stomach.]*

MARY: What are you?

[She laughs.]

Everybody wants to know what you're gonna be. *[Pause.]* I'm scared. You hear that?

[She laughs nervously.]

Your mama's scared. *[Pause.]* What do you think about that?

*[*FRANCINE *enters.]*

FRANCINE: I think you need to crawl back up into that bed.
MARY *[turning around at the sound of* FRANCINE'*s voice]*: Hey.
FRANCINE: What are you doin' up on your feet?
MARY: Just looking out the window.
FRANCINE: Ain't nothin' out there worth lookin' at. Come on and get back in the bed. You ain't missin' nothin'.
MARY: How you doin'?

[They embrace.]

FRANCINE: I'm all right.
MARY: I tell you, it's like being on detention in here.
FRANCINE: I hear you.
MARY: So, what do you plan on doing now? Mama tells me you quit your job. The Taco Bell one.
FRANCINE: I don't know. I'm thinkin' about maybe takin' some classes.
MARY: Oh, yeah? In what?
FRANCINE: I don't know. I might go to the beauty academy.
MARY: Ooooll, that would be nice.

[She touches her own hair.]

You think you could do something with this?

FRANCINE: Shoot, I ain't learned nothin' yet.

MARY: I mean when you get in there.

FRANCINE: Yeah, you know I'ma hook you up.

MARY: Em, I need to sit down.

[*She makes her way to the chair.*]

FRANCINE: Come on, let me help you in the bed.

MARY: Em, em. Every time I lay down seem like the baby wanna slide out.

FRANCINE [*helping her sit*]: Maybe that's what you need to do so you can get out of here.

[*Pause a beat.*]

What's all this talk about you losin' your mind?

MARY: Mama said that?

FRANCINE: Yeah. Real serious-like.

MARY: Oh. It ain't nothin'. Just tired of bein' all cooped up.

FRANCINE: She said you won't let them do what they need to do. What's up with that?

MARY: Did you come on your own to see me? Or did she send you down here?

FRANCINE: She ain't send me nowhere. I just wanna know what she meant, that's all. You don't wanna let me in on your little secret, that's fine. [*Pause.*] I'm use to secrets.

[*She laughs.*]

We keep havin' these glorified family meetings to discuss our problems and then we go right back to our secret little lives. If you don't wanna share your problems with me, then that's fine. It ain't a problem.

MARY: It's nothing that I really want to talk about right now.

FRANCINE: All right. [*Pause.*] When I came in here, I heard you say somethin' about bein' scared. You wanna talk about that?

MARY: No.

FRANCINE: All right. [*Suddenly upbeat*] Hey. Tell me somethin' about Noah.

MARY: What do you wanna know?

FRANCINE: I don't know. Anything. Somethin' about y'all. [*Pause.*] Just the two of you. Somethin' that you all did that was special.

MARY: Hum. We did a lot of things, mostly family. Everybody.

FRANCINE: But didn't he spend some time with you? Take you anywhere?

[MARY *smiles*.]

What?

MARY [*laughs*]: Nothing.

FRANCINE: No, come on, tell me.

MARY: He use to help me with my homework. My math.

FRANCINE: No, I wanna hear about y'all goin' to the park or somethin'. Layin' out on the grass late at night lookin' up at the stars.

MARY: Never anything like that.

FRANCINE: All right. Go ahead and tell me your math story.

MARY: When I was about seven or eight, I was in the second grade and I use to make my nines like this.

[*She demonstrates, gesturing in the air.*]

The first time he saw me do that, he smacked me on the back of my head [*demonstrating*], *pap!* Just like that. He wanted me to make my loop the other way.

[*She laughs.*]

Said I was doing it backwards.

FRANCINE: What's special about gettin' whacked upside your head?

MARY: When he died, I was numb. And what bothered me the most was that I never thought that I would ever laugh again or to even be able to smile. And then one day, about two months after he passed, I was writing out a check and when I made my nine, the right way . . . a smile came over my face. I felt that little thud on the back of my head all over again. I walked around beaming all day with the biggest smile stuck on my face.

[FRANCINE *smiles*.]

We never did much, just the two of us. We could have, but it was always all of us together.

[*She laughs.*]

Ham use to stay so close to him. He adored him. When he died, I think a part of Ham died too. He was never the same. He shut down. Just drifted off into his own world. [*Pause.*] You miss your father?

FRANCINE: Yes.

MARY: He's still alive.

FRANCINE: I know. I'm thinkin' about goin' to see him.

MARY: You should. He's not a bad man. He just made some bad choices.

FRANCINE: I just wish he could have been here while we was growin' up.

MARY: There ain't nothing wrong with the way you were raised. Nothin' to be ashamed about. Mama always did her best. You can't keep beating yourself up about what you didn't have. You think he's not hurtin'? You think it doesn't pain him that he couldn't be there for you? Francine, you two need each other. You're punishing him by trying to block him out. [*Pause.*] And you're punishing yourself in the process.

[*Pause of several beats.*]

FRANCINE [*teary-eyed*]: I'ma go.

[*She starts to exit.*]

MARY: OK. [*Pause.*] Hey! Thanks for the visit.

[FRANCINE *nods and exits.*]

I'm going to love you, little child of mine. [*Pause.*] No matter what happens.

[*The lights fade.*]

SCENE 2

[*The lights come up to a darkened living room and kitchen.* REBECCA *sits in the living room chair staring straight ahead.* LARRY *enters through the front door and turns on the light. We can now see that the TV is missing as well as the stereo.*]

LARRY: Mom? [*Pause.*] Mom?

REBECCA: [*Pause.*] Huh?

LARRY [*moving closer*]: Mama, is you all right?

REBECCA: Yeah, I'm fine.

LARRY: What's goin' on with Mary?

REBECCA: I don't know.

LARRY: You don't know?

REBECCA: I don't know.

[LARRY *sits down on the couch across from her.*]

LARRY: Mom, what is wrong wit you?

[*He picks up the remote and aims it at nothing.*]

You actin' all weird. [*Pause.*] Where the hell the TV at?

[*He stands up.*]

    Pig! He back to his old ways again?

[*He starts toward the door.*]

    And where the ster—?

[*He sighs.*]

    Mom, he been back up in here with that—

[PIG *enters.*]

    Man, where is our shit at?
PIG: What shit you talkin' about?
LARRY: The shit you took up out of here!
PIG: I don't know what the hell you talkin' about.
LARRY: OK, yeah, all right.

[*He sighs.*]

PIG: Look, man, I said I don't know what you talkin' about.
LARRY: *Look around, man, look around!* You see somethin' different about
    what's goin' on up in here?
PIG [*staring right at him*]: Why don't you just tell me?
LARRY: The motherfuckin' TV, all right? *And the stereo!* Where that shit at,
    huh?
PIG: Why don't you ease up with all the cussin' round Mama, all right?
LARRY: Oh, so now you with that *Seven Hunerd Club* shit too?

[PIG *grabs* LARRY *up.*]

    Get off me! Get off me! Get the hell off me!

[PIG *throws him down to the ground.* REBECCA *rises from her chair.*]

PIG [*leaning down with his hand around* LARRY's *throat*]: I told you I ain't know
    nothin' 'bout what happen to the stuff that was in here. Now you need to
    ease up before I beat your little ass.

[PIG *stands.* LARRY *jumps up, still feisty.*]

LARRY: You took the shit and sold it! You know you did. Just like you sold my
    Nintendo! Yeah, I ain't forgot about that shit. Niggah, you ain't changed!

They told me! [*Almost a whisper*] Yeah, they told me you still be gettin' high. [*Back to normal tone*] And I knew it! I knew damn well the first time I set foot in there. Saw all the shit they be doin'. I said to myself, "There's no way Pig gonna be able to handle this shit!" And on top of that, some of them say they be givin' you stuff for free.

[PIG *looks over at his mother.*]

Yeah, yeah, yeah, you don't wanna talk about that. Do you?

PIG: Shut up!

LARRY: No! You shut up! You a sorry motherfucker.

[LARRY *exits.* PIG *stands at the door, unable to confront his mother's stare.*]

REBECCA: Ham. [*Pause.*] Ham.

PIG [*pausing*]: Yes?

REBECCA: I know you didn't take those things.

PIG: How you know that?

REBECCA: Don't you worry. [*Pause.*] Ham.

PIG: Yes?

REBECCA: What I don't know, and what scares me is, are you still clean?

PIG [*after several beats*]: Yes, Mama, I am.

REBECCA: Well, what was your brother talking about? Why would he—

PIG: Mama, look. I'm clean, all right. That I can promise you. I'm clean, I really am. You got to trust me with what I'm tellin' you.

REBECCA: He said men in there are giving you drugs. Is there any truth to that?

[PIG *looks up at his mother and then back down to the floor and walks about.*]

PIG: Mama, it ain't like it look.

REBECCA: *I ain't asking you about how it looks!* I wanna know whether it's true or not.

PIG: All right, yes! Yes, it's true. They be givin' me a little here and there. *But I don't use it!* I don't get high no more. You gotta believe me, Mama.

REBECCA: Well, then what do you do with it, huh? Flush it down the toilet for 'em? Sell it to your friends after your meetings?

PIG [*looks up sharply at his mother and after a pause replies*]: Yes.

REBECCA: What?

PIG [*coldly*]: That's exactly what I do. I sell it right to their sorry asses. I think about all the money I done ran through, all the cars and fancy clothes I done contributed to around this here neighborhood, and I want a damn rebate! I knew it was wrong from the very beginning. I knew it. But what'n nobody there to tell me . . . no. Everybody round me was sayin' . . . it's OK. But it grabbed hold of me, Mama. You just don't know. It's gotta strong grip. And it takes a real strong person to break free from it. But the drugs . . . Mama, they make you so damn weak. But I broke loose. And I'm clean. Now look, I've been workin' my ass off. Doin' stuff I'd never do. Smilin' while they tell their stupid-ass office jokes. I stand there and watch all these nerds spray cologne on themselves just so they can go back out there and stand in the corner and stare. Yeah, Ma, I sell it to 'em. I sell back to the white boys in the club too. And guess what? Soon, so will Larry. I ain't proud to say it. But that's where we at. There's cats that come into those meetings that ain't never gonna turn themselves around. And you know what? It ain't my problem. The hell with them! The hell with all of them!

REBECCA: You ain't no better. Can't you see it's a trap? Ham, you more than anyone else should be able to see that.

PIG: Mama, we was born in a trap. Life ain't nothin' but one big ol' maze for the black man, and we, we like mice steady tryin' to find our way out. And the white man. The system. They busy tryin' to find ways to gather us up and put us right back in there. Jail, rehab, psychiatric wards. Think about it. Free cheese.

[*He laughs.*]

REBECCA: You should be ashamed of yourself.

PIG [*quickly*]: I am. I'm real ashamed of myself. But the truth of the matter is [*pointing*] that it's a cold world out there. You can turn the heat up all you want. There still gonna be some out there that gonna freeze to death. You can't save 'em all.

[*They stand there silently.* REBECCA *turns away in thought.* FRANCINE *enters through the front door.*]

FRANCINE: We still havin' a meetin'?

[PIG *walks over and kisses* REBECCA *on the forehead.*]

PIG: It's over.

[*He exits through the front door. The lights fade.*]

SCENE 3

[The lights come up on the living room. It now looks worse than before. Empty glasses line the table. Old pizza boxes are strewn on the floor. LARRY *enters from stage right, coming through the hall from his bedroom offstage. He looks about the living room, kicking pizza boxes aside.* REBECCA *enters the living room from stage left, coming through the hall from her bedroom offstage.]*

LARRY: You see, ah, my backpack?

REBECCA: Yeah.

LARRY: Where?

REBECCA: I think it's in the bathroom.

LARRY: What's it doin' in there?

[He marches down the hall stage right. REBECCA *sits in a chair.* LARRY *returns.]*

Hey, there some things missin'. Did you see—

REBECCA: What? Your stash?

LARRY [*pausing*]: Yeah, where it at?

REBECCA: I sold it.

LARRY: You what?

REBECCA: Your rent's paid through September.

LARRY [*laughing*]: Wait a minute. You jokin', right?

REBECCA: No, I'm not joking.

LARRY: Are you serious?

REBECCA: Yes.

LARRY: Oh, hell no! You sold my stuff? To who?

REBECCA: Well, I don't know everybody's name, but I know Luke. He bought the most. You know, you got a real good business goin' on there.

LARRY: What chu give Luke? And for how much?

REBECCA: Let's see. I sold to him four times . . . he just kept coming back. Look at this telephone he gave me.

[She picks up a phone.]

LARRY: That's probably his mama's phone!

REBECCA: Not no more, it's your mama's now. Shoot! Where can we get some more of that stuff?

LARRY: We?

[He paces back and forth.]

Francine's right. You are crazy. You have lost your damn mind?

REBECCA: I'm crazy? I'm not doing no different than what you do.

[LARRY *exits, slamming the door.* REBECCA *walks over to the window and looks out of it. After several moments, she rushes back to the chair and sits.* FRANCINE *enters wearing a backpack and carrying a small beauty academy case. She is dressed more professionally. She looks about the room in disgust. She places her case on the couch, opens her backpack, and removes a box of trash bags. She opens the box, removes a bag, and starts to pick up trash. Several moments elapse.*]

FRANCINE: You still workin' on him?

REBECCA: Yes.

FRANCINE: I think you're wastin' your time. Unless someone around here hit the lotta, he ain't ever gonna turn that loose. They out there makin' too much money.

REBECCA: What am I suppose to do?

[*The front door opens, startling both women.* LARRY *angrily enters.*]

LARRY: You cut the price on my shit?! Mama, what the hell is wrong with you? You done went and messed up my business and everyone else's.

[*He points toward the door.*]

Now all them heads out there is demanding lower prices. They out there right now asking for you by name!

[FRANCINE *laughs.*]

And you! I know damn well you told her. Tryin' to get back at me.

FRANCINE: I—

REBECCA: *Larry!* It don't matter who told me.

LARRY: You're right! It don't matter, it's too late, you done went and already fucked everything up!

FRANCINE: You said you wasn't gonna sell no crack anyway!

LARRY: What it matter to you, huh?

FRANCINE: It matters, Larry. It matters a whole lot.

LARRY: At my new job. Them fools is givin' me the stuff for damn near free. What you think I'ma just turn around and tell 'em "Naw, that's all right" or throw it away? Hell no! I ain't! I'm makin' eight hunerd percent profit.

[*He reaches into his pocket and pulls out a clear plastic bag full of crack.*]

This! This the best thing ever came my way. Now, Mama, I done tried to do it on the up-and-up. Went in there and smiled and passed out paper towels and took my little dollars and even went and bought you a TV. A brand spankin' new one. And what happened? It just up and disappeared. Don't nobody know nothin'. Look, I ain't blind. I see what's out there. Now the door done swung open for me and I'ma take whatever I can get before it closes back up.

REBECCA: Yeah, well the door opened for me too. And I saw an opportunity to try to get through to you, and I took it. Now you might not like the outcome, but there's a whole nother set of circumstances that could easily just as well have taken place. That door, Larry, the one you talking about. It's gonna close again. You can best believe that. And the way you goin', it's gonna close right in your face. And you gonna wind up sittin' in there . . . right next to your daddy.

FRANCINE: Eatin' potato chips.

LARRY: Shut up!

REBECCA: Larry. You're not doing this around here no more.

LARRY: What?

REBECCA: You ain't sellin' . . . no more [*pause, pointing to the bag*] of that *shit*! Around here. And if you try, I'ma make damn sure that everybody out there know my name. And everybody downtown know yours.

LARRY: What you think you in some gospel play or some shit? You know what, you crazy. I oughtta go sign some papers right now and have them take you away.

REBECCA: Take me away?

[*She laughs.*]

Who gonna come in my house and take me away?

LARRY: Oh, they can do it!

REBECCA: Ain't nobody taking me nowhere.

LARRY: They come in here and see this junky-ass crib and you in here lookin' and actin' like a crackhead, they gonna snatch your ass right up. You lucky we old as we is. Yeah, you keep messin' with me, you hear.

REBECCA: Messin'? [*Pause.*] I can make a phone call right now and have them take your butt away.

LARRY: For what?

REBECCA: *For sellin' drugs!* Larry.

LARRY: Yeah, well, you gonna be right there with me.

REBECCA: You shut your dumb mouth and listen! You think it's OK, to do what you do, and it's a crime for me to attempt to keep my family together? You done got so comfortable in your ignorance that you feel you can just waltz your way through life?

LARRY: What else we got to do? What else is out there for us?

REBECCA: What? You give up? You think that's all that life got to offer?

LARRY: What life? We ain't got no damn life.

REBECCA: Don't you speak for me. Life . . . is what you make it.

LARRY: Yeah, I know all that, but I'm tired of tryin' to just make it. We ain't got the resources to make it out here legally. I ain't tryin' to work some bullshit-ass job my whole life just so I can say to the world, "I did it! I made it through life—legally." I don't want to wander down that long road, Mama, 'cause ain't nothin' at the end of it but a coffin and some dirt. It ain't easy. We can't make nothin' out here, not in this world. We gotta take what we can get. And this is what they give us. Drugs and guns! We fucked up, Mama. This is what our culture done evolved into. We got to take what we can put our hands on and make the best of it. And you gonna try and mess that up for me. You know how long it took me to set up my business? Damn near a whole month! I had to go out and buy all this expensive gear, so that they would know I had it goin' on. Set that image up in their mind. Then I had to figure out who I could trust. Who I could have sellin' for me. Who the snitches are and who's willin' to go all out. It's a process, Mama. It ain't for just anybody. What you did was simple. You could of got your head beat in out there. Please . . . don't play no more games with my shit.

REBECCA: *You* . . . are . . . my . . . shit! Do you know how long it took me and your father to set you up? Hum? Nine times longer than it took you to put yourself out there like that. It took love, commitment, and understanding. Changing the way I eat. Being careful about the air I breathed. Goin' to the clinic . . . on the bus. Buying our clothes at the Salvation Army. Bein' thrifty and dealin' with that image. You ain't got a clue what I been through for you. I carried you, Lawrence. I kept you inside of me for a long time. I went through a whole lot to bring you into this world. There's a long list of things that I hold near to me that represent you. [*Pause.*] Don't . . . don't make me add regret . . . to that list. I know it's not easy out there. But me and Lloyd. We made you . . . and ain't you somebody?

LARRY: Mama, that sound good and all but—

REBECCA: *Niggah!* I love you.

[*The lights fade.*]

SCENE 4

[*The lights come up in the living room. It's Thursday. After several moments, some-one is heard in the outer hallway opening the door.* PIG *enters, talking on his cell phone.*]

PIG: Yeah, man, look, I told you it wasn't gonna be no problem. Yes, I know him, he's in there just about every night. [*Pause.*] We'll, what's it gonna hurt to ask him? Huh? Now, all you got to do is talk to Rush. Try to get him to back you on your end. [*Pause.*] No!

[*He walks into the kitchen and proceeds to make a sandwich.*]

Look, I done told you, you ain't got to say nothin' about me. He don't need to know I'm in on it 'til I deliver. [*Pause.*] Man, would you quit bein' so damn paranoid! What you think he gonna say? If you was him, what would you say? [*Pause.*] Well, act like you him. Listen, man, it ain't that hard. You wanna be like Wayne and Donnie? How you think they got to where they at, huh? [*Pause.*] Jail? Man, prison what'n nothin' to them. That's all part of the game. [*Pause.*] Do you wanna be in charge of this? [*Pause.*] All right, then, look, all you got to do is do what I tell you. Now I ain't tryin' to sound all bossy or nothin', but somebody got to be in charge of this thing, and you got to have some trust in that person. I trust you, but you tellin' me you don't wanna be in charge. So, who that leave? Me. Right? [*Pause.*] You trust me? All right, then act like it. You got to stop questioning everything I'm tellin' you. Look, what did I just get done sayin'? [*Pause.*] So what? If it don't work, it don't work, and we deal with the consequences. [*Pause.*] Then that's where we wind up. You been down there before. What you scared of? [*Pause.*] What we got right now, huh? What you got? [*Pause.*] Dog, dog look, now, right now, we little fish. We been sittin' round watchin' the big ones swim around us . . . all . . . our . . . lives. But now I done been out there at the club watchin' them sharks.

[*He sits at the kitchen table and eats.*]

Now believe it or not . . . they share. So you got to trust me on this. [*Pause.*] I don't know, man, I can't explain it. They just roll up on me and be like, "Here." And I know they ain't cops 'cause they be gettin' high as hell right in front of me. You hear me? I see 'em. One cat opened up his shirt just to show me he wasn't wired. Talkin' 'bout "Come on man, it's cool." Gave me some shit that would of cost 'bout two hunerd dollars out in the street. [*Pause.*] You know what I'm startin' to think? I'm thinkin' it's that white guilt people be talkin' about. I think it's their way of sayin' "Here, take this dime or this ounce as a peace offering." [*Pause.*] Could be. So . . . you ready to go swimmin' in the deep end? [*Pause.*] All right, then, you hook up with him, and let me know what's up. [*Pause.*] Hey. [*Pause.*] I'll see you at the top.

[REBECCA *enters from stage left, coming from her bedroom, and is startled by his presence.*]

You too, man. [*Pause.*] Later.

[*He hangs up his phone.*]

REBECCA: How'd you get in here?

PIG: I used my key.

REBECCA [*after a pause of several beats*]: How long have you been here?

PIG: Not too long. Jus' stopped by to see what was goin' on. Where everybody at?

REBECCA: They went to go see their father.

PIG: Is that right?

REBECCA: Yeah.

PIG: Why you actin' so cold?

REBECCA: 'Cause it's a cold world.

PIG: Yeah, you figurin' that out, huh?

REBECCA: I've got it all figured out.

PIG: You do?

REBECCA: Yes, I do.

PIG: Well, Mama, look. I don't know what the problem is. I don't know what's eatin' at you. I just stopped by to see what was goin' on. I ain't tryin' to start no trouble. I'm just stoppin' by.

REBECCA: You are?

PIG: Yeah, why? What's the problem? I can't stop by here whenever I want?

REBECCA: I'd prefer you call first, instead of just showing up.

PIG: Mama, what is you talkin' about? You ain't never had no problems with me comin' by here before.

REBECCA: Things aren't like before.

PIG: Now what that s'pose to mean?

REBECCA [*after a pause of several beats*]: You know the last time you came up in here, making yourself something to eat, was before you started that job of yours. What, you not working there no more?

PIG: Yeah, I'm still in there. [*Pause.*] It's just slow, that's all. [*Pause.*] *Damn!* I should of went to that new joint! Everybody then up and rolled over there. We done lost three bartenders to them since they opened. That's where all the tips is.

REBECCA: And your free drugs.

PIG: Ha, ha. Yeah, that too.

[*He laughs.*]

But hey, I heard you was the connection now. What's up with that?

REBECCA: I was just trying to teach your brother a lesson.

PIG: I almost had to whip somebody's ass. Niggah's out there callin' you a crackhead. Well, you don't hafta worry about me sellin' nothin' else.

REBECCA [*shaking her head, looking not at him with her hand outstretched*]: Give me my door key.

PIG: What? Why?

REBECCA: Give . . . me . . . my . . . key.

[*He takes out his keys and tries to remove her key from the ring.*]

PIG: Here, I'ma give it to you. I don't know why you trippin'.

REBECCA: Me? I'm trippin'? It's always me. I'm the one that's crazy. I am so sick of this drug culture bullshit! I just wanna smack y'all upside y'all heads 'til that nonsense comes pouring out. You ain't changing up none. You think you gonna just keep on comin' in my house telling me your lies and expect me to close my eyes?

PIG: Mama, what is wrong with you? Didn't you just hear me tell you I wasn't doin' that no more?

REBECCA: That's what you say . . . to me. While you here. But I know damn well it's a whole nother story once you hit them streets. And you know what? I don't even give a damn about what you do anymore.

[*She extends her hand. He reluctantly hands her the key and exits. She locks the door behind him. After several moments, the phone rings. She picks it up.*]

Hello? Oh, hey, baby. [*Pause.*] What? [*Pause.*] Are you sure? No, no, no that's, that's fine if that's what you want to do. [*Pause.*] Well, honey, I just think that you oughtta stay put, that's all. [*Pause.*] Well, yeah, that does make a difference. OK, then, what day are we talking about? [*Pause.*] Saturday? [*Pause.*] What time? [*Pause.*] Oh, couldn't it be later? [*Pause.*] Mary, the morning is bad for me. [*Pause.*] I have a program to attend. [*Pause.*] Just some thing that's going on at my job. [*Pause.*] No, I can't get out of it. It's something I have to do.

[FRANCINE *and* LARRY *enter noisily.*]

LARRY: What I tell you! Huh?

REBECCA [*into the phone*]: OK, look. Let me see what I can do. I'll call you later on. [*Pause.*] I love you too. Good-bye.

[*She turns toward her children.*]

How did it go?

LARRY: Marvelous! It felt good, didn't it, 'Cine? Didn't it? Come on, tell the truth, tell the truth, didn't it?

FRANCINE: All right, yeah! I done told you already.

LARRY: I just want Mama to hear you say it.

FRANCINE [*looking at her mother and talking like a zombie*]: It felt good seein' my daddy.

LARRY: That's what I'm talkin' about! It's better than not seein' him, ain't it?

FRANCINE: Yes.

REBECCA: OK. I hate to be a spoilsport here. But there's just something I have to say.

LARRY: What? Kick it.

REBECCA: There's something that's going on right in front of your eyes, and I want to try and help you to see it.

LARRY: Well, then, go ahead. Kick it.

REBECCA [*slowly and methodically*]: The reason why your father is in that cage and not here, home with us, and to be able to do all the things that husbands and fathers do, is because he was high. The same kinda high all these other fools out here is gettin' and they be gettin' it off of fools like you and your brother. And you fools are getting it off of them fools that are partying and having themselves a good ol' time . . . at our expense. *So!* It may feel good for you to see him . . . but it hurts me. I'd rather be able to feel, not just set my eyes on him in that condition. Francine, I understood you not wanting to go down there. That's why I never pushed you. It hurts, and you have to know I know how much it hurts. But Larry, it hurts even so much more to see you and your brother trying to make it in that game. You're gonna lose. Eventually, everybody does. Even the ones watchin'. [*Pause.*] Do you see . . . what I'm sayin'?

LARRY: Yes . . . I see.

[FRANCINE *nods her head yes.*]

REBECCA: Good.

[*She pauses a few beats and then takes a deep breath.*]

That was Mary on the phone.

FRANCINE: What's wrong? Is she all right?

REBECCA: Yes, she's fine. She just wants to come home on Saturday.

LARRY: Why don't she just wait 'til she have the baby?

REBECCA: Her insurance company suggested she go home until she's ready.

FRANCINE: I thought they were gonna induce labor?

REBECCA: She doesn't want them to.

FRANCINE: Why not?

REBECCA [*sighs*]: She's got her reasons. Can you two pick her up?

LARRY: Yeah, no doubt, no doubt. What time on Saturday?

REBECCA: At noon.

LARRY: OK, we'll get a jitney and go grab her.

REBECCA: Good.

FRANCINE: Where you gonna be at?

REBECCA: I have an appointment that I can't get out of.

LARRY: Don't even sweat it. We got it covered.

REBECCA: Listen. I'll be home around four. I'd like very much if we could have our meeting a little early.

FRANCINE: What time?

REBECCA: Right when I get back.

FRANCINE: That'll work. We can get out of here a little early.

LARRY: That's what I'm talkin' about. What's the big deal? This the way it's always gonna be?

REBECCA: I'm just trying a little something different. I wanna see what kind of effect it has.

LARRY: I'm feelin' it already. I'm out.

[*He stands near the front door.*]

REBECCA: Larry? I want it to stop. When you go out there, I want you to empty your pockets. I don't want you to ever touch or bring any drugs into this house ever again. 'Cause if you do, I'm going to make a phone call. Do you understand?

LARRY: Yes.

REBECCA: And you make sure your brother knows the same?

LARRY: Yeah. Yeah, I'll do that.

REBECCA: And, tell him about the meeting.

LARRY: OK, I will. I'll see y'all later on.

[*He hugs his mother and exits.*]

FRANCINE: I think you may have gotten through.

REBECCA: You think?

FRANCINE: Yeah.

[FRANCINE *exits stage right, heading toward her bedroom.* REBECCA *smiles to herself. The lights fade.*]

SCENE 5

[*The lights come up in the living room. It's Saturday afternoon, time for the family meeting. Some commotion is heard outside the front door.*]

FRANCINE: *Watch what you doin'! Be careful!*

LARRY: *You be careful! How the hell I'm gonna open the door if I don't turn around?*

[*The front door swings open and* LARRY *enters walking backward, holding* MARY'*s arms.* FRANCINE *follows behind, carrying several bags.*]

MARY: Larry, why do you have to make things so difficult all the time?

LARRY: What? I don't even know why you bother even comin' home. Your due date like, tomorrow!

MARY: It's not. It's not 'til Tuesday.

LARRY: Mary, that ain't but three days from now. What sense it make to come all the way back here?

[*They help* MARY *into the chair stage right.*]

FRANCINE: Larry, get her back. What difference does it make? We're already here, all right. Besides, Mama say she got a surprise for us and she wants us all to be here for the meeting.

LARRY: Shoot! We could have had it at the hospital long as we had to wait for her to get discharged.

[*He pulls out his cell phone and looks at the time.*]

We just barely made it. It's almost four o'clock. You know Mama said—

[*There is a knock at the door.* LARRY *opens it, and* PIG *enters.*]

PIG: Hey. How's everybody?
LARRY: We all right, we all right. What's up with you?
PIG: Nothin'. You said to come on over.
LARRY: Yeah. We s'pose to be havin' the meeting early.
PIG: Hey, Mary. How are you feelin'?
MARY [*surprised by his interest*]: Ah, fine. I'm feeling a lot better.
PIG: Well, where's Mom at?
FRANCINE: She said she be here at four.

[PIG *looks down at his watch.*]

PIG: I heard y'all went and saw y'all old man the other day.
LARRY: Yeah, we did.
PIG: How's he doin'?
LARRY: He's all right.
FRANCINE: He say he gonna try and get them to do some DNA testin'.
LARRY: Yeah, you know like they be doin' now. Gettin' cats off on technicalities.
PIG: They can do that with his case?
LARRY: I don't know. He just say that's what he's gonna try to do. Try to find out who was chokin' who.
FRANCINE: They can do it with anybody if they want. Hey, Pig, we gonna start savin' up so we can get him a real lawyer.
PIG: Well, count me in.

[*He pulls out an enormous wad of money and hands several bills to* FRANCINE.]

Here. Here go two hundred. Put that toward it.

[*Everyone is quiet as they stare at him. He notices this, stuffs his money back into his pocket, and attempts to make some sense of his fortune.*]

Ah, ah, hey, check it out. I'm startin' this masonry apprenticeship program on Monday over at the Impact building. And check this out. You get paid while you're trainin'. About nine dollars an hour.

LARRY [*moves toward* PIG]: What? You ain't, you know . . . doin' your thing no more?

PIG: Hell naw! I was gettin' it for pennies and makin' a ton. But that connection dried up when everybody migrated to your joint.

LARRY: My joint? Shoot! Ain't you heard?

PIG: What?

LARRY: Man, they was workin' an undercover sting operation up in there. Somebody tipped me off. And I wasn't 'bout to be bumpin' into no light switches. They rolled up in there and I was outie! The LCB s'pose to be shuttin' the place down.

PIG: Huh? I ain't hear about all of that.

LARRY: How you hook up that gig you got?

PIG: There's opportunities out there.

MARY: You got in there through your program.

PIG: Yeah, I did! So what, what difference do it make. It's a job, ain't it?

MARY: Yes. I'm sorry, Ham. It is an opportunity.

LARRY: That's all right. Nine dollars! Shoot! That ain't no chump change. What else they got over there?

PIG: They got electrical wirin', insulation, you know, weatherproofin'?

LARRY: I know what insulation is!

PIG: Carpentry, small appliance repair. They got all kinds of stuff.

FRANCINE: You probably have to be in his program to get in.

PIG: Yeah, yeah, you right. You do. But look, I can come back here and show you what I learn.

LARRY: What? Naaaw, I don't want no hand-me-down skills. I'm tryin' to be straight-up certified!

PIG: Mary, what's up with the baby? I hear you ain't want it to come out. [*Laughing*] What's up with that?

[*Everyone is silent for several beats.*]

FRANCINE: The baby's gonna come when the time is right.

LARRY: Yeah, she ain't due 'til Tuesday. [*He laughs.*]

PIG: Yeah, well I ran into Roy.

MARY: Oh, you did?

PIG: Yeah. And from what he say, seems like he wasn't the only one creepin' around.

LARRY: What? Man, what is you talkin' about?

PIG: Ol' Mary here come back home layin' the sleepin'-with-the-enemy guilt trip on Roy and here she done went out and done the same damn thing.

FRANCINE: Mary, what is he talkin' about?

LARRY: What? Is you serious?

PIG: There's always two sides to every story. Ain't that right, Mary?

MARY: It's not like it sounds.

FRANCINE: Mary, you was messin' around too?

LARRY: Wit some white boy?

MARY: He was a friend from work. We only went out once. [*Starting to cry*] I just wanted Roy to see me out like I saw him, so he can see how it felt.

PIG [*laughs*]: Yeah, that was all it took for him to drop that Ecstasy on your ass!

LARRY: Daaaaam! That's who knocked you up?

MARY [*crying*]: It wasn't suppose to . . . We went back to his place . . . and I fell asleep. It wasn't supposed to be this way.

FRANCINE [*comforting* MARY *while talking to* PIG]: Roy told you all of this? Where's he at?

PIG: I don't know. He around. What difference do it make? Ain't nobody gonna know nothin' 'til she have it anyway?

[*He laughs.*]

Gonna have a baby on Father's Day . . . and don't even know who the father is.

FRANCINE: Where'd you see Roy? He needs to be here with her.

PIG: She shouldn't of never had left! Mary, you shoulda stayed your ass down there instead of bringin' all your mess up here. Talkin' all that Jesus shit all the time and here you are puttin' yourself out there like that. I'm glad the tables finally turned on your ass! You made my life miserable when I was strugglin', Mary. You thought you was helpin'? Pointin' your finger at me the way you did. Lookin' down at me . . . your own brother! Like I was trash! You hurt me, Little Sis. I ain't never gonna forget that shit. I hope that little motherfucker come out lookin' like Michael Jackson on crack! I hope his hair is red, his skin is white, and his eyes are deep blue! Hell, you oughtta try and have him on Monday. It's Flag Day!

[MARY *gets up and quickly exits stage right toward her bedroom.*]

LARRY: Come on, man, ease up. That's some cold shit.

PIG [*pausing a beat*]: Brother . . . you ain't seen cold.

[REBECCA *enters wearing a cap and gown.*]

LARRY: Daaamn, Ma! What the hell?

FRANCINE: Mama, what's up with all that?

[REBECCA *spins around, showing off her gown.*]

REBECCA: How do you like this outfit?

[FRANCINE *looks at* LARRY.]

LARRY: Mama, what you been up to?
REBECCA: You are looking at a college graduate.
LARRY: What?
REBECCA: I just completed evening classes at Temple.
FRANCINE: What?
LARRY: I knew you what'n workin' no two jobs!

[MARY *reenters and* REBECCA *hands the diploma to her.*]

REBECCA: I have a bachelor's degree in elementary education.
MARY [*looking at it*]: You went back and finished?
REBECCA: Yes! I even took some classes in the Theater Arts Department. I got extra credit for writing an essay on being a stripper, a drug dealer, and a drug addict.
LARRY: Yeah, and you ruined my livelihood in the process.
REBECCA: I'm proud of that.
LARRY: Ain't nobody ever gonna trust me to move their stuff no mo'.
REBECCA [*moves toward him and hugs him*]: If it was only contagious.
LARRY: What?
REBECCA: Don't you all see? All those changes I went through. They were for you, and you, and you. And even you, Mary. I called Roy. I ask him to come in. I got him a ticket.

[*Pause of several beats.* REBECCA *spins around.*]

And I didn't sell the TV or any of those things.

[*She takes her cap off and places it on the top of* PIG's *head and removes a pawn ticket from her purse.*]

They're over at Wolenskies.
LARRY: You pawned them?
REBECCA: Yes.
PIG: Why?
REBECCA: I needed somewhere to keep them until all this . . . until this moment.

LARRY: What about all my stuff you took?

REBECCA: I did sell that. I'm not proud of it, except for the effect that it had on you.

FRANCINE: But you ain't have to put on that outfit and do what you did down the Poodle. That was straight-up ridiculous.

REBECCA: Your former customers didn't seem to think so. Matter of fact, Mr. Cicero just called me the other day, wanting to know if he could book me for a bachelor's party.

PIG: Aw, y'all need to stop that now.

LARRY: So, you gonna be a teacher now?

REBECCA: Yes, I am. I'm even planning on going back again, so one day I can be a principal. Maybe some of us can take classes together.

LARRY: Well 'Cine, I guess Mama our new role model.

[FRANCINE *runs over and hugs her mother, followed by* LARRY *and then* MARY.]

PIG: Well, you know what?

[PIG *pulls out his wad again and removes several bills.*]

Congratulations! Here you go.

[*He attempts to hand her some money. She stands there silently, staring at him.*]

What? You don't want this money?

REBECCA [*shaking her head*]: I don't ever want that kind of money.

PIG: What is you talkin' about?

REBECCA [*to* LARRY]: Did you give him my message?

LARRY: Yes.

PIG: What?

REBECCA: All of it?

LARRY [*pausing*]: Yes.

REBECCA [*to* PIG]: Larry says he gave you my message.

PIG: Yeah, I'm here, ain't I?

REBECCA: He told you about the drug-dealin' part?

PIG: Aw, Ma, come on now, you messin' up the celebration. Here, take these dollars and get yourself somethin' nice. Now, go on, take it now.

[*He takes her hand and places the money in it and folds her fingers around it.*]

Come on, you deserve it.

[REBECCA *stands there silently. With tears welling up in her eyes, she slowly walks toward the phone and picks it up, releasing the money in the process. She dials.*]

REBECCA: Yes, Officer. I'd like to report a crime. Yes, a crime in progress. [*Pause.*] My name is Rebecca Pratt. [*Pause.*] 756 Marshall Street, Apartment 3B. [*Pause.*] There's a drug dealer in my home threatening my family and I—Yes, yes . . . yes.

[*She hangs up the phone.* PIG *stands center stage in shock, staring at his mother. He then slowly makes his way to the front door, staring at his mother the entire time. He stands at the door momentarily. He looks at his brother and sisters, removes the cap and lets it fall to the floor, and then exits. Blackout.*]

THE DIVA DAUGHTERS DUPREE

Kim Euell

Second-Place Winner

2001–2002

Diva: A black woman who gives a consistently strong performance, with or without an audience or stage.

—Saundra Sharp

When people talk about the strength of black women . . . they ignore the reality that to be strong in the face of oppression is not the same as overcoming oppression, that endurance is not to be confused with transformation.

—bell hooks

For my mother, Grace Euell, and my recently departed cousin, Ruby Crump

PLAYWRIGHT'S STATEMENT

The Diva Daughters DuPree is my riff on cultural assimilation and consumerism. Race is an artificial construct so far as identity is concerned. Within a few generations, racial identity can be altered. And we all know people who are outwardly identified with a race that they obviously despise. The essential defining question has become: What culture do you identify with? I'm asking: What value do you attach to your cultural identity?

Many Americans aspire to the American Dream version of success: the large house, the status cars, the designer clothes, the trophy spouse. Consumerism has emerged as a new form of enslavement. The media constantly broadcast the dual message that buying "stuff" is the key to happiness and that everyone can have it all if they are willing to play the game. The assimilation game. I am posing the question: *What are you willing to give up for material success?* Your hairstyle? Your dialect? Your political views? Your cultural identity? Where does one draw the line? And what are the hidden costs?

Do we value our African American culture and heritage enough to retain it and pass it on to the next generation? For me, this is the essential question that lies at the heart of this play. I believe that if African American culture is going to survive as a distinctly identifiable culture, those of us who identify with that culture have to ask ourselves these questions on an ongoing basis. In today's world, cultural assimilation is a universal issue. Everyone lives under some degree of pressure to assimilate into the mainstream. As the character Uri points out in the play, "Lots of [Jews] eat pork, even in Israel."

PRODUCTION HISTORY

The Diva Daughters DuPree, by Kim Euell, was originally developed in the Robey Theatre Company's Playwrights Lab and subsequently at the Mark Taper Forum. It premiered at the Plowshares Theater Company in Detroit,

Michigan, on May 4, 2002. This production was directed by Gary Anderson, with set design by Mark Magni, costume design by Leslie Littell, lighting design by Neil Carpentier-Alting, and sound design by Lumumba Reynolds II. Janet Cleveland was the stage manager.

Sarah DuPree	Sonya Carswell
Abbey DuPree	My-Isha Cason-Brown
Spencer Thompson	Andrew Dawson
Billie DuPree	Iris Farrugia
Zak	Bryan Sanger
Uri	Mark Schock

The play was subsequently produced by the Penumbra Theatre Company in Saint Paul, Minnesota, in February 2004. It was directed by Lou Bellamy, with set design by Jason Allyn-Schwerin, costume design by Jean Williamson, lighting design by Mark Dougherty, sound design by Malo, and properties design by Sharon Selberg. Mary K. Winchell was the stage manager. This production was awarded "Outstanding New Show of 2004" by critics at the *Minneapolis–St. Paul Star Tribune* in their year-end review.

Billie DuPree	Ericka Dennis
Zak	Brent Doyle
Uri	Dylan Fresco
Spencer Thompson	Rob Manning
Abbey DuPree	Kimberly Morgan
Sarah DuPree	Thomasina Petrus

CHARACTERS

Billie DuPree, forty-year-old successful financial planner and a type A personality. The eldest sister but looks younger. About three sizes larger than her svelte siblings but carries it well. Coiffed and very Saks Fifth Avenue, a card-carrying member of the black bourgeoisie. High-strung, she can turn on a dime. Compulsively busy. A fast talker and a loose cannon. A woman on the verge, she's more hysterical than angry.

Zak, forty-year-old American of European descent; Billie's husband. A nice guy, but a little short on ambition, or perhaps his ambition is to be supported by his wife. Think Woody Harrelson entering a midlife crisis.

Sarah DuPree, thirty-four-year-old light-skinned African American; Billie's sister. History professor at a prestigious New England university. Cerebral and characteristically understated but prone to passionate outbursts under stress.

Grandmom, voice-over only. A feisty, elderly woman.

Abbey DuPree, very youthful twenty-five-year-old African American with flowing dreadlocks; Billie's sister. Prep school education, college dropout. Earthy/airy feminist hippie girl with her own unique worldview. A child of privilege. A ditzy "diva in training," she is just learning to assert herself with her two older sisters.

Uri, twenty-five-year-old recent Israeli immigrant, with thick accent and all the enthusiasm of a newcomer; Abbey's husband. Earnest, well-intended, but highly emotional. Abbey is the sun around which he revolves.

Spencer, twenty-seven-year-old dark-skinned African American, approximately six foot three and very self-assured. A graduate student at the university where Sarah teaches. A former athlete and an aspiring poet. From the hood but a country boy at heart. His dialect reflects his family's southern roots.

STAGING

This play is not a realistic drama! It is a comedy of manners with a farcical edge, hence purely naturalistic direction is not the way to go. The play is driven by the underlying tension emanating from the impending anniversary of the death of the parents. This tension periodically pushes the sisters into such heightened states that they display various compulsive behaviors including ranting and behaving like caricatures of themselves (think Coen Brothers: *Barton Fink*). It is vital that the appropriate tone and pace be established from the very top of the play.

The play is set in late 1995 in the DuPree family home, a gracious two-story, single-family dwelling in Chestnut Hill, a wealthy, predominantly white suburb of Philadelphia.

The Diva Daughters DuPree can be produced with either a realistic set or an impressionistic set as long as it conveys the impression of a tasteful upper-middle-class home. In either case, the portrait of the three sisters in their youth is of paramount importance and should be large enough for the audience to read the girls as the seeds of the women they have become.

ACT 1

PROLOGUE

[*The lights fade in to reveal a large framed portrait of three girls, aged fourteen years, eight years, and six months old.* BILLIE, *the eldest, is the smiling personification of a "good girl." In her lap is the baby,* ABBEY, *staring openly and curiously into the camera.* SARAH, *the middle child, stands next to her older sister wearing a serious expression. The portrait is hanging askew. On a table below the portrait is a telephone with an answering machine. The phone rings. The answering machine picks up the call. The recorded greeting begins with* BILLIE *singing a line from a sentimental pop tune about home.* BILLIE *has a great voice and could have been a professional singer had she not opted for a more dependable road to financial security.*]

> *Voice-over,* BILLIE: Greetings! You've reached the DuPree household. Leave a message and Billie or Zak will call you back.
> *Voice-over,* MATTHEW: Hey Zak, hey Billie. It's me, Matthew. I'm sorry we won't be able to get together on this trip, but I hope you guys have a great time. Send me a postcard, will ya? And give a call when you get back. Bye now.

[*Lights fade out.*]

SCENE 1

[*Lights fade in.* ZAK *enters through the back door into the kitchen, loaded down with* BILLIE's *luggage. Exhausted, he sets it down and then goes out and returns with more. After a third trip, there is an immense pile of expensive luggage in the kitchen. At this point* BILLIE *sweeps in. The tension is thick between them. Finally, in an effort at levity,* ZAK *speaks.*]

ZAK: Home sweet home.

BILLIE [*erupting, on the verge of hysterics*]: Why, why, why didn't you call the airline before we left?

ZAK: Not fair, Billie! You can't blame me for a tropical storm. I understand that being stranded here at this particular time of the year is very stressful for you, but we just have to make the best of it. So let's just try and see the bright side.

BILLIE: Bright side? Bright side?!!!

ZAK: Well, now we can spend some time with Matthew, while he's in town—

BILLIE: We? You mean you can—

ZAK: It's not like I get to see him that often. And we can spend some time with Sarah too.

BILLIE: After she stood us up last night?

ZAK: She called and canceled. That doesn't count as a stand-up.

BILLIE: I bought those veal chops especially for her. Veal isn't cheap, you know.

ZAK [*looking out window*]: She should've been here by now. I hope she won't be disappointed 'cause she won't have the place to herself.

BILLIE: It'll be good for her. She's too used to getting her way all the time.

ZAK: In that case, I'll let you tell her.

[*He heads toward the door.*]

BILLIE: Where are you going?

ZAK: I left Bertha out.

[*He races outside. The moment* BILLIE *is alone, she reveals a much more vulnerable side. We see that she is on the verge of tears, but she resumes her armored stance as soon as she hears* ZAK *approaching. He reenters carrying a surfboard overhead. He props it up against the wall.*]

BILLIE: What did you bring that thing in here for?

ZAK: Just for a minute.

BILLIE: Do you see an ocean in here?

ZAK: I'm gonna put her back in the garage; just let me have a few last moments.

BILLIE: Zak!

ZAK: Sweetheart, you need to relax. Come here; let me rub your shoulders for you.

[*She does.*]

Ooh, so tense. [*Pauses a beat.*] Now that we're gonna be in town, why don't we invite The Matthewman to come stay with us?

BILLIE: There's no place for him to sleep.

ZAK: What about Abbey's room?

BILLIE: I wouldn't put anyone in there without a major cleaning. Besides, Sarah will be here. I think Matthew will be more comfortable in his Rittenhouse Square hotel.

ZAK: I just thought it would be fun if we had a whole house full of people. Like the holidays.

BILLIE: Fun for you maybe, not for the rest of us. And don't forget that I'm due to start ovulating any day now.

ZAK: Yeah, yeah, Zak's stud service. How could I forget?

[ZAK *abandons the massage effort and goes to the refrigerator and gets himself a beer.*]

BILLIE: That's no way to talk about it! I don't want to feel like I'm in this alone.

[*He grabs a rag from under the sink and begins polishing the surfboard.*]

Zak?

ZAK: Look, I've done everything the doctor said. I even switched to boxers, as if that's gonna make a difference.

BILLIE: I hope you're not planning to spend every evening with Matthew, now that we're going to be home.

ZAK: I gotta be hospitable.

BILLIE: I need you at home!

ZAK: Come on, Billie—

BILLIE: Why don't you take him out tomorrow night and then maybe we can get Sarah to show him around one evening. Just because our trip has been postponed doesn't mean we can afford to miss another opportunity.

ZAK: What if Sarah has plans?

BILLIE: She won't. [*She pauses a beat.*] The car! I forgot about the car.

ZAK: What car?

BILLIE: My car!

ZAK: What's the problem?

BILLIE: Listen, while Sarah's here I want to leave it in the garage, with the door locked. We'll just use your car, OK?

ZAK: Why?

BILLIE: You know how she gets. If she sees it, she's gonna start.

ZAK: So you're gonna try to hide the fact that you have a new car from her the entire time she's here?

BILLIE: I don't need the added stress of arguing with her about what kind of car I drive while I'm trying to conceive.

ZAK: Just tell her it's what your clients expect.

BILLIE: When she gets on her soapbox I can't—she starts—she—oh, never mind, why am I trying to explain it to you?

[*She puts her coat on.*]

ZAK: Where are you going?
BILLIE: To park it in the alleyway behind the old firehouse. It'll be fine.
ZAK: Billie, you're taking this thing too—

[*She exits, slamming the kitchen door behind her.*]

far.

[*He goes over to the surfboard and puts it down on the floor. He climbs on, pretending that he's surfing. The phone rings; he answers it.*]

Hello? Abbey? Where are you? Is everything all right? [*Pause.*] Maybe you should talk to Billie, she'll be right back. [*Pause.*] C'mon, Abbey, help me out here, I'm having a gnarly time here with your sister. [*Pause.*] I see. [*Pause.*] All right, all right. I'll tell her. [*Pause.*] Drive safely. Bye.

[*At this bad news, he decides to fix* BILLIE *a drink. He puts a lot of vodka in her Bloody Mary, among other things . . .* BILLIE *reenters.*]

You actually hid your car?
BILLIE: Look, I don't want Sarah thinking I have a lot of money. She'll tell Abbey, and the next thing you know we'll be fronting money for that immigrant husband of hers to get his green card, and then his entire clan will be here and we'll be expected to house them, 'cause Abbey and Uri will probably have an efficiency. You watch.

[*She grabs a broom and begins sweeping angrily despite the fact that the floor is spotless. She rants to herself.*]

I'm so disgusted with her I don't know what to do. All that money we spent on her fancy prep school education only to have her drop out of college halfway through, and now she's gone off and married some fresh-off-the-boat—
ZAK: Plane.
BILLIE: What?
ZAK: They come on planes now.
BILLIE: Why is that surfboard still here?
ZAK [*taking the broom from her*]: Here, I fixed you a drink.
BILLIE: The question still stands.

[*She knocks it back, draining the glass, which she sets down decisively.*]

ZAK: How was it?

BILLIE: Strong.

ZAK: But how'd it taste?

BILLIE: All right.

ZAK: Just all right?

BILLIE: Well, it didn't blow my dress up.

ZAK: The way you downed it, I thought—

BILLIE: All right, Zak, it was the best Bloody Mary I ever had. OK? Are ya happy now? Are ya satisfied?

ZAK [*after pausing a beat*]: I got some news.

BILLIE: It better be good news.

ZAK: That depends. C'mon and sit down so I can finish rubbing your shoulders.

BILLIE: That doesn't seem like good news.

ZAK: It's not bad news. C'mon.

[*She sits; he massages her aggressively.*]

BILLIE: Not so hard!

ZAK: Is that better?

BILLIE: Yeah. [*She pauses a beat.*] So what's the neutral news?

ZAK: Abbey just called. Her and her hubby are coming for a visit. Sounds like they're planning to stay a while.

BILLIE: She's planning to stay? Here?

ZAK: That's what she said.

BILLIE: She hasn't spent a night in this house since my parents died.

ZAK: She said they'd be here tomorrow. She thought we were in Hawaii. Looks like we'll have a full house after all.

BILLIE: That's just great. I'll have to go grocery shopping in the morning. And that room needs to be aired out and dusted and vacuumed.

ZAK: You don't have to do everything yourself, you know.

BILLIE: Who's gonna help me? You?

ZAK: You know I'll help.

BILLIE: Yeah, right.

ZAK [*after pausing a beat*]: Someone's pulling into the driveway.

BILLIE: Where're you going?

ZAK: To help Sarah with her bags.

BILLIE: She can manage. C'mon.

ZAK: But—

BILLIE: Finish me.

ZAK: It'll only take—

BILLIE: You don't want me *tense*, do you?

ZAK: All right. All right.

[*He resumes the massage. A moment later,* SARAH *enters cautiously, wearing a black leather motorcycle jacket, with a backpack slung over one shoulder, carrying a pizza box. She has a pair of scholarly looking glasses pushed up onto her head. She also wears a guarded expression, but seeing the luggage puts her more at ease.*]

Hey now!

SARAH: Hey guys.

[*She kisses* ZAK *and* BILLIE, *who offers her cheek.*]

BILLIE: So, you finally made it.

SARAH: Yep.

BILLIE: Brought your own dinner, I see.

SARAH: I just picked this up for the drive down. There's plenty left if you want some?

BILLIE: Humph. I saved you your dinner from last night.

SARAH: You did?

BILLIE: And just what was so important that you couldn't make it yesterday like we planned?

SARAH: I wanted to watch the coverage of the Million Man March. It's a historic—

BILLIE: Couldn't you tape that?

SARAH: I wanted to be part of history in the making, not after the fact.

ZAK: I know what you mean. I don't like watching a game after I already know the outcome. Takes all the fun out of it.

[BILLIE *begins making her shopping list.*]

Did you see the fight?

SARAH: Yeah, what a snore.

ZAK: They just danced around each other for twelve whole rounds.

SARAH: I swear, boxing is going right down the tubes. Where's all the talent? I remember when there used to be lots of greats fighting at the same time, Sugar Ray Leonard, "Marvelous" Marvin Hagler, Tommy "Hit Man" Hearns—

ZAK: "The Motor City Cobra."

SARAH: Right, and I even liked that nasty little Panamanian brawler, you know, what's his name? *"No más"*?

ZAK [*shouting*]: Duran! Roberto Duran!

BILLIE [*overlapping* ZAK]: Can you guys keep it down?

SARAH: These guys fighting today have no style, no personality, and very little talent.

ZAK: They don't even have good nicknames anymore.

BILLIE [*to* SARAH]: Abbey eats fish and chicken, doesn't she? Or is it only fish? [*She pauses a beat.*] Sarah?

SARAH: Fish. [*To* ZAK] There's "Macho" Camacho, but I always thought that name made him sound more like a wrestler than a boxer, don't you think?

BILLIE: Enough sports talk already, you're giving me a headache!

[SARAH *shoots her a look.*]

ZAK: I didn't know you wear glasses.

SARAH: Oh, these? They're not prescription. Just part of the professorial uniform.

ZAK: No! Really? You have to wear fake glasses?

SARAH: You'd be surprised what a woman has to do to be taken seriously by her male colleagues.

ZAK: Put 'em on.

SARAH: Nope.

ZAK: Let me see.

SARAH: No way.

BILLIE: Leave her alone, Zak, she doesn't want to.

ZAK: Aww, c'mon, Four-Eyes. Be a sport. I won't laugh.

SARAH: You better not.

[*She complies.*]

ZAK [*impressed*]: Wow! You do look smarter.

SARAH: *Tres chic* amongst the intelligentsia.

[*She flings the glasses down.*]

Elitist assholes, makes me wanna puke.

BILLIE [*looking up from her list*]: Girlfriend, what's up?

SARAH: Work has really sucked lately, that's all.

ZAK: I thought things were going good, you got that award and—

BILLIE: Is it the tenure thing? Did you find out something?

[SARAH *gestures that she doesn't want to discuss it.*]

ZAK: Sarah? What's wrong?

[*The following rant by* SARAH *is one of those heightened moments in the play that should be played over the top and dripping with sarcasm.*]

SARAH: Dinosaurs! The history department is full of dinosaurs that don't even have enough sense to lay down and die. These guys are still trying to teach history the way they did when our parents were in college. Propagating lies like colonialism developed Africa and that slavery was an aberration, a mere footnote in the glorious American past. I'm the only one in my department who delves into the dirty laundry. Then they wanna act surprised when all the students flock to my courses. "Must be because I grade easy," they say. The students work harder in my courses because I challenge them. But let's not talk about all that. Let's talk about your trip.

[BILLIE *and* ZAK *exchange glances.*]

I wish I could afford to get away. I could use a break right now, but I guess I'll get that while I'm here. *Some solitude.*

[*She looks at them expectantly.*]

Whoa, is that a surfboard?

ZAK: Yeah. I thought it was time to get her out of mothballs.

SARAH: How long since you've been on one of those things?

BILLIE: Too long. He thinks he can just jump up and ride it like he's still a teenager. I'm scared he's going to really hurt himself.

ZAK: Surfing is like riding a bike. Once you get the hang of it, you never forget. Besides, I'm still in good shape. I swim almost every day.

BILLIE: Swimming and surfing are two totally different activities.

ZAK [*beginning an overlapping exchange with* BILLIE *that builds in intensity*]: They're related.

BILLIE: I know that you have this need to prove to yourself that you can still do everything you could do when you were twenty-two—

ZAK: Plenty of guys my age still surf—

BILLIE: —but you can't and I don't want to have to spend my vacation in some emergency room—

ZAK: Billie, will you just get off it? Jeez!

BILLIE: —just because you are having a midlife crisis! [*End of overlap.*]

ZAK: Why can't you be more like your sister?

[*Awkward pause.*]

SARAH: So . . . what time's your flight?

[ZAK *and* BILLIE *glare at one another before turning to face* SARAH. *Lights fade out.*]

SCENE 2

[*Lights fade in.* SARAH *sits in her room, meditating. Lighting gives the effect of the room spinning, while she sits completely still, in a lotus position, eyes closed. The entire scene's dialogue is played through voice-overs.*]

Voice-over, SARAH: Breath in, breath out. Breath in, breath out. You should just get in your car and drive straight back to Connecticut. Right now. If you stay here there will be no peace. But what about Abbey? You'll see her at Thanksgiving. But what if they move before then? And what if . . . Oh, I'm supposed to be—breath in, breath out. Breath in. You see how stressed you're getting already? You can't even concen—breath in, breath out. And where does she get off interrupting your conversation like that? She talks to you like you're five years old! Breath in. Better head back right now. But I'm tired. That's a long drive. And what about Spencer? He's coming. Yeah, right. If he shows. And how are you two gonna resolve anything anyway, with the whole damn family here? Breath! Observe breath. Breath in, breath out. OK. You're tired. Spend the night and then head back after breakfast. But, she's gonna take it personally if you leave right away. You saw how she acted when you didn't come for dinner. That's not your issue! You've got some real problems to solve. You have no money saved. Yeah, but right now I'm supposed to be focusing on my breath. Breath in, breath out. Breath in, breath out. Breath in, breath out.

[*At this point* SARAH *achieves mental stillness and the room stops spinning. The lights shift to soft motionless lights focused on* SARAH.]

Voice-over, GRANDMOM: Sarah? Sarah? Can you hear me?

Voice-over, SARAH: Grandmom?

Voice-over, GRANDMOM: Sassy Sarah!

Voice-over, SARAH: Oh, Grandmom. I miss you so much.

Voice-over, GRANDMOM: Baby, what's wrong?

Voice-over, SARAH: Everything. My life, it's spinning out of control.

Voice-over, GRANDMOM: We're never in control. You know that.

Voice-over, SARAH: Yes, but—

Voice-over, GRANDMOM: Tell Grandmom what's got you so upset.

Voice-over, SARAH: Well, I did something dumb. I got involved with this—I don't know where to begin, everything's such a mess, I—

Voice-over, GRANDMOM [*commanding*]: Tell it!

Voice-over, SARAH: I didn't get tenure.

Voice-over, GRANDMOM: Tenure? What's that?

Voice-over, SARAH: It's a job for life.

Voice-over, GRANDMOM: Ain't that what they used to call slavery?

Voice-over, SARAH: It's not slavery, it's freedom. You can say and write whatever you want, and they can't fire you. Now I'm going to have to find another job and start all over again somewhere else. And it's so unfair. My classes are more popular than anyone else's in the whole department. And my book was nominated for—

Voice-over, GRANDMOM: I imagine that's why they don't want you around. You're raisin' the bar too high for the rest of 'em.

Voice-over, SARAH: I never thought of that.

Voice-over, GRANDMOM: Well, you have to look for the open door.

Voice-over, SARAH: What?

Voice-over, GRANDMOM: A door never closes without another one openin'. Didn't you want to spend more time writin'?

Voice-over, SARAH: Yeah, but I need money to pay the bills while I write, I can't just—

Voice-over, GRANDMOM: Of course you can. Chile, you are divine right *now!* Besides, my baby ain't no fat dog on a leash; you're the lean hungry wolf who's got her freedom. Now cut your losses and move on.

Voice-over, SARAH: But how will I—

Voice-over, GRANDMOM: When your back's against the wall, you have to surrender. Let it go, Sarah. Look for the signs. When I was a girl growin' up on our farm, we knew to look for the signs. When the cows come home early, it means a storm's coming. So pay attention to the signs. Ah'm here for you. Your dad, your ma, we're all here for you to stand on our shoulders. Now stop your worryin' and go'n do what ya gotta do.

Voice-over, SARAH: OK, Grandmom. I love you. [*Pauses a beat.*] Grandmom? You still there? [*No answer*] Don't go yet. [*Pauses a beat.*] Breath in, breath out. [*Whispered*] Bye.

[*Lights fade out.*]

SCENE 3

[*Lights fade in. At the dinner table, the following day.* URI *and* ABBEY *have arrived.* ZAK *and* SARAH *hover while* BILLIE, *in her element, moves about purposely.*]

ABBEY [*to* ZAK]: Too bad about your vacation being postponed. I love it there, especially the smaller islands, Maui, Molokai . . .

ZAK: Yeah, it's so beautiful, it's hard to believe it's part of the U.S.

SARAH: That's called imperialism, Surfer Dude.

ZAK: Guess you would know, Four-Eyes.

BILLIE [*to* ABBEY]: I'm so glad you got here in time for dinner. Not like some people who just show up when the mood strikes, carrying a pizza box . . . [*To* URI] I hope you don't mind eating in the kitchen; we only use the dining room at the holidays. Zak, you're here; Abbey, you sit here; Uri, you sit across from Abbey; and Sarah, you sit there. OK. We're ready. [*Pause.*] That's a nice top, Abbey. Is it a designer's?

ABBEY: Huh?

BILLIE: Whose label is it? It looks like Donna Karan.

ABBEY: I don't know. I got it at a thrift shop.

BILLIE [*disappointed*]: Oh. [*She pauses a beat.*] Well, come here, let me see the label.

[ABBEY *gets up but* SARAH *stops her.*]

SARAH: Did you guys find any cities you think you want to live in?

ABBEY: We liked the Bay Area, especially Berkeley and Oakland.

BILLIE: Abbey, come here!

[ABBEY *goes to her and* BILLIE *examines the label.*]

URI: I did not like San Francisco. I had to wear a big heavy coat in the summertime, and so many people begging us. Spare change? Spare change? Do I look like this Rockefeller?

ABBEY: I liked Seattle.

SARAH: Seattle? I find that place depressing. All that rain, and the people of color there seem so disempowered. All those black folks and they don't even have a radio station.

ABBEY: But I like that mountain.

ZAK: Florida's nice. Did you try Florida?

ABBEY: Too humid.

[ZAK *begins helping himself.*]

BILLIE: Let's say grace.

[*All bow their heads.*]

Heavenly Father, we give thanks for this food we are about to receive and for the safe return of our sister. Amen.

[*Everyone begins serving the food.*]

SARAH: Has it ever occurred to you that God may not be male?

BILLIE: Well, actually it has, but when I asked Reverend Ballard, he told me that God created man in his image, so in Christianity, God is male. Pass the greens, please.

SARAH: One more reason not to be a Christian.

BILLIE: You're not a Christian? Since when?

SARAH: Why would I practice a religion that was used to justify the enslavement of my ancestors?

BILLIE: Jesus didn't sanction slavery—

SARAH: But Christians did—

BILLIE: Slavery is over, Sarah, stop living in the past.

SARAH: Slavery never ended, it's just taken subtler, more insidious forms. Remember what Daddy used to say—

BILLIE: Don't start—

ABBEY: Billie, these greens are really good, aren't they, Uri?

URI: Huh?

ABBEY: The collard greens, taste good, don't they?

URI: Oh yes. I've never had so good. How you say—colored? Colored greens?

ABBEY: Collard, dear, not colored. [*To* BILLIE] I was hoping you could show me how to make a few new dishes while we're here. I want to start cooking more.

BILLIE: How long are you planning to stay?

ABBEY [*shrugs*]: A year or two.

BILLIE: What? A year?

ABBEY: Or two.

BILLIE: Why didn't you call me?

ABBEY [*shooting* ZAK *a look*]: Didn't you get my message? We're broke. Pass the potatoes, please.

BILLIE: After all these years of staying away, you suddenly decide to move in without talking to me first?

SARAH: We all own the house equally, Billie. She doesn't have to ask permission to move in.

BILLIE: It's just common courtesy to let people know what you're planning. Well? [*To* ABBEY] What are your plans?

ABBEY: To get jobs, save some money, you know. Uri wants to start his own business. I want to start a family, after we get our own place, of course.

URI: In Berkeley or Seattle.

SARAH: But that's so far away. Don't you want to be closer to family when you have kids?

ABBEY: Maybe.

BILLIE: Abbey, you and I will have to discuss this further.

[*The microwave buzzer goes off.*]

I almost forgot.

[*She jumps up from the table and fetches the veal chop from the microwave and sets it down in front of* SARAH.]

SARAH: What's this?

BILLIE: It's your dinner from the other night. I saved it for you.

SARAH: But, what is it?

BILLIE: Veal.

SARAH: I don't eat red meat.

BILLIE: Veal is white meat. And what are your plans while you're here?

SARAH: I'm staying a night or two to visit with my sister here and then I'm heading back to Connecticut. Why?

BILLIE: Zak has a friend in town that we thought maybe you'd like to show around. You two could have dinner tomorrow and then maybe you could take him downtown to hear some jazz at the Zanzibar. He likes jazz, doesn't he, Zak?

ZAK: Yeah, he used to play a little.

SARAH: I don't think so.

BILLIE: Why not?

SARAH: I'm just not up for it. I came here for some quiet time, but since that's no longer possible, I'm staying the night, and then I'm out.

BILLIE: You haven't tasted your veal. I fixed it especially for you.

SARAH: Billie, I don't eat veal.

BILLIE: Since when? It was your favorite when you were a kid.

SARAH: You mean, twenty-five years ago?

BILLIE: You met Matthew before. He was here around the Thanksgiving holidays, that year we had the early snow.

SARAH: I'm afraid I don't recall.

ZAK: Tall? Lanky? He hunches his shoulders.

BILLIE: Would you just try one bite? One bite won't hurt.

SARAH: Am I speaking Sanskrit? *I do not eat red meat!*

BILLIE: I told you, it's white meat! Never mind, just pass it down to me, I'll eat it myself!

[SARAH *passes it down.*]

SARAH [*slowly and deliberately as* BILLIE *begins eating; throughout this speech,* BILLIE *ignores* SARAH *and savors the veal chop as though it's the tastiest thing she's ever eaten*]: Veal may appear to be white meat but that's only because the animals are anemic because they are fed only milk, so their flesh, lacking healthy red blood cells, becomes pale. They're kept half starved in pens that are too small to move around in, so their muscles don't develop properly. Eventually they can't even stand up, they're so weak. And that's when they are slaughtered. So what you are eating, dear sister, is the decomposing flesh of an abused animal. An innocent calf who was tortured all of its brief life, all for the sake of capitalist agribusiness. Bon appétit.

[*All eyes are on* BILLIE *as she pushes the plate away, unable to eat another bite.*]

BILLIE: Cooking always ruins my appetite. [*To* SARAH] And don't flatter yourself that your little mind games work on me. I wear fur!

SARAH [*rising*]: If you all will excuse me—

BILLIE: Where are you going?

SARAH: Out!

BILLIE: What time is Matthew coming, Zak?

ZAK [*hesitantly*]: Uh—what time should I tell him?

BILLIE: Sarah?

SARAH: Why are you asking me?

ZAK: Why don't I just take Matthew out?

URI [*excited*]: I have idea. We could all have reggae experience.

ZAK: A reggae what?

URI: In Israel sometimes when old friends come, we light candles and incense, put on Bob Marley songs, and sing and dance together.

[ABBEY *looks embarrassed.*]

BILLIE [*to* ABBEY]: Where did you find him?

ZAK: I'll just take him out and show him a good time. It's not that big of a deal, Billie.

BILLIE: When's the last time you went out on a date?

SARAH: That's none of your business.

BILLIE: I just don't understand why you won't do us this one favor?

[SARAH *leans over the table and gets right in* BILLIE'S *face.*]

SARAH: Because I don't date white men, that's why.

[BILLIE *gasps.*]

No red meat. No white meat.

[*Utter silence, only* ABBEY *continues eating mechanically.*]

Any further questions?

ABBEY: What's for dessert?

BILLIE: Ice cream. [*Through clenched teeth*] Vanilla!

SARAH: I don't eat that either.

[*She turns and strides toward the door.*]

BILLIE: Well, hail Caesar!

SARAH: Don't wait up.

[*She slams the door behind her. Lights fade out.*]

SCENE 4

[*Lights fade in.* URI *is pacing back and forth in* ABBEY'S *bedroom when* ABBEY *enters and heads straight for the dresser and begins searching for something.*]

ABBEY: Honey, have you seen the pictures from the trip, I want to show Zak—

URI: No! I have not seen.

ABBEY: What's wrong?

URI: I am disturbed. Did you not hear what your sister said?

ABBEY: Which one?

URI: Sarah!

ABBEY: What did Sarah say?

URI: She said [*dramatic pause*] that she does not date white men!

ABBEY: And?

URI: Abbey . . . you have racism in your family.

ABBEY [*shrugs*]: We're Americans.

URI: This is not for joking!

ABBEY: Honey? Honey? Don't you think you're overreacting a bit? I really don't think what Sarah said was racist; I think that's called umm, umm, cultural nationalism.

URI: She *said* that she does not date white men, like she has a policy. That sounds to me like discrimination because of race, which is racism!

ABBEY: I think that what she meant to say is that she doesn't date outside of her race. So it's not like she's singling out white men, she doesn't date Asians or Latinos either.

URI: That is still discrimination, Abbey.

ABBEY: She didn't say she doesn't hire them or rent to them, she said she doesn't date them! It's her prerogative! Sarah's black. We're black. She wants to marry a black man. What's wrong with that? [*Pauses a beat.*] I married who I wanted to, why can't she?

URI: I just feel—[*softening*] I don't know, I feel that she does not approve of our marriage. That she does not want me here.

ABBEY: Honey, that's just not true—

URI: I can't help—

ABBEY: Look, all of your brothers married Jewish women, didn't they? Is that discrimination?

URI: Of course not.

ABBEY: Did they date any Christians or Arab women?

URI: You don't understand, in Israel these things are governed by tradition.

ABBEY: Well, it's traditional for black women to marry black men in this country. Sarah's just being traditional.

URI: I thought I was getting away from all that when I left Israel.

[BILLIE *bursts into the room without knocking.*]

BILLIE: Your sister is such a bitch—

ABBEY: Really? Which one?

BILLIE: Sarah!

[*A beat elapses while she figures it out.*]

What do you mean by that?

ABBEY: I really don't like that *B* word, Billie. It reeks of misogyny. If you must use a pejorative, why don't you do like Mommy and just call her a hussy?

BILLIE: Because she's a bitch!

ABBEY [*to* URI]: Honey, I'm getting a headache. Would you please do me a favor and go downstairs and make me some tea? You know, the kind for headaches, there's a bag of it in the car. Please?

URI: But when can we—

ABBEY: Later! Honey, please.

URI [*heading for the door while muttering under his breath*]: Why do I feel like I'm back in Haifa?

[*He exits.*]

BILLIE: I don't understand why you're taking her side when she just slapped us all in the face like that.

ABBEY [*delicately*]: I don't feel like I got slapped; you, on the other hand, were asking for it. She obviously wasn't interested in going out with Zak's friend, but you just kept on pushing her.

BILLIE: The question is: Why isn't she interested in going out with Zak's friend? Huh? Huh?

ABBEY: Duh! Didn't she just tell us?

BILLIE: That's my point. She's just blowing smoke, with this business about marrying a black man. Where's she going to find an eligible black man at her age?

ABBEY: She could. God, you're so cynical.

BILLIE: And you're naive. Think about it. When's the last time Sarah's had a man?

ABBEY: She stopped dating to focus on her career—

BILLIE: Right, that was her last excuse, but now her career's established, so she's got to come up with a new one, and what better excuse than she's holding out for a black man?

ABBEY: Excuse? What're you—are you trying to say that Sarah's gay?

BILLIE: Ding, ding, ding, ding, ding, ding, ding!

ABBEY: Based on what?

BILLIE: Abbey, Abbey, Abbey, just look at how she dresses.

ABBEY: She's casual. So am I. So what?

BILLIE: She dresses way more butch than you.

ABBEY: Oh, so now *I* dress butch?

BILLIE: No, you're more andronomys—

ABBEY: Androgynous?

BILLIE: Yeah, yeah, right. I just wish you'd let me take you shopping some-times, you're a pretty girl, if only you'd fix yourself up. And when are we going to do something about those things on your head?

ABBEY: They're called dreadlocks.

BILLIE: And I certainly dread seeing them.

ABBEY: I'm waiting to hear the real reason why you think Sarah's gay.

BILLIE: Well, just look at her car. She's still driving that old Jeep she's had since she was in grad school. I can't believe that she actually drives that thing to work.

ABBEY: I drive a VW camper.

BILLIE: You've got a man and she doesn't!

ABBEY: Billie, trust me, Sarah is not gay. If she were, she would have come out to me a long time ago.

BILLIE: Come out? Of what?

ABBEY: The closet. [*She pauses a beat.*] You know, she would have declared herself.

BILLIE: Well, you certainly seem to know a lot about it, the lingo and all.

ABBEY: I have lots of gay friends.

BILLIE: Lots?

ABBEY: Several. And so do you, you probably just don't know it.

BILLIE: Because they haven't come out?

ABBEY: Right.

BILLIE: Well, they can just stay in as far as I'm concerned. Not everything needs to come out.

ABBEY: OK, Billie. I read you loud and clear. But I think that if it's that im-portant to you, you should just ask Sarah.

BILLIE: She wouldn't tell *me*.

ABBEY: Sarah's the most straightforward person I know.

BILLIE: That's why *you* should be the one to ask her.

ABBEY: So that's what this is all about.

BILLIE: So will you?

ABBEY: I don't know, Billie. I really don't want to get involved in gay-baiting.

BILLIE: Well that's just like you, isn't it? You just took off after Mom and Dad died, leaving me and Sarah to sort out everything—

ABBEY: I was only fifteen, what was I supposed to do?

BILLIE: Stay and support your family! That's what.

[ABBEY *covers her ears and begins singing "Row, Row, Row Your Boat" to drown out* BILLIE'S *words. It does not work.*]

But no, you always have this "I don't want to get my hands dirty" attitude, so off you go to boarding school, *prep* school no less, and I don't know why you even wasted your inheritance on that only to turn around and drop out of college halfway and to top that now you've gone and married some immigrant foreigner and brought him home for me to support. Who do you think is going to hire him? He can't even speak proper English. And you don't even have a degree. How are you two going to—

ABBEY: All right, Billie, all right, I'll speak to Sarah, OK?

BILLIE: When?

ABBEY: Soon!

BILLIE: How soon?

ABBEY: Soon, I said. *Soon!* Now if you don't mind, I'm very tired and I have a headache.

BILLIE: OK, honey. Get some rest.

[*She kisses her.*]

I'm glad you're home.

ABBEY: Me too. But Billie, would you do me a favor?

BILLIE: Anything, darling, what is it?

ABBEY: Please knock before you enter our room. I know that you still think of me as your baby sister, but I'm married now, and with married couples, you never know what you might walk in on.

BILLIE: Of course. I'll try to remember. Sweet dreams.

[*She backs out, closing the door behind her.*]

ABBEY [*to herself*]: I'll try. We know what that means, don't we?

[BILLIE *bursts into the room again.*]

BILLIE: Listen, let's just keep this conversation between us, OK?

ABBEY: You mean you don't want me to mention to Sarah that *you* think she's a lesbian?

BILLIE: I want you to find out; just don't tell her that I put you up to it. You know me; I don't want to start anything.

ABBEY: Whatever.

BILLIE: Did you enjoy your dinner, Sweetie?

ABBEY: Well now that you mention it, the—

BILLIE: Anything in particular I can fix you for breakfast?

ABBEY: What I'd really like is for you to remember to knock before you enter my room.

BILLIE: I got it.

ABBEY: You did it again, just now.

BILLIE: Oh, right. Next time.

[*She exits only to stick her head in again.*]

And see what you can find out about the tenure thing. [*Sweetly*] Good night.

[*Lights fade out.*]

SCENE 5

[*Lights fade in. The next day.* SARAH *approaches the door of* ABBEY's *bedroom and knocks.*]

ABBEY [*from inside the closet*]: Sarah?

SARAH [*entering*]: How'd you know it was me?

ABBEY: Billie never knocks. I gotta get a lock for that door.

SARAH: Busy?

ABBEY: Just cleaning out my closets.

SARAH [*pausing a beat*]: So, how's it feel to be back?

ABBEY: I waited until I was really ready.

SARAH: To clean out your closets?

ABBEY: Exactly. I guess getting married does that. Makes you want to reconnect. Next, I want to go up in the attic and go through some of Mom and Dad's things.

SARAH: What things?

ABBEY: You know, photos, scrapbooks—

SARAH: You never used to like to go through the photo albums.

ABBEY: There are no baby pictures of me in there.

SARAH: That's ridiculous.

ABBEY: Look, I've got the one from the living room right here. Just look at all those photos of you and Billie when you were little. They had studio shots made of you guys, candid shots, butt-naked-on-a-bear-rug shots, and the only picture of me when I was a baby is that portrait of the three of us that's hanging downstairs. So looking at the family albums was always a hurtful reminder of how disappointed they were that I wasn't a boy.

SARAH: Abbey, don't go down that road; they loved us all.

ABBEY: I feel like I never got a chance to really get to know them, as people. They were always so busy with their careers. So now I have to search for clues.

SARAH: Clues to what?

ABBEY: Who they were. What they wanted for us. Why they named us like they did?

SARAH: You know who they named us after.

ABBEY: I know that Daddy named us after his favorite singers, but why? Did he want us all to sing? Like the Jackson Five or something? The Three DuPrees?

SARAH: I don't think it's that deep.

ABBEY: There's clues in this house. Somebody's got to find them.

SARAH: You realize what the day after tomorrow is, don't you?

ABBEY [*firmly in denial*]: No.

SARAH: The ten-year anniversary?

ABBEY: Ohh, no wonder . . .

SARAH: Billie always goes away around this time, and I'm usually here alone. This'll be the first time that we've all been together. I just hope things don't get too weird.

ABBEY: Do you think we should all go put flowers on their grave or something?

SARAH: Well that would be the normal, well-adjusted thing to do.

ABBEY: Right; we're not ready.

SARAH: Let's not say anything to Billie unless she mentions it. She'd insist on us all going to the cemetery together. That would make for a very long drive.

ABBEY: Mum's the word.

SARAH [*pauses a beat*]: So, you're moving back home. Think you can live under Queen Billie's rule?

ABBEY: She is getting to be a bit much, isn't she?

SARAH: She's morphing into some surreal, whacked-out version of Mommy on amphetamines.

ABBEY: Scary.

SARAH: I told her it was a bad idea for her to move back home like she did right after the accident. And to move right into their bedroom. But she never listens to me. Now look at her. She acts like she's trying to be our mother. And did you notice that veal chop tyranny she tried to pull? She came this close to gettin' that thing shoved up her nose.

ABBEY: She's so homophobic. And sexist. I can't stand it when women call each other bitches.

SARAH: Next time she does it, just roll your eyes and say, "Must you use that word? It's so 'ghetto.'" She'll drop it like a hot rock.

ABBEY: That's worth a try. [*She pauses a beat.*] Why is she so obsessed with appearances?

SARAH: She gets that from Mommy.

ABBEY: I don't remember Mommy being like that.

SARAH: Abbey, please. Mommy used to pay the pest control people extra to come in unmarked vans. And then there was the time when Cousin El-lice got drunk and turned a cartwheel down the aisle at Aunt Winifred's wedding; Mommy almost—

ABBEY: Who's Cousin Ellice?

SARAH: You know, the one who used to give us those sets of panties with the days of the week embroidered on them.

[ABBEY *looks blank.*]

Come to think of it, she probably died while you were still in diapers. [*She pauses a beat.*] You know Zak's out of a job again.

ABBEY: What happened to the video venture?

SARAH: His partner pulled out. He was the one with the financing. Zak was the people person.

ABBEY: What's he going to do now?

SARAH: Drift probably until something else comes along. I love Zak like a brother, but leave it to Billie to marry the one WASP in the world with no ambition. Not that everyone has to be a wage slave, but at least do something constructive with your time.

ABBEY: Wait a minute, he teaches handicapped children how to swim.

SARAH: He hasn't done that in years. That's what I'm trying to tell you, Abbey. Life with Billie has transformed Zak into a sports-channel-surfing couch potato.

ABBEY [*pauses a beat*]: When did she put on all that weight?

SARAH: It started when she quit smoking.

ABBEY: Knowing her, she's probably ultrasensitive about it.

SARAH: Sensitive? Billie?

ABBEY: Well, don't say anything to her about it. You know how she gets. And you know you have a way of saying things that really undoes people.

SARAH: *Moi?*

ABBEY: *Oui, toi.* Uri was very upset by your proclamation about not dating white men.

SARAH: Why should he care who I date?

ABBEY: He's such a drama queen sometimes. "Abbey," he says, "you have racism in your family."

SARAH: He called me a racist? An Israeli?

ABBEY: Calm down. He didn't call you anything. It was just his way of expressing his insecurities. He thinks you don't approve of our marriage.

[*Silence.*]

Well?

SARAH: It's not that I disapprove; I'm sure he's very nice to you. I just wish he was a brotha, that's all!

[*She continues, launching into another of her over-the-top rants.*]

I mean, what if you have kids and Zak and Billie have kids and all of your kids, who will all be half white, what if all of them married white? There won't be any black DuPrees left! Think about it, Abbey. We could be just one generation away from being whited out!

ABBEY: Look, Sarah, you know as well as I do that I gave "the brothas" a chance. I bent over backwards to make things work with Malik, but it just wasn't going anywhere. I don't want to be like Billie, pushing forty and childless. I want to have children while I'm still young enough to enjoy them. Uri is hardworking, he values family, and he's *devoted to me.* He would never, ever desert his family. I know that.

SARAH: Daddy did not desert us, he was killed

[ABBEY *covers her ears.*]

by a drunk driver!

ABBEY: I wasn't talking about Daddy.

SARAH: You better not be—

ABBEY: Why, you gonna beat me up?

[*She lights a joint and takes a couple of quick hits as* SARAH *watches disapprovingly. Then she puts it out.*]

SARAH: He was a good father. He provided for us and raised us to have some consciousness and—

ABBEY: My kids will have a black consciousness. Don't worry.

SARAH: But you can't expect them to deny their father—

ABBEY: It's not like I'm the first one in the family to choose a mate that's not black. How else would you end up looking like you do?

SARAH: OK. All right. You know, I never really saw myself getting married, but you chicks are forcing me not only to consider it but to marry the blackest man I can find. Somebody's gotta keep some color in this family!

ABBEY: I never saw you look twice at a brother who wasn't dark-skinned. So don't try to hang that on me, that's just your preference. Admit it. C'mon. Just lick your lips and say, "I like dark meat!"

SARAH: Shut up! [ABBEY *laughs*.] You're not funny! I read a book recently, nonfiction. Written by a woman who decided to search for a branch of her family that decided to pass. Her mother was the darkest one in the family, and they all deserted her, cut her off like with no explanation. So forty years later the daughter decides that she going to try to reunite the family while her mother is still alive. And eventually with the help of a private detective she finds her mother's only remaining sister and her family and brings them all together. Afterwards she wrote, "All those years I'd been looking for black people who were passing for white, but what I found was black people who had actually become white." [*She pauses a beat.*] Nonfiction, Abbey. Nonfiction.

ABBEY: But that happened way back when people had to pass to get ahead. As long as we raise our kids to have pride in their heritage, things will be fine.

SARAH: It's still much harder to be black in this country, and I don't see that changing anytime soon. Mark my words. Nonfiction!

ABBEY: I just don't see what I can do about any of that. I'm married and I actually like my husband.

SARAH: Like? Like? You're jeopardizing the future of this family for someone you like?

ABBEY: I haven't been with him long enough to love him, but that'll come.

SARAH: Just how long did you know him before you married him?

ABBEY: A few weeks, I mean, months. [*Off her look*] He's good company. I can work with him.

SARAH: You are incorrigible. Did you tell Malik you got married?

ABBEY: I wrote him a letter.

SARAH: What about his sister? You write her one too?

ABBEY: Fuck you.

SARAH: Now, now. I'm not criticizing. I actually admire people like you.

ABBEY: What's that supposed to mean? People like me.

SARAH: Free spirits. People who take their freedom. I'm still trying to buy mine. So, now that you're married, does that mean you've given up girls?

ABBEY: For the time being.

SARAH: What do dat mean?

ABBEY: I always thought I'd find a nice woman to settle down with, you know, after the kids are grown.

SARAH: What about Uri?

ABBEY: Men don't live that long.

SARAH: Really, Abbey, how can you be so insouciant?

ABBEY [*assuming her "ditzy diva" posture*]: I don't know what you mean.

SARAH: Yeah, right. [*She pauses a beat.*] So what's his position on the Palestinian homeland question?

ABBEY [*defensively*]: He supports it.

SARAH: Did he tell you that before or after you slept with him?

ABBEY: That's not fair! How would you like it if people in other countries judged you based on the actions of the U.S. government?

SARAH [*shudders*]: Good point. [*She pauses a beat.*] Abbey, I didn't get tenure.

ABBEY: You want some of mine?

SARAH: Tenure, Abbey. Tenure! I'm out of a job at the end of the school year.

ABBEY: Good for you. You can get on unemployment and go traveling, like Uri and me.

SARAH: I'm afraid I'm way past the age where I enjoy camping out. I like warm, cozy bed-and-breakfast inns.

ABBEY: Oh. Well, do you have any savings?

SARAH: I'm still paying off ten years' worth of student loans.

ABBEY: What're you going to do?

SARAH: I want to come home for a while. I want to work on my new book without any outside pressures, like having to pay rent.

ABBEY: Did you tell Billie?

SARAH: Of course not. You know, this house is not big enough for all of us. Since me and you and Uri need a place to live, I think Billie and Zak should move.

ABBEY: Whoa! You sound like that Tracy Chapman song, talking 'bout a revolution.

SARAH: It's our turn, Abbey. Mom and Dad left it to all of us, equally. She's had ten years of rent-free living. And you know she makes way more than I do teaching. Plus she's got investments. She can afford to buy her own house. So, are you with me? We can do this if we work together.

ABBEY: I don't know. This feels like the kind of thing that could create bad blood.

SARAH: It's only fair.

ABBEY: You said Zak isn't working.

SARAH: He's never working. But this could help motivate him to get off his butt.

ABBEY: I need to think about it.

SARAH: I'm going to settle this before I leave.

ABBEY: Well, if you think this can be settled peacefully—

SARAH: I'm all for diplomacy. I'm Buddhist.

ABBEY: Promise?

SARAH: What did I say?

ABBEY: OK, Kayo, what's the plan?

SARAH: There is no plan, but I do have a strategy. We have to change the way we deal with Billie. You have to stop giving in to avoid conflict. Start standing up to her. You don't have to get angry, just stand your ground and assert yourself.

ABBEY: I do!

SARAH: Well, don't let her overwhelm you. And when she starts getting irrational, question her. Stay calm and ask her penetrating questions that force her to stop and think. And keep the pressure on until she realizes how irrational she's being. That'll throw her off balance, weaken her defenses.

ABBEY: OK. I'll try.

SARAH: Don't try, just do it.

ABBEY: What about you? What are you going to do differently?

SARAH: That's the part I haven't figured out yet.

[Lights fade out.]

SCENE 6

[Lights fade in. Later that same day, in the kitchen. URI and ABBEY are at the table having a cup of tea. SARAH enters and goes to the refrigerator.]

SARAH: God dang it! Will you look at this—some jerk ate all my pizza and left the crusts in the refrigerator for me to find. Do we have to start labeling things around here?

[*She tosses the box into the trash and goes back into the refrigerator.* URI *whispers something to* ABBEY.]

ABBEY [*heading toward the door, followed by* URI]: Uh—We're going out for a while.

SARAH: Hold it. You're not expecting me to clear away your dishes, are you?

ABBEY: You don't have to act so—

[URI *stops her and then proceeds to clear the dishes. As* ABBEY *and* URI *exit,* ABBEY *throws her sister a look.*]

[ZAK *enters from outside.*]

SARAH: Hey now.

ZAK: Hello.

SARAH: I was just heating up some leftovers. Want some?

ZAK: No thanks.

[*He starts to exit the kitchen to another part of the house.*]

SARAH: Uh, Zak. Can I have a word with you?

ZAK: Yeah?

SARAH: About last night—

ZAK: Yeah?

SARAH: You remember the confrontation at the table? Me and Billie?

ZAK: Yeah?

SARAH: I hope you weren't offended by anything I may have said to Billie—

ZAK: Oh, you mean the part about not dating white guys?

SARAH: Right. I want you to know that statement wasn't directed at anyone at the table.

ZAK: Yeah?

SARAH: What I mean is that that argument was not about what it seemed to be about on the surface. Billie was once again trampling all over my established boundaries and I guess I just went for shock value to try to get her to back off.

ZAK: Does this mean that you would date a guy who looked like me?

SARAH: I think we're digressing, Zak. The point is that I'm trying to apologize in case I may have said something inappropriate at the dinner table. I—I was insensitive, and I just want you to know that I'm sorry. [*Silence*] It was just unresolved sister stuff. Nothing to do with you or Uri. I've been under a lot of stress lately and—

ZAK: Your job?

SARAH: Right.

ZAK: You wanna talk about it?

SARAH: *No!*

ZAK: OK. If that's how you feel.

[*He starts to leave.*]

SARAH: Wait, Zak. I didn't mean it to come out like that. I'm just not ready to go public yet, but—

ZAK: What?

SARAH: Well, promise me that you won't tell Billie.

ZAK: I promise.

SARAH: Swear.

ZAK: I swear I won't tell Billie.

SARAH: I didn't get tenure. Theoretically I have eighteen months to find another job, but there's no way I could possibly stick it out that long. I feel like hiring a moving company to go pack up my apartment and letting them find someone else to teach my overenrolled courses.

ZAK: Where would you go?

SARAH: I've been thinking about moving back home for a while.

ZAK: Well, I could come up and help you pack everything up and move it for you. Depending on how much stuff you have, you might have to put some in storage, but there's room in the basement.

SARAH: You'd really do that?

ZAK: Sure. I'm not that busy during the week.

SARAH: Thank you, Zak. I really appreciate that. [*She sighs.*] I guess I've been really stressing over this—

ZAK: Sarah, you can always come to me if you need anything. Anything.

SARAH: Thank you. That means a lot to me.

[*The doorbell rings.*]

ZAK: Come here, Four-Eyes.

[*He pulls her into an embrace but holds her a little longer and a little closer than is comfortable. When she starts to disengage, he kisses her. She responds with a martial arts move that lands him on his butt.*]

SARAH: Zak! Have you lost your mind? Or maybe you've seen too many Woody Allen movies?

BILLIE [*from offstage*]: Sarah!

ZAK: I'm sorry, Sarah. Honestly, I don't know what came over me.

SARAH: That didn't happen, Zak. It never happened. Do you understand?

ZAK [*getting to his feet*]: Yeah, Sarah. Sure. Whatever you say.

BILLIE [*yelling, still offstage*]: Sarah! There's someone here to see you!

SARAH [*ignoring* BILLIE]: Didn't I just tell you that I have way too much drama in my life right now? I can't let my guard down around here for a second!

[BILLIE *bursts in.*]

BILLIE: Sarah! Didn't you hear me calling you? There's a young man here to see you. Says he's a student at your school?

SARAH: Oh God.

BILLIE: Why didn't you tell me you were expecting company?

SARAH: I wasn't sure he was coming. Anyway, you're supposed to be in Hawaii.

BILLIE: What's wrong?

SARAH: Nothing.

BILLIE: You look upset.

SARAH: I just—I get wicked PMS. Excuse—

[SPENCER *enters.*]

SPENCER: Hello, Sarah.

SARAH: Spencer.

SPENCER: Have I come at a bad time?

SARAH: No. No. Not at all. You met my sister Billie? And this is my brother-in-law, Zachary. Zak. Spencer's a friend of mine from school.

BILLIE: And you said that you're a student up at—

SPENCER: Graduate.

BILLIE: Huh?

SPENCER: I'm a graduate student.

BILLIE: Oh, right. Are you one of Sarah's students?

SPENCER: Ah'm takin' an independent study with her, but ah'm not in history. Ah'm in education.

BILLIE: I see.

SARAH: Spencer's on his way back to Connecticut from the march in D.C. I invited him to stop—

SPENCER: Sarah, maybe this isn't the best time. Maybe you should call me when you get back in—

SARAH: No! I want you to stay. It's no problem, really. Besides, it's getting late. You don't want to have to drive all the way to New England tonight.

BILLIE: Really, Sarah. We do have a full house. Don't you think you should discuss it with me before—?

SARAH: He's my guest, Billie. Where are your manners?

BILLIE: For your information, Missy, the sofa bed in the study is broke. Where's he going to sleep?

SARAH: With me!

[SPENCER looks pleasantly surprised, ZAK looks uncomfortable, and BILLIE looks totally exasperated. Blackout.]

SCENE 7

[Lights fade in. A short time later in SARAH's room.]

SARAH: How was the march?

SPENCER: Incredible. Inspiring. Life changin'. I wrote a poem. Wanna hear it?

SARAH: Sure.

[SPENCER turns away briefly to assume his performance persona and then recites the poem from memory.]

SPENCER: One million strong, we stand, we breathe;
　　Hearts in our one million black bodies,
　　We stand beating, the million of us;
　　Our bones calling back, calling the bones of the ancestors,
　　Our bones calling up the souls, which shine white under the earth,
　　A bright thing that lights the way for us, together as one;
　　The path on the sea floor, beneath the Atlantic,
　　Made by the curl and suck of each rare body;
　　They light the way through the mud-grit of memory
　　　　of our murdered leaders and freedom fighters
　　Our leaders take to the air in sound, in waves they prophesy;
　　We gather their lyrics together in our arms,
　　Gather the words of our leaders like sun, like thirst;
　　On this day the million is planted, our feet sink down into the mud;

Each moment of air, the pith of it, is full,
We are God calling back to God;
As the air into our lungs is ripening us, we remember,
On this day we testify our pride is in Technicolor today,
On October 16, 1995, we remember crowns;
On this day we stand together as one.

SARAH: That was so impressive. So powerful. I'm overwhelmed.

SPENCER [*modestly*]: I was on a mission down there after I wrote it. I tried to get to the podium to recite it, but I never made it past the guards. The Fruit of Islam run a tight ship.

SARAH: Did you recite it for them?

SPENCER: Yep. They said, "That's real good, brotha, but we still can't let you back here."

SARAH: Oh well, next time.

SPENCER: Ah'm so high off that march I feel like I can do anything.

SARAH: Well, that won't last. With midterms coming up, you TAs are going to be buried.

SPENCER: Ought to be illegal to work us like they do.

SARAH: You all should organize. If the teaching assistants went out on strike just before finals, the administration would be forced to negotiate. The faculty wouldn't be able to grade all those tests and papers.

SPENCER: Strikes can last a long time. Most of us can't afford it. That's why we take those jobs in the first place. [*He pauses a beat.*] So, yo' sista didn't make her flight?

SARAH: Nobody did. Their airport's closed. There's a typhoon or a monsoon or something.

SPENCER: You and her get along?

SARAH: Not really.

SPENCER: Thought I felt some tension.

SARAH: Why didn't you call?

SPENCER: I tried to. Some white guy answered the phone, so I thought I wrote the number down wrong.

SARAH: I wasn't sure if you were coming or not.

SPENCER: I said I was.

SARAH: You said you'd "try." I'm no rookie. I know what it means when a man says he'll "try." Especially under these circumstances.

SPENCER: And what circumstances are these?

SARAH: Trying to reach closure.

SPENCER: Sarah, I been thinkin'. I don't think we need to stop seein' each other.

SARAH: What?

SPENCER: I thought about it while I was in D.C. A lot. I know that there's some differences, but I feel real comfortable with you. I can't quite put my finger on it, but there's something about you jes' agrees with me. [*He pauses a beat.*] You look confused.

SARAH: I feel like I'm being yo-yoed.

SPENCER: What's that mean?

SARAH: You know.

[*She gestures.*]

Pushed away, yanked back. Like I'm on a string. Yo-yoed.

SPENCER: Ah'm sorry about what happened before I left. I wasn't sure then. But I am now.

SARAH: Things have changed for me too since I saw you last. I met with Dean Kraft on Friday. I didn't get tenure.

SPENCER: Naw! Dey can't do that! You the most popular professor they got up there.

SARAH: They seem to be holding my popularity against me. I can see it all clearly now. I was just a "diversity hire" for my department. I never had a chance at tenure. It was all a setup.

SPENCER: We're not gonna take this.

SARAH: "We"?

SPENCER: We have to fight this.

SARAH: What "we"?

SPENCER: You, me, the Black Student Union, the Graduate Student Union, the entire student body.

SARAH: What're you saying?

SPENCER: "Where there is no struggle there is no progress." I say we demonstrate, we boycott, we take over Dean Kraft's office if we have to.

SARAH: Bring the university to its knees. I like it. I like it a lot. But you know, if we do this, we have to be clear; it's not about me. It's about the way they use the subjectivity of the process to keep qualified women and people of color out of tenured positions.

SPENCER: I feel ya.

SARAH: We can't be rash. There's too much at stake. Let's think about it.

SPENCER: That's a good idea. Let's sleep on it.

SARAH: Come on. I'll show you to your room.

SPENCER: You said I was sleepin' wit you.

SARAH: I just said that to antagonize my sister. [*Off his look*] She's never liked me.

SPENCER: Why not?

SARAH: Oh, something about me being born.

SPENCER: C'mere.

[*He pulls her to him and traces her lips with his finger.*]

I like how you talk.

[*They kiss.*]

SARAH: Something about you agrees with me too. [*More kissing*] But—you're still not sleeping with me.

SPENCER: Why?

SARAH: We need to think things through.

SPENCER: I thought 'em through while I was marchin'.

SARAH: Well, now I need a chance to do the same. With a clear head. Sex is a drug, you know.

[*He kisses her again.*]

Stop it, Mr. Heroin.

[*She nudges him toward the door.*]

Your room's across the hall. There's sheets and towels in the closet.

SPENCER: She said the sofa bed is broke. You gonna make me sleep on the floor?

SARAH: Nice try, but I seem to recall that you keep a futon in the back of that Bronco of yours. Make yourself at home.

[*He starts to leave.*]

Spencer? I'm glad you came.

[*He leans in to kiss her one last time, but when she leans in, he teasingly pulls back and exits.* SARAH *leaps and falls onto her bed. Lights fade to black.*]

ACT 2

SCENE 1

[*Lights full up. The next morning.* BILLIE *is in the kitchen, smoking in front of an open window. When she hears footsteps, she hurriedly extinguishes the cigarette and fans the air with her hand.* SARAH *enters from outside wearing a running suit.*]

SARAH: Good morning.

[*She sniffs the air.*]

Ah. There's nothing like the smell of early death before breakfast.

BILLIE: Where's your friend? Or should I say your student?

SARAH: He'll be down shortly.

BILLIE: So Professor DuPree, just what kind of lessons are you giving him?

SARAH: Oh, I'd say that our relationship is more collaborative in nature.

BILLIE: Thought you said he was sleeping with you?

SARAH: Are you doing bed checks now?

BILLIE: Well, I saw a light on in the study. [*Off* SARAH's *look*] I thought somebody had left a light on.

SARAH: And?

BILLIE: He was getting undressed.

SARAH: And?

BILLIE: Nothing. I said "Excuse me" and left.

SARAH: Umm hmm.

BILLIE: What?

SARAH: I'm just waiting for the rest of it.

BILLIE: That's it.

[SARAH *pours herself a cup of coffee, adding an unhealthy amount of sugar.*]

So where'd he get that body? The penitentiary?

[SARAH *slams down the sugar bowl but then speaks in a calm and controlled manner.*]

SARAH: I don't know where he got his body, Billie. Maybe you should ask him. Of course, then he might ask you where you got your body—

BILLIE: There's nothing wrong with my body!

SARAH: Did I say there was?

[*She exits, passing* ZAK *as he enters.*]

Morning.

ZAK: Good morning, Sarah. [*To* BILLIE] Umm. Sweet potato pancakes. [*Hugging her from behind*] What did I ever do to deserve a wife like you?

BILLIE: I'm just waiting for Abbey to get back with the syrup. She must be tapping the sap from the trees, it's taking her so long.

ZAK: I'll set the table.

BILLIE: What's gotten into you?

[ABBEY *and* URI *enter;* URI *is loaded down with grocery bags,* ABBEY *empty-handed.*]

Took you long enough. I was getting worried.

ABBEY: The first two stores we went to didn't have real maple. And I wanted to get the milk that doesn't have growth hormones in it.

BILLIE: So you went to the farm and milked the cows yourself.

ABBEY: No, we found a natural foods store. I got a gallon plus a few other things. And then there was that man who was lying in the driveway. That's what took so long. When can we eat?

BILLIE: Wait a minute. Back up. What was a man doing lying in our driveway?

ABBEY: I didn't ask him all that. I just asked if he could scoot to one side so I could back out around him because you were waiting for the syrup.

BILLIE: That makes no sense, Abbey. We don't have street people in our neighborhood.

ABBEY: He wasn't a street person. He was very well dressed. You would have approved.

BILLIE: Well, is he still out there?

ABBEY: No, he was gone when we got back. So he must've worked it out. Can we eat now?

BILLIE: Yeah. Go call Sarah. [*Yelling*] Sarah!

[SARAH *and* SPENCER *enter.*]

SARAH: You don't have to yell, I'm right here. Abbey, I want you to meet my friend Spencer. My sister Abbey. The world traveler of the family.

ABBEY: Oh! You're the one who was lying in the driveway.

SPENCER: I was checking out something under my truck.

ABBEY: Of course. Nice to meet you. This is my husband.

[URI *extends his hand.*]

URI: Spencer? I'm Uri.

[SPENCER *looks* URI *up and down before shaking his hand.*]

SPENCER: Nice to meet you.
BILLIE: That's your seat, Spencer.

[*They serve themselves in silence.*]

ZAK [*to* SPENCER]: Did you catch that game the other night?

[*He mimes shooting a basket.*]

SPENCER: Naw. [*Pointedly*] I was watchin' PBS.
ZAK: I see.

[*Awkward pause.*]

URI: Do you live here in Philadelphia?
SPENCER: No, I'm going to school in Connecticut.
URI: Is that where you are from?
SPENCER: No, ah'm from California, originally.
URI: I see.
BILLIE: Spencer is one of Sarah's students, right, Sarah?
SARAH: Well, not exactly. I'm supervising a project he's doing. That's all.
BILLIE: I see. And did you sleep all right, Spencer?
SPENCER: Very well, thank you.
BILLIE: And you, Sarah, did you sleep well?
SARAH: Come on, Billie. We're all adults here.
BILLIE: What's that supposed to mean?
SARAH: You tell me what it means, Billie.

[*Awkward pause.*]

SPENCER: The pancakes are delicious.
BILLIE: Thank you.
SPENCER: They have sweet potatoes in 'em?
BILLIE: Right. It's an old family recipe. [*Pause.*] Has Sarah told you about our
    family's history?
SPENCER: Not really.
BILLIE: Well, our people have been in this area for many generations. We
    have a great-great uncle named W. D. Matthews, *Captain* Matthews, who
    was a stationmaster on the Underground Railroad. This area was a very

important stop for fugitive slaves, being the first major city *north* of the Mason-Dixon Line.

SPENCER: That so?

BILLIE: Captain Matthews owned and operated a restaurant and boarding-house that served as his cover. During the Civil War he was appointed captain, one of only two African American officers in the Union army.

SPENCER: Only two?

SARAH: Billie, do we have to bore Spencer with the family album right now?

SPENCER: I like family stories.

BILLIE: We have another ancestor, Thomas Carney, who fought in the Revolutionary War under George Washington.

SPENCER: Naw! Really?

BILLIE: Bayoneted seven *of the enemy.*

SARAH: Billie's a regular Daughter of the American Revolution.

BILLIE: Yes. We have a lot of achievers in our family. And so far as we know, there's never been anyone in our family who's been on welfare or in jail.

SARAH: Oh, Billie, stop talking noise. We're one generation removed from the ghetto and you know it.

BILLIE: I don't know what you're talking about.

SARAH: Daddy showed me where he and Mommy lived while they were saving for their first house. You know, when you were a baby. Looked like the projects to me.

BILLIE [*shouting*]: That's a goddamn lie! Those weren't projects, they were garden apartments!

SARAH: Umm hmm. And I know we have relatives who've been in jail.

BILLIE: Name one! Name one relative that you know who's been in jail!

SARAH: Well, I don't know them personally, but I'd bet money that they exist. Growing up way out here, we don't know most of our relatives anymore.

BILLIE: Well, that's what I said, none that we know of.

[SARAH *gestures to* SPENCER *indicating that* BILLIE *may not be playing with a full deck.*]

I saw that!

SARAH: And?

ZAK: Ladies, ladies. We have company.

[BILLIE *pauses a beat while she recovers her composure.*]

BILLIE: So, tell us about *your* family.

SPENCER: Mah people went out west from Mississippi. M'uncle got caught messin' with this white girl when he was a boy, you know, jes' kids rollin' in the hay really, but her father found out about it and he rode up on a horse demandin' to know where my uncle was. Told my grandfather that he was gonna kill 'im. Dey started arguin' and the cracker struck my grandfather wit a whip, but my grandfather had just finished cuttin' some sugarcane for the kids so he grabbed his machete. Pretty soon all my kin knew they had to leave real quick. But my grandfather's brother, Hannibal, he stayed behind to head 'em off. And that's how we come to settle down in Bakersfield.

URI: What's a cracker?

[*Utter silence.*]

ZAK: It's a bigoted southern white person. Usually of a lower class.

URI: Bigoted?

SARAH: Historically speaking, "cracker" was a term used by slaves in this country to describe the overseer, the one who cracked the whip.

URI: I see.

ABBEY: What happened to Hannibal?

SPENCER: Dey killed 'im. Chopped his body up and threw it in the river. My grandfather never got over that. Couldn't stand to have a white man set foot on his property. An' when he got old, he used to sit and call his brotha's name, over and over, 'til my grandmother would tell me to go touch him and say, "Grandpa, Hannibal is dead." It always hurt me to have to do that.

BILLIE: And just what did your people do in California?

SPENCER: Farmed mostly. That's what they knew how to do. Dey was sharecroppers back in Mississip, on a cotton plantation. And my grandmama ran a juke—

BILLIE: Your folks picked cotton?

SARAH: That's enough, Billie!

SPENCER: My grandpa told me he used to pick over eight hundred pounds of cotton in one day. [*To* SARAH] I'm just as proud of my folks as she is a' yours.

[SARAH *reaches across the table and takes his hand.*]

SARAH: Welcome to the family.

[SPENCER *looks at* BILLIE; *she looks away.*]

BILLIE [*clears her throat*]: So, what are your plans for today, Abbey?

ABBEY: I want to finish going through some boxes in the attic.

BILLIE: What for?

ABBEY: I just wanted to go through some of Mom and Dad's old things. You know, their yearbooks, Dad's scrapbook. I like looking at their things.

BILLIE: Don't you think it's time you started *looking* for a job?

ABBEY: We have the rest of our lives to work, Billie.

BILLIE: That top—I know that's a Donna Karan! Come here and let me see the label.

[ABBEY *starts to comply, but she sees* SARAH *shaking her head no vigorously. Instead she quickly removes it and passes it to* BILLIE *and continues eating in her undershirt.*]

Really, Abbey, that wasn't necessary.

[*She examines the label.*]

DKNY! I knew it. That's Donna Karan's youthful line. Here.

[*She passes it back.*]

Is that undershirt a Calvin Klein?

ABBEY: You want me to take this off too?

[BILLIE *sucks her teeth and turns her attention to her other sister.*]

BILLIE: What're your plans, Sarah?

SARAH: I was thinking about going for a walk later on. Spencer and I have some plans to discuss.

BILLIE: Oh?

SPENCER: Actually, Sarah, I was hopin' I could get to an auto supply shop. There's a part on my truck that needs changin' before I drive the rest of the way back.

SARAH: No problem.

SPENCER: You don't mind if I change my fuel pump in your driveway, do you, Billie?

[*Her jaw drops.*]

BILLIE: How long will it take?

SPENCER: Could take a couple of hours, dependin' on if I have all the right tools.

SARAH: It's fine.

BILLIE: Wait a minute, Sarah. I'm not comfortable with this. I mean, what will the neighbors think if they see a strange man fixing a truck in our driveway?

SARAH: I know I didn't just hear you say, "What will the neighbors think?"

BILLIE: Well you just zoom in and out of here whenever you please, but I actually live here and I have to think about these things. The people around here are very particular and—

SARAH: We're talking about a couple of hours at most.

BILLIE: But what if somebody shoots him?

SPENCER: If it's a problem—

[SARAH *kicks him under the table.*]

Oww.

SARAH: All right. Let's take a vote. We all own the house equally, we each get a vote. One for, one against; Abbey, you're the tiebreaker. What do you say?

ABBEY: I don't see anything wrong with it.

SARAH: Done!

BILLIE: Well, I think that since I pay the taxes, I should have a bigger say.

SARAH: That doesn't matter in a democracy. One woman, one vote. It's settled.

ABBEY: Why don't you help him, Uri?

URI: Me?

ABBEY: You've been saying you want to learn more about cars. You can help him while I'm up in the attic.

URI: OK. All right. Sure.

[*He slaps* SPENCER *on the back.*]

Hey, Spencer.

[SPENCER *looks unenthused.*]

SARAH: Billie, what are your plans for today?

BILLIE: You know very well what my plans are. I'm going to my office. Somebody in this family's gotta make some money.

[*Lights fade out.*]

SCENE 2

[*Lights fade in.* ABBEY*'s room, soon after breakfast.* ABBEY *is propped up on her bed twisting her locks;* URI *is painting her toenails.*]

URI: Why you call your sister Kayo?

ABBEY: My dad used to call her that 'cause she used to get in a lot of fights when she was a girl.

URI: I do not understand "Kayo." It's a word or a name?

ABBEY: The letters *K-O* stand for "knockout." Daddy always said she "coulda' been a contenda'."

URI: But why she was fighting?

ABBEY: I think it all started when my family moved south. My dad's job transferred him to their aerospace plant in Daytona Beach; it was a big promotion. I was just a baby, but Sarah became the first black student to attend the all-white elementary school in the district where we lived. So sometimes the white kids would call her names, and my parents had told her to ignore them, but one day a girl was following her—taunting her, saying that all niggers are dumb or something to that effect, and I guess Sarah had had enough 'cause she swung around all of a sudden and punched the girl so hard that she knocked her down and gave her a black eye. I think they left her alone after that.

URI: That's good she won.

ABBEY: Yeah, but I think the experience left some scars. She's still got some major anger management issues. Once I saw her get into it with some lady over a parking space when the woman called her "stupid—"

[BILLIE *bursts into the room.*]

BILLIE: The nerve of her! Bringing some homeboy straight out of the hood into our home and telling him "welcome to the family"! I think your sister's lost her mind.

URI [*to* ABBEY]: You want I go make the tea?

ABBEY: You might as well stay. You're in it now.

BILLIE: Letting him fix his truck in our driveway—

ABBEY [*overlapping*]: It's a sport-utility vehicle.

BILLIE: This time that bitch has gone too far!

ABBEY: Billie, must you use that word? It's so ghetto.

BILLIE: That hussy has gone way too far!

ABBEY: I would've thought you'd be relieved since you obviously found the idea of having a lesbian in the family so undesirable. You were really barking up the wrong tree with that idea, weren't you?

BILLIE: All I know is that I want her and her Mississippi homeboy out of here!

ABBEY: Why?

BILLIE: Because I said so, that's why!

ABBEY: What's your reason?

BILLIE: Didn't you hear him say that his grandfather was a murderer! She's got no business bringing him here. This is my house and—

ABBEY: No, Billie, the house belongs to all three of us.

BILLIE: But it's my home—

ABBEY: It's my home too. And Uri's.

BILLIE: I just don't think it's right for her to be layin' up with some young buck in our parents' house.

ABBEY: You said he slept in the den.

BILLIE: He's her student, Abbey. I may not know everything that you and Sarah know, but I know that professors are not supposed to have personal relationships with their students. It's not right. She can't do that!

ABBEY: Why can't she?

BILLIE: What?

ABBEY: Listen, Billie. Kayo can do whatever she wants. And so can I. And so can you. We can all do what we want. It's not a crime.

BILLIE: You mean—

ABBEY: We can all do what we want.

[BILLIE *reacts visibly to this but tries to cover.*]

BILLIE: You think I don't know that? I don't know who you think you're talking to. Tryin' to tell me—

[URI *opens the door for her to exit.*]

And this is my house!

[*She turns abruptly and exits, swatting* URI *on her way out. Once she's outside the door, she stops.*]

I can do what I want. I can do what I want.

[ABBEY *peers into the hall to make sure* BILLIE's *gone.*]

ABBEY: Yes!

[*She turns to* URI.]

Did you see that, honey? I think I won.

[*He goes to her and embraces her. Lights fade out.*]

SCENE 3

[*Lights fade in. Later on that afternoon, in* SARAH*'s room. She is doing seated bicep curls.* SPENCER *knocks and enters.*]

SPENCER: Hey.

SARAH: Hey. Did you get your car parts?

SPENCER: Yep.

SARAH: Uri go with you?

SPENCER: Yep. [*He pauses a beat.*] So . . . Wassup wit yo' sistas? They don' like brothas?

SARAH: Oh, that. You noticed.

SPENCER: Did you think I wouldn't? One of them I could maybe understand, but both of 'em?

[SARAH *puts down the weights and begins to pace and gesture, continuing to do so throughout the following rant.*]

SARAH: I just don't know what to do. Your sisters meet someone they think they can be happy with, you want to support them. You want them to be happy and it's almost as though it's taboo to even notice that their fiancé happens to be of a different race, but call me reactionary 'cause I just can't help thinking about how their choices could alter the future of our family. Our family as we know it, as an African American family, could cease to exist within two generations. I read a book about a family where every-body decided to pass except for the youngest sister, who was possibly too dark, or maybe just too black-identified to want to pass—

SPENCER: I know, baby, nonfiction.

SARAH: Right. I keep asking myself, what's to become of us?

SPENCER: I didn't mean to pick at your scabs.

SARAH: And I don't want to sound like a racist, but I do want my family to stay black. I mean, after all that our ancestors went through, I feel that we owe them that much. Don't you think?

SPENCER: Ah'm startin' to think you only want me for my melanin.

SARAH: That's not funny!

SPENCER: Ah'm sorry. [*He pauses a beat.*] Come over here.

[*She gives him a look and resumes her bicep curls in silence.*]

So what happened—wit yo' sistas? They jes'—fell in love?

SARAH: I guess. [*She pauses a beat.*] Actually Billie was a rebounder. She was engaged to some brother she met in college, but they ended up calling it off. And then when my parents died, we all came home, and that's when she got hooked up with Zak.

SPENCER: What? He was the boy next door?

SARAH: Literally. An outcome that I don't think my folks anticipated when they moved us out to the burbs.

SPENCER: What did she see in him?

SARAH: They were good for each other at first. He was there for her when my folks died. It was really hard for us, you know, losing both of them like that. Plus he used to be able to get her to lighten up.

SPENCER: And Abbey?

SARAH: Abbey's a love mercenary. She'll take on anybody, s'long as they're willing to worship at the altar of Abbey. [*Pause.*] Third daughter syndrome. She grew up feeling neglected when the novelty of a baby girl wore thin. She always used to say she was raised by the maid.

SPENCER: Y'all had a maid?

SARAH: Housekeeper. [*Off his look*] Only when my mother worked.

SPENCER: And what about us? Was that "welcome to the family" meant for me, or jes' to antagonize yo' sista?

SARAH: What are you chasing me for, anyway?

SPENCER [*offended*]: Chasin' you? I don't see you runnin'.

SARAH: What state are you in?

SPENCER: Pennsylvania.

SARAH: And who arrived here first?

SPENCER: All right. You made your point. But what I want you to tell me is: Who's being yo-yoed now?

SARAH: I know you think—

SPENCER: Answer the question, Sarah.

SARAH: But I—

SPENCER: Answer the question!

SARAH: I will if you let me! For years I've been on a tenure track, and now I've been derailed. And it would be oh-so-easy just to fall into your big strong arms and take refuge from the world that's wronged me, but that's just not who I am.

SPENCER: Maybe it's time for you to expand your repertoire. Look at me. I've been a student and a coach. An athlete and a poet. Maybe you should open up to the possibility of being a warrior and a lover. No pressure, though. Jes' something to think about.

SARAH: Touché.

SPENCER [*sitting down on the bench facing* SARAH]: Here, let me show you a few things. I used to be a personal trainer.

SARAH: I'd never know to look at ya.

SPENCER: Try this.

[*He demonstrates a new arm exercise, which she tries.*]

That's good. You have good form. See how that works your delts and your trapezius at the same time?

SARAH: Umm hmm.

[*He removes his warm-up jacket and begin to stretch and flex in his tank top.* SARAH *finds this very distracting, but they both continue to exercise through most of this scene.*]

Where *did* you get that body? Did you special order it . . . for me?

SPENCER [*pleased*]: In my neighborhood you had to have a body like this, for survival.

SARAH: I see. A strategy of deterrence.

SPENCER: That's right. Deterrence. When I was growin' up I was bookish. I liked to read, to draw. Stuff like that was considered girlish. So I *had* to play sports, get into weight trainin'. I wasn't always six foot three, ya know. Back in the hood, in the summertime brothas used to go around bareback, walkin' pit bulls. "It's like a jungle sometimes; makes me wonder how I keep from goin' under."

SARAH [*joins in on*]: "How I keep from goin' under." [*Pauses a beat.*] Did you think about what we talked about last night?

SPENCER: I think we should move forward.

SARAH: Good. I have an idea. I think we should link the tenure issue to the struggle that the teaching assistants have been waging around reduced workloads and better pay. I think you guys should unionize. I know it sounds radical, but if you joined forces, say, with the Teamsters, and you went out on strike, they would honor the picket lines. That would mean no deliveries to the campus. No food for the cafeterias, no office supplies, no textbooks. That's power.

SPENCER: Ah'm scared of you.

[*He begins to do sit-ups.*]

SARAH: No need for that, long as we're on the same side. So if we enlist the
graduate teaching assistants and the Teamsters as allies and wage a war of
attrition, we can bring the university to its knees.

[*She comes over and perches on his knees.*]

Show Dean Kraft how it feels having your face shoved in the mud. You
know that's how the Union beat the Confederates.

SPENCER: Yeah?

SARAH: The South had the superior army.

[*She straddles him, completely unaware of the effect she's having.*]

Up until the Confederates seceded, Southerners dominated the U.S.
Army. Still do. But the North had the ability to wage a sustained effort,
a war of attrition. They prevailed through nontraditional strategies. Basi-
cally they starved them out.

[*She gets up to get a towel, leaving* SPENCER *disappointed.*]

I was thinking that we should stage the takeover of Dean Kraft's office
for publicity purposes. Alert the media just before we do it and have a list
of demands. Of course we'll have to plan it carefully; his office is pretty
heavily guarded.

SPENCER: A challenge. I like challenges.

[*He embraces her.*]

You're quite a troublemaker, you know that?

SARAH: And you like trouble, don't you?

SPENCER: Did I ever tell you about when I used to be a bouncer?

[*They kiss, but then comes a knock at the door, and they separate.*]

SARAH: *Entrez!*

[ABBEY *comes in.*]

ABBEY: Uri and I were wondering if you guys might want to go with us to
the movies later on?

SARAH: What's playing?

ABBEY: I haven't checked yet. But I'm sure there's something. I thought it might be a good idea to let Zak and Billie have an evening to themselves.

SARAH [*to* SPENCER]: Sounds good to me, what do you think?

SPENCER: Sure.

ABBEY: Should we plan to eat out?

SARAH: Better check with Billie. I don't want her getting bent out of shape 'cause she'd planned to cook. Remember the infamous veal chop incident.

ABBEY: Right. I'll check on it. Hope I wasn't interrupting anything?

SARAH: No, we were just plotting how to take over Dean Kraft's heavily guarded office.

ABBEY: Him? [*Jokingly*] He makes cheese.

SARAH: Really, Abbey, you gotta stop smoking that green stuff. There's a reason why they call it dope.

[ABBEY *makes a face at her and exits.*]

SPENCER [*starts to embrace her again*]: I sure do like the way you talk.

[ABBEY *sticks her head back in.*]

ABBEY: Oh, I have something to tell you. About Billie. I did what you said. It worked!

SARAH: Good. Good for you. We'll talk—

ABBEY: Later.

SARAH: Let's go for a walk.

[SPENCER *sits down on the bed.*]

SPENCER: I'm comfortable here.

SARAH: I want to get some fresh air.

SPENCER: What are you scared of?

SARAH: You said no pressure.

SPENCER: I'll tell you what I was scared of. Bein' an athlete, ever since I was in high school, I've had females tryin' to trap me. You know, figurin' me for a meal ticket out the ghetto. Now I'm the first person in my family to go to college and I want more out of life than the people around me had. And I'm not talkin' 'bout material things, 'cause even though we lived in the hood, we always had things. I'm talkin' 'bout wanting to travel. Africa. Europe, see what's between the East and West coasts, even. I might even want to go for my PhD. So I decided a while back that I needed to stay to myself because I didn't want any kids until I'd had a chance to do what I wanted to do. My mama had all three of us by the time she was twenty-one. I'm not sayin' there's anything wrong with that. It's just not what I want to do. Now when we started gettin' close, it kinda scared me, not because I think you're tryin' to latch onto me, I know that you've got things you want to do too, I just wasn't used to bein' close like that with a woman. But when I was marchin' in D.C. I realized that my fear had nothin' to do with us. I thought about how much I like bein' around you and how much I admire you. So that's why I'm here, sleepin' on your floor. If somebody hadda told me I'd be in this situation, I woulda told them dey was crazy. But here I am.

SARAH: That happened to me.

SPENCER: What?

SARAH: People after me for the wrong reasons. Men wanting me because I'm light-skinned. Took me a while to figure it out—why most men who asked me out never seemed interested in getting to know me. But after a while I could tell what they wanted by checking out the kind of car they drove. If it was a show-off car like a Mercedes, I knew that all they cared about was how I was gonna look on their arm. So I guess that's another reason why I started putting up walls. Problem is, once that becomes a habit, it's hard to take them down.

SPENCER: I never came at you like that.

SARAH: I know. You liked me in spite of: "She's pretty cool for a high yella." Bet your mama's gonna love me.

[SPENCER *guiltily breaks eye contact.*]

Right. I'll be about as welcome as a rich white girl.

[SARAH *turns away.* SPENCER *tries to embrace her but she rebuffs him.*]

SPENCER: Hey, this ain't nothin' we can't get through.

[*She turns and faces him.*]

SARAH: You don't understand. I'm not good at . . . I don't know how to make people like me for me.

[*He caresses her face.*]

SPENCER: You made me like you for you.

[*After a beat, he takes her hand.*]

Come on. Let's go get some air.

[*She follows him out of the room. Lights fade out.*]

SCENE 4

[*Lights fade in. Later that same day.* ZAK *is in the kitchen making a sandwich.* SARAH *and* SPENCER *enter; he's laughing, and she's scowling.*]

SPENCER: I wish I could see their faces when dey read what you wrote.
SARAH: Hey Zak.
ZAK: Hey guys. What you been up to?
SARAH: Should I tell him?

[SPENCER *shrugs.*]

These people around here, I swear—
SPENCER: Is there a bathroom down here?
SARAH: Off the front hall, on your left.

[SPENCER *exits.*]

Lemmings. That's what they are, mindless little consumer lemmings.
ZAK: What are you talking about?
SARAH: We were out taking a walk when we came upon a shiny, brand-new, top-of-the-line navy blue Mercedes-Benz. Some idiot left it parked in the alley behind the old firehouse—
ZAK: Uh, Sarah—

[BILLIE *silently enters the kitchen and stands behind* SARAH, *listening.*]

SARAH: As if it wasn't enough to spend all that money on such a gratuitous, ostentatious display of wealth and consumerism, they had the audacity to pick navy blue. Navy blue, Zak! Of all the conservative Ronald Raygun Republican colors. Navy fucking blue. So I took out my trusty little marker and wrote across the shiny clean windshield, "Just say no to conspicuous consumption."
BILLIE: You wrote on my brand-new car?
SARAH: Your car?
BILLIE: That's right, my car! My car! Goddammit!
SARAH: How was I supposed—?
BILLIE [*overlapping with* SARAH's *line*]: You stupid bitch! I oughtta—

[ZAK *grabs her from behind and struggles to restrain her.*]

SARAH [*starts taking off her earrings*]: Stupid? Who parked an overpriced status symbol in a deserted alley? Let her go, Zak.

BILLIE: Let go of me—

ZAK: Go upstairs, Sarah.

BILLIE: You let go of me this instant—

SARAH: I'm not going anywhere.

[*She executes a couple of martial arts kicks to warm up.*]

BILLIE: You're nothing but a selfish, self-righteous bitch, and I'm sick of your shit!

SARAH [*overlapping* BILLIE]: You could be buying your freedom instead of blowing your money on an overpriced car. So who's stupid?

BILLIE: Sleeping with students and you expect to get tenure?

ZAK: Sarah, please, she's wearing me down, I can't hold her much longer.

SARAH: Good. She wants a piece of me, let her try.

[SPENCER *enters unseen, assesses the situation, and scoops* SARAH *up in his arms and takes her upstairs over her protests.*]

Put me down, Spencer. Right now! You let go of me, you have no right—

[*A moment later they enter* SARAH's *room, where he drops her onto her bed and bars the door.*]

How dare you manhandle me! Who told you to interfere in my family's business?

SPENCER: You really expected me to stand there and let you and your sista go at it? I know I always said I wanted to be with a strong black woman, but y'all is jes' takin' it way too far!

SARAH: She started it!

SPENCER: Sarah, you need to take a time-out.

SARAH: Ooohhh! [*Through clenched teeth*] You're right, of course.

[*She pauses a beat while regaining some self-control.*]

That wasn't very Buddhist of me. Did you hear what she wanted to fight about?

SPENCER: Nope.

SARAH: That was her car I wrote on.

SPENCER: Why'd she leave it in that alley like that?

SARAH: I gave up trying to figure her out a long time ago. I think I need to go meditate.

SPENCER: I got a better idea.

SARAH [*exploding*]: Would you just give it a rest! Is that all you ever think about?

SPENCER: How long do you expect me to wait?

SARAH: We shouldn't be sleeping together right now. We can't jeopardize our plans like that.

SPENCER: But what we're planning is bigger than us, you're talking about the teaching assistants, the Teamsters, and the tenure issue. Nobody's going to care if we're sleeping together!

SARAH: You said no pressure. Back off!

SPENCER: I think you're just punishin' me 'cause I didn't come see you before I left for the march.

SARAH: Oh, you mean the time *you stood me up*?

SPENCER: When we was jes' foolin' around, you wanted me up in your bed every night. Now that I'm sayin' let's be serious, you got me sleepin' 'cross the hall on the floor. What kinda shit is that?

[*He gets up to leave.*]

SARAH: Where are you going?

SPENCER: To change my fuel pump. If I hurry, I can be on the road while it's still light.

SARAH: So now you're leaving?

SPENCER: This is gettin' too frustratin'. You need some space; I'm gonna give you what you think you need.

[*He exits.* SARAH *throws her pillow at the door as he closes it. Blackout.*]

SCENE 5

[*Lights swirl to give the effect of the room spinning.*]

Voice-over, SARAH [*in meditation*]: Breath in, breath out. Breath in, breath out. You know he's trying to manipulate you, don't you? He's not going anywhere. He's bluffing. Trying to get his way. Typical male shit. What if he's not bluffing? Let him go. You don't need him. But I want him. Breath in, breath out. Listen to yourself. "I want him." Give in now and it'll be a slippery slope. Be strong, black woman! Breath in, breath out. Breath in, breath out. That's right, concentrate on breath in, breath out.

[*Lights shift to still, soft focus on* SARAH *just before* GRANDMOM's *voice-overs begin.*]

Voice-over, GRANDMOM: Sarah? Baby? Can you hear Grandmom?

Voice-over, SARAH: Yes, Grandmom. I can hear you.

Voice-over, GRANDMOM: Chile, what are you doin'?

Voice-over, SARAH: Meditating.

Voice-over, GRANDMOM: I know that. But what was you fussin' wit Billie about?

Voice-over, SARAH: A car! She tried to accost me over a stupid car. She went out and bought a ridiculously expensive car, then hides it in an alley so I won't see it. She went off on me because I wrote something on the windows. How was I supposed to know it was hers?

Voice-over, GRANDMOM: What was you doin' writin' on somebody else's car?

Voice-over, SARAH: I—I, I guess I got carried away because of what it symbolizes. It was a Mercedes, Grandmom. A top-of-the-line, navy blue Mercedes-Benz. Navy blue. Don't you think that's excessive?

Voice-over, GRANDMOM: You always did have a peculiar dislike for navy blue. It's just a color, Sassy.

Voice-over, SARAH: And I suppose you think that a Mercedes is just a car?

Voice-over, GRANDMOM: Mercedes? Now, is that a Ford or a Chevy?

Voice-over, SARAH [*laughing*]: I love you, Grandmom.

Voice-over, GRANDMOM: I love you too, but baby, what is you doin' plannin' all this protestin' and so forth?

Voice-over, SARAH: Well, I just don't think I should give up without a fight.

Voice-over, GRANDMOM: But you don't want to stay there!

Voice-over, SARAH: But it should be my choice to leave.

Voice-over, GRANDMOM: Tha's your ego talkin' now, Sassy. If you didn't get your tenure, that means you're not supposed to be there. God's got other things in mind for you. Now you're about to make things a lot worse by trying to swim against the tide. I'm going to say this one last time, Sarah. Look for the open door!

Voice-over, SARAH: But how will I know?

Voice-over, GRANDMOM: Let go of the past. Stop strugglin'. Learn how to walk away from a fight. And when help comes your way, don't swat it away wit a baseball bat. Dat boy's tryin' to court you. He seems like a nice young man, why don't you let him?

Voice-over, SARAH: I don't know. [*She pauses a beat.*] I don't want to feel vulnerable right now. [*She pauses another beat.*] I don't feel safe.

Voice-over, GRANDMOM: The open door!

Voice-over, SARAH: OK. OK. The open door. Grandmom? Are you there? Grandmom! You never give me a chance to say good-bye.

[*Lights fade out.*]

SCENE 6

[*Lights fade in. In the kitchen.* BILLIE *is fixing dinner.* SARAH *enters.*]

SARAH: I need to have a word with you.

[BILLIE *nods.*]

I want to apologize for what I did earlier. It was immature and irresponsible. I already cleaned it up.

BILLIE: Is that it?

SARAH: Well, there's one other thing. I did not get tenure. I am out of a job come the end of the school year.

BILLIE: Well, well, well. I'm not surprised.

SARAH: Really? And why is that?

BILLIE: You didn't try hard enough. You just don't dress the part of a successful university professor.

SARAH: You should see how some of my colleagues dress—

BILLIE: But I bet they already have tenure.

SARAH: The point is that I'm out of a job! I thought about fighting it, but I'm realizing that what I really want and need is some time out. My new book proposal was accepted, but the advance is too small to live on if I have to pay rent. Therefore I need to move back here for a while. Abbey needs to live here while she gets her situation established, and we all know that this house is not big enough for all three of us and our significant others. You and Zak have had full run of the place for ten years. Let me and Abbey have our turn.

[*Long pause.*]

Well?

BILLIE: I have to think about it.

SARAH: What is there to think about?

BILLIE: You are asking me to move, which I had not planned on doing for another couple of years—

SARAH: Aren't you trying to start a family? Don't you think you should have your own place for that?

BILLIE: Yes, but Zak and I have financial goals we wanted to reach before we take on a mortgage. Besides, he's in a career transition right now and—

SARAH: He's been in a career transition since you married him.

BILLIE: Well, I have to investigate and see where we stand financially.

SARAH: You're a financial planner, Billie. You make good money, enough to carry you and Zak, plus with not having to pay rent all these years— I know you, Billie. I know you've got plenty of money squirreled away somewhere. Probably millions.

BILLIE: That's not true. You just don't know how much it takes to run a household, and until Zak gets situated—

SARAH: What Zak needs is some responsibility. If you all had a mortgage to pay, that might give him some incentive to get up off his ass and start contributing.

BILLIE: You don't understand—

SARAH: I do understand: Zak is lazy. And living here has enabled him to persist in his pattern of prolonged adolescence. As soon as he moved out of his parents' house into our parents' house, his parents sold theirs and high-tailed it to Florida. Now he's living off the fruits of our parents' labors. You need to put your foot up his butt.

BILLIE: Who are you to try and tell me how to run my marriage? You don't even have a husband.

SARAH: Neither do you. You have a son. If Daddy could see what's going on up in here, he'd be turning over in his grave.

BILLIE: You're one to talk. You had to go to the ghetto to find someone. Mommy's the one who's spinning.

SARAH: The will says the house belongs to all three of us equally. You've had it to yourself for ten years. It's time to share the wealth.

BILLIE: I've paid the taxes and the upkeep—

SARAH: Which Abbey and I will happily assume.

BILLIE: I can't give in to you on this, Sarah. I cannot.

SARAH: Why?

BILLIE: Because. Because you, you, you—you've always gotten your way on everything. Ever since we were kids, you've always gotten exactly what you wanted, and I'm sick of it. You can't make me move, and I won't until I am good and ready.

SARAH: What have I gotten my way about, *besides tenure*?

BILLIE: You got the prom dress that you wanted—

SARAH: I never went to the stupid prom!

BILLIE: And you and Abbey always had nicer clothes than I did when you were kids. You think I didn't notice? Saks Fifth Avenue, B. Altman's, Best and Company, while all I got was J. C. Penney's and Sears. And then there was the time when you got to go to the white school in Florida, while I had to go way 'cross town to that dilapidated school for the colored. How do you think that felt, huh?

SARAH: You think I wanted to go to the white school? You think it was fun being called "nigger," being ostracized and having to fight my way through? You think I wanted that abuse? And to make matters worse, I still had to fight the neighborhood kids when I got home because they thought that because I was light and went to the white school, that I thought I was better. And the ultimate irony was that I was being sacrificed for them. Years later I found out that some of the parents had asked Mom and Dad to enroll us in the white school because they figured that with Dad having such an important job, they wouldn't refuse his kids entry into their precious segregated school system. I was sent to pave the way.

BILLIE: But why did you get to be the one? I had good grades. I was the oldest.

SARAH: Mom and Dad were trying to protect you. They thought you would be more of a target because you're darker and that it would be harder on you because you were older. And they figured elementary-school kids wouldn't be as vicious.

BILLIE: How do you know that's why they picked you?

SARAH: 'Cause I asked. I ended up with three sets of enemies: the white kids at my school who didn't want me there, the black kids on our block, and you—the one I should have been able to count on to defend me. And about the dresses, Mom and Dad had more money by the time we came along. That's all it was.

BILLIE: So you're gonna stand there and try and tell me that things weren't easier for you because you're lighter?

SARAH: There's been times when it's worked to my advantage, but there have been just as many times when it's worked against me. Like with you. You're my sister. Don't you think I wanted some kind of meaningful relationship with you?

BILLIE: You mean, all these years—[*pauses a beat*] I never knew.

SARAH [*gently*]: You never asked.

[SARAH *exits. This scene should cross-fade seamlessly into the next.*]

SCENE 7

[*In the kitchen a short time later.* BILLIE *is whipping cream by hand.* ABBEY *passes through and peeks into the pots on the stove.*]

ABBEY: What time is dinner? I'm starved.
BILLIE: Well, if it isn't Mrs. Pac-Man.

[*She makes a gobbling gesture with her hand.*]

So what else is new?

[ABBEY *exits.* ZAK *enters.*]

ZAK: You still whipping that cream?
BILLIE: Umm hmm.
ZAK: Why don't you use the electric?
BILLIE: S'broke.
ZAK: Aren't your hands getting tired?
BILLIE: Yes. Yes they are. My hands are tired. I am tired. I am very tired of whipping this cream. And you know what this reminds me of? Us, Zak. It reminds me of our marriage. How I keep spinning my wheels but nothing is solidifying. After all these years, I feel like I need some clarity here. If I have to do everything myself, I can do that. That's exactly what I've been doing. But I don't want to keep pretending that there's a partnership here when we both know that there isn't.
ZAK: So, what're you saying?

[BILLIE *dumps the whipping cream into the garbage can, bowl and all.*]

BILLIE: We're moving.
ZAK: Moving?
BILLIE: Moving. You know, the men drive up and take all your belongings and put them on the big truck.
ZAK: When? Where? What's this all about?
BILLIE: Sarah didn't get tenure. She wants to move back home and none of us feels that this house is big enough for all of us; I've decided that it's time for us to move on.
ZAK: But this is our home.
BILLIE: No, Zak, it's our home, the DuPree family home, it belongs to me and my sisters.
ZAK: Well, all right, but I am your husband. Don't you think you should've discussed it with me?

BILLIE: That's what I'm doing now.

ZAK: But you've already made up your mind.

BILLIE: That's right.

ZAK: I see. And just where have you decided we're moving to?

BILLIE: Well, that's where you get to decide. I'm thinking of renting a place, a small place of my own. I need some space.

ZAK: You mean a separation? I don't understand. Yesterday you wanted to make a baby. What did I miss?

BILLIE: I realized that I'm not ready to be a single parent, and that's just what I would be at the rate things have been going.

ZAK: I thought you wanted to be in charge.

BILLIE: Not all the time, Zak! Sooner or later even I get tired. I'm running a business, taking care of my clients' needs, paying all the bills, managing the household, and cooking and cleaning for all you ungrateful Negroes. From now on, the kitchen's closed. Go git yourself a Happy Meal 'cause I'm on vacation!

[BILLIE *exits.* ZAK *stands there stunned. Lights fade out.*]

SCENE 8

[*Lights fade in. The next morning, in* SARAH's *room.* SPENCER *is asleep in her arms. She blows in his ear to wake him. He slowly stirs.*]

SARAH: Wake up, Buttercup.

SPENCER: Who you callin' Buttercup?

SARAH: That's how my Grandmom used to wake me up when I was little.

SPENCER: What time is it?

SARAH: Time to get up.

SPENCER: Why?

SARAH: This hotel doesn't serve breakfast anymore. We gotta cook it ourselves. C'mon. You can cook, can't you?

SPENCER: 'Course I can.

SARAH: Good. If there's one thing I can't stand, it's a man that can't cook.

SPENCER: My grandmother taught me how to cook when I was little. I can cook better than anybody in my family.

SARAH: Well, I can cook better than anybody in my family 'cause my grandmother taught me too. Billie learned from my mother, I learned from my grandmother, and Abbey, well she learned from the housekeeper. You know, I just thought of something: we won't have to sneak around anymore when we go back to Connecticut. I mean, what are they going to do, fire me?

SPENCER: Sarah, there's something I think I should tell you. And I hope you won't take it the wrong way.

SARAH: What? [*Pause.*] What? Spit it out.

SPENCER: Marriage.

[*She freezes like a deer caught in the headlights.*]

Bein' here with your family and all, it's hard not to think about it. I always saw myself getting married, but I never saw myself doing it before I was thirty-five.

SARAH: "Mah-ridge." What a peculiar word. What is that, Greek?

SPENCER: I love how you talk.

SARAH: Good, 'cause I have something to share with you that I hope you'll understand.

SPENCER: What?

SARAH: I don't want to protest my tenure denial.

SPENCER: What! Why? You deserve it.

SARAH: That's why I don't want to fight it. I know that I did the best job that I was capable of. So maybe the universe is trying to give me a promotion.

SPENCER: But how do you know?

SARAH: I don't. But I'm trusting. All I know is that when I woke up in your arms, I just felt like letting all that stuff go.

SPENCER: My grandmama used to say, sometimes you jes' gotta go wit' your gut. Now, tell me, why does your sister call you Kayo?

SARAH: 'Cause I'm a knockout. Haven't you noticed?

SPENCER: Why do you think I'm here? [*He looks away and says, awkwardly*] I love you, Sarah.

SARAH [*just as awkwardly*]: I love you, too.

[*Lights fade out.*]

SCENE 9

[*Lights fade in. In the kitchen.* SARAH *and* SPENCER *are cooking breakfast.*]

SPENCER: Biscuits are in the oven, you doin' the home fries and the turkey sausage, what else?

SARAH: You know how to make coffee?

[*He gives her a look.*]

I'm not trying to insult you. I don't drink it, so I never learned how to make it, OK?

SPENCER: Where's the coffeepot?

SARAH [*pointing*]: In there.

[*He starts making coffee.* ZAK *enters.*]

ZAK: I thought I smelled breakfast.

SARAH: Spencer made biscuits. How soon will they be ready, honey?

SPENCER: 'Bout fifteen minutes.

SARAH: Is Billie up?

ZAK: I don't know. I slept in the study. [*To* SPENCER] I used your futon. Hope you don't mind.

SPENCER: I'm just glad I wasn't sleepin' on it.

[URI *enters.*]

URI: Good morning.

SARAH: Good morning. Is Abbey up?

URI: She went up to the attic.

SARAH: Again?

[URI *shrugs.* SPENCER *puts the coffee on and goes to set the table.*]

URI: Sarah, I have confession. I am the guilty one who ate your pizza, while everyone was sleeping.

SARAH [*laughs*]: I never suspected you.

URI: No?

SARAH: It had sausage on it. I thought Jews don't eat pork.

URI: Lots of us do, even in Israel. I thought you didn't eat meat.

SARAH: I don't eat red meat. And I only consume swine-laden pizzas when I'm under stress.

URI: Well, I'm sorry I ate it and left the crusts. Abbey said it was "a subconscious passive-aggressive."

SARAH: Act?

URI: Sorry?

SARAH: You needed a noun.

URI: Abbey said it was because I was angry with you.

SARAH: What did I do?

URI: I thought you didn't like white men, but Abbey explained me, she said you want a traditional marriage.

SARAH: Oh, no. Abbey's misinformed. I don't want any kind of marriage. You won't find me signing up to be on anybody's leash.

URI: Leash? What is—?

SARAH: Bad choice of words. Uri, I hope you and Abbey will be very happy.

URI [*visibly moved*]: Thank you. We're thinking about going dancing tonight, there's a reggae band. Maybe you and Spencer—

SARAH: I don't think so.

[*He looks disappointed.*]

Uri, you have to remember that Billie and I are a lot older than you and Abbey.

URI: How old are you?

SARAH: Almost thirty-five. And Billie's forty.

URI: No! You're joking me. Really? Sure?

SARAH: I'm sure.

URI [*shaking his head*]: Abbey has a saying—"black don't crack." Now I get it.

[URI *goes over to* SPENCER.]

I think I figured out why the truck wouldn't start last night.

SARAH: 'Cause I removed the spark plugs.

[*They both look at her.*]

Just kidding.

URI: I think we may have put that, how you call it—I think we may have put it backwards.

SPENCER: Think so? Let's go check it out.

[URI *and* SPENCER *start to exit;* SPENCER *pauses at the door.*]

[*To* ZAK] You comin'?

ZAK [*surprised*]: Uh, yeah.

[*The men exit.* BILLIE *enters.*]

SARAH: Good morning.

BILLIE: Is it?

SARAH: You tell me.

BILLIE: I want you to know that I thought about what we discussed and I checked out the finances. When were you thinking of moving in?

SARAH: Oh, say, mid-June. I'm going to finish out the school year.

BILLIE: Well, I don't think there'll be any problem with that. In fact, I may move out ahead of schedule.

SARAH: Really?

BILLIE: Something Abbey said made me realize that I'd really like to have a place of my own for a while.

SARAH: Well, if that's what you want, why not?

BILLIE: That's what I thought, why the hell not? I might even trade in that Mercedes. I always wanted a sports car, a cherry red convertible. [*Pauses a beat.*] Where would you like me to sit?

SARAH: There.

[*She points to* BILLIE's *usual place at the head of the table.*]

Unless there's some other seat you'd rather have.

BILLIE: No, no, this is fine.

[*She sits.*]

So, where's Mandingo?

[SARAH *clenches her fist reactively, but then she makes a different choice.*]

SARAH: Outside, with Surfer Dude and the Immigrant.

[*Silence for a beat, then* BILLIE *laughs; after another beat,* SARAH *joins in.* ABBEY *enters.*]

ABBEY: You guys, you won't believe what I just found! What's so funny?

BILLIE: You're late. Ya missed it.

SARAH: What did you find?

ABBEY: A letter from Dad.

BILLIE: What?

ABBEY: A letter from Dad. It's addressed to us.

SARAH: Let me see.

[*She tries to take it from* ABBEY, *but* ABBEY *holds it out of her reach.*]

ABBEY: Just listen. "My Darling Diva Daughters," that's us.

SARAH: Just read it.

ABBEY: "My Darling Diva Daughters, I've been thinking, wondering about what could be the most important thing to pass on to you? As you know, my father died when I was a boy, so I never got the benefit of his wisdom, his experience in life. I'm sure that you all know that your mother and I have worked hard to secure your future. We want you to have opportunities that were, for whatever reason, denied to us. I myself would've loved to have pursued a career as a musician, a vocalist. But I came along at a time when opportunities for a man of color in this country were limited. Nat King Cole got my gig, and truth to tell, he had the better voice. But, I did have the good fortune to come along when other windows of opportunity were opening. Corporate America, which up to this point had only employed men who looked like me as janitors and elevator operators, was now hiring managers. Just a few. But if we did well, then a few more and so on. So I want you to know that if I'm not around as much as you'd like, it's not from any lack of love or devotion, but out of a sense of responsibility, first to my family, to do an outstanding job so that you will never have to go without. But secondly to my race. To do an outstanding job so that more will gain the opportunity to secure a place for their families. But above all, I wish for your happiness and that you all lead long, productive, fulfilling lives. My recipe for a fulfilling life is this: Love, wonder, imagine, dream, question, reflect, demand justice, spread truth, work hard, save your money, invest in stock—blue chip! [BILLIE *chimes in on "blue chip"*], *buy your freedom!* [SARAH *chimes in on "buy your freedom"*]— always give something back, count your blessings, see the world, cherish family, think before speaking, practice forgiveness, follow your heart—it will always lead you home, live life with abandon, sing!

"I love you. Your Devoted Father."

And listen to the date: May twenty-eighth, 1969. That's my birthday. I was born just after midnight. So he must've written this after I was born. Don't you see? He doesn't sound the least bit disappointed that I wasn't a boy! He was happy to have three daughters. Three "Darling Diva Daughters."

[*They are all having a group-hug moment when the guys reenter.*]

ZAK: What happened in there?
SPENCER: I don't know, but I think we'd best leave 'em be.

[*They quietly back out of the kitchen. Lights fade to black.*]

[*The curtain call should reprise the idea of a family portrait, both with and without the men. And the portrait of the sisters as girls is finally hanging straight.*]

AFTERWORD

Chuck Smith

Thank you for reading this anthology. I must also thank the playwrights and my editorial staff, who have donated all royalties to Columbia College Chicago's Theodore Ward Prize for African American Playwriting. This volume is the second in a series that will be published every three years. Seven Black Plays *was the first. Its primary markets are African American theater students and theater professionals across the nation. I mention the students first because each of the first-place winning plays included received its first full production on a college stage. Also keeping our new black theater students in mind, beginning with this volume, certain monologues and scenes are referenced on page 223.*

CLASSROOM SWAN SONG

It was the worst of times; it was the best of times. I know that isn't the way it was originally penned, but that's the way it really was for this editor since writing the afterword for the first volume of black plays from the Theodore Ward Prize competition. I have been honored to be the coordinator for this competition for black playwrights since 1988 and have been a proud participant in Chicago's black theater scene since the 1970s. There have been ups and downs over the decades, but 2005 was an exceptionally unhappy year.

At the 2005 National Black Theatre Festival in Winston-Salem, North Carolina, one of the board members of the Chicago Theater Company privately informed me that the company, which I had helped put together twenty years earlier, was about to go under. I wish I could say that the shortness of breath that I experienced on hearing the news went away once it all sank in. However, such was not the case, and in Chicago a few weeks later, I was diagnosed with congestive heart failure. I was hospitalized for a few weeks and had to go on sick leave from my fall semester teaching post and give up a choice directing assignment at the University of Wisconsin. I had never been seriously ill and, unconsciously being a naughty patient, things got worse. My heart doctor put me under house arrest and wouldn't even allow me to attend the funeral of August Wilson. It was a bad time. Earlier in April, my aunt Lois passed in New York; fortunately I was there. A few days later I rolled my Jeep over on Chicago's Outer Drive. Physically I got away clean from the accident, but mentally I still recall each horrific second. It also caused me to miss the closing of my production of *The Story* by Tracey Scott Wilson at the Goodman Theatre. At midnight on December 31, 2005, I breathed a sigh of relief. A bad year for me, 2005, was over.

The doctor let me go back to work in the first week of January 2006, and I began rehearsals for the twentieth anniversary Theodore Ward Prize–winning play, *The Etymology of Bird*, by Zakiyyah Alexander, at Columbia College Chicago. It opened in February and—with its young subject matter, rap, and break dancing—was a wildly popular show, especially with students and young adults. Many came back to see it twice, and it sold out quickly. The Goodman Theatre and the History Makers presented an evening interview with me on February 6. My friend Harry Lennix took time out from taping his TV drama, *Commander in Chief*, in Los Angeles to host. A few weeks later, my church, Saint Columbanus, honored me with a special Mass. It was a great Black History Month. The year 2006 was looking, and feeling, better. I went to work on a new play, *Stick Fly*, by my friend Lydia Diamond, at Congo Square. The show opened in late March and set a box office record for the company. In late May, I opened a production of *Crumbs from the Table of Joy*, by Lynn Nottage, at the Goodman Theatre that was extended. While in rehearsals for that production, the League of Chicago Theatres honored me with a lifetime achievement award. My friend Woodie King came in from New York to present, and friends in the audience included playwright Charles Smith from Ohio University and Lou Bellamy, artistic director of Penumbra Theatre in St. Paul, Minnesota; Ella Joyce and other members of my *Crumbs* cast; and my cousin and daughter. It was another great event. During my acceptance speech, I announced that I would be leaving Columbia College Chicago after the 2007 spring semester. I have been at the college well over twenty years and now want to focus on producing outside of Chicago.

The summer of 2006 found me, for the fifth consecutive year, at the Timber Lake Playhouse in Mount Carroll, Illinois, where I directed *Ain't Misbehavin'*,' the company's first all-black show. Choreographed (really codirected) by Lili-Anne Brown, the production was a sold-out winner that closed the Timber Lake season with fun and class.

In October, *Two Trains Running* opened Columbia College Chicago's

2006–2007 theater season. The department had never presented an August Wilson drama as part of its mainstage season, and directing the first one knowing it would be my last production as a faculty member provoked a wild mix of emotions. A few years ago, members of Columbia's Black Actors Guild made it clear that while working on the premiere production of the Theodore Ward Prize–winning play each year was a great honor and a learning experience, they wanted to perform other established plays from the black theater canon as well. They had a point. Unfortunately, we currently do not have a sufficient number of African American students in the nation's largest theater department to warrant more than one black show per season, and for the past twenty years, that play has been the Theodore Ward Prize winner. This season, thanks to a grant from the Boeing Foundation, the prize-winning play, *Like a Cow or an Elephant,* by Kara Corthron, will be presented at DePaul University, allowing room in Columbia's season for *Two Trains Running.* Next year, the winning play returns to Columbia College, and I hope this will begin a rotation of producing the prize-winning play at a venue outside of Columbia every other season. Black shows made a significant mark at the Jeff Awards (Chicago's equivalent of the Tonys) in 2005 and 2006. Congo Square took home several awards in 2005, including best production for their *Seven Guitars,* and in 2006, Court Theatre did the same with *Fences.* Ella Joyce won best supporting actress for her performance in the Goodman's *Crumbs from the Table of Joy,* and the show's Nambie E. Kelly received a nomination as best actress. Lydia Diamond's *Stick Fly* and *Voyeurs De Venus* both received nominations for best new play, with the *Venus* production at Chicago Dramatists winning the award. Somehow overlooked was Congo Square's stunning world premiere of *Deep Azure,* my own personal choice as best "everything."

Despite the loss of the Chicago Theater Company, black theater in Chicago remains in good health. The ETA and Black Ensemble companies are ever so much closer to building new venues. MPAACT is now firmly entrenched at the Victory Gardens Greenhouse space, but Congo Square will again be looking for a home or making a deal with the new owners of the Duncan YMCA space (God bless the child . . .). Charles Smith's powerful new play *Denmark* opened the beautiful new Victory Gardens Theater season at the restored Biograph Theater mainstage. On opening night, I was thrilled to watch three of my former Columbia College acting students (A. C. Smith, Kenn E. Head, and Anthony Fleming III), now seasoned professionals, seamlessly perform in this fascinating new drama.

I leave the Columbia College classroom in May 2007 but will stick around to facilitate the Theodore Ward Prize and edit future volumes of this anthology until a replacement is chosen. By the end of summer 2007, I will have completed productions for Roosevelt University (my first opera), Teatro Vista at the Goodman Theatre, DePaul University, Eclipse Theatre Company, and my beloved Timber Lake Playhouse.

The year 2006 was a joy, and 2007 is looking good.

CONTEST GUIDELINES

Columbia College Chicago's Annual Theodore Ward Prize for African American Playwriting

Sponsors

Columbia College Chicago Theater Center
Sheldon Patinkin, Chair, Theater Department
Paul Carter Harrison, Playwright in Residence
Chuck Smith, Facilitator

Goals

1. To uncover and identify new African American plays that are promising and producible.
2. To encourage and aid playwrights in the development of promising scripts.
3. To offer an opportunity for emerging and established playwrights to be exposed to Chicago's professional theater community through staged readings and/or fully mounted productions.

Eligibility

1. All entrants must be of African American descent and permanent residents within the United States.
2. Only full-length plays addressing the African American will be considered. One-act plays and musicals are not accepted (with the exception of a play with music).
3. Adaptations and translations are not eligible unless from works in the public domain.
4. All rights for music or biographies must be secured by entrant prior to submission.
5. One completed script per playwright will be accepted.

6. Scripts that have received professional productions are ineligible. "Professional" includes Equity Showcase and Waiver productions but does not include amateur and college productions.
7. All manuscripts must be typed and bound. Please include a brief personal résumé (with a telephone number), a short synopsis, and a script history. The script history should include information about any prior productions or readings.
8. Staff and faculty of Columbia College Chicago are not eligible. Winners cannot win in successive years.

Submission

All manuscripts must be typed, securely bound, copyrighted, and mailed to Chuck Smith, Columbia College Chicago, Theater Center, 72 East Eleventh Street, Chicago, IL 60605. Only scripts with self-addressed envelopes will be returned.

Prizes

The first-place winner will receive two thousand dollars and a fully mounted production in the New Studio season. The performance space is a seventy-seat black box theater that is a part of the Theater Center of Columbia College Chicago. The prize also includes transportation (within the continental United States only) and housing (maximum one week) during rehearsal period and performances.

The playwright must be willing to sign a contract with the college that obligates the playwright to (1) travel to Chicago during production; (2) acknowledge prize in future programs and publications; and (3) grant publishing rights to Columbia College Chicago. The playwright will receive future royalties of 1 percent (three-year time limit).

The second-place winner will receive five hundred dollars, a staged reading at Columbia College Chicago directed by a faculty director, and an audiotape of this reading.

Columbia College Chicago and the Theodore Ward Prize Advisory Board reserve the right to withhold the awards should the Advisory Board so recommend.

Deadline

Scripts will be accepted from April 1 to July 1. All scripts must be postmarked no later than midnight on July 1.

Columbia College Chicago

Columbia College was founded in 1890. In 1947, Mike Alexandroff became its president and instituted the principles Columbia is based on today, the use of professionals as teachers giving up-to-date and practical instruction, aiming toward success in the field after college. Today, President Warrick Carter carries on that proud tradition.

Columbia's Theater Department, chaired by Sheldon Patinkin since 1980, offers a program aimed at equipping its students with the skills needed to fully develop their careers. Performance is considered the key to progress.

The faculty and staff are all working professionals, active and prominent members of Chicago's lively theater community. The department stresses intensive one-on-one training in all aspects of the profession and supplies a multitude of opportunities for applying this learning in performance situations.

The Theater Department produces a six-show subscription season for general audiences. At the four-hundred-seat Emma and Oscar Getz Theater, fully mounted productions of two large-cast plays, or musicals, and one concert featuring our Faculty Ensemble as directors and designers are presented. In the seventy-seat New Studio, the season is rounded out with full productions of two smaller plays and one musical or concert. In addition, many all-student-directed workshop productions and recitals are presented each semester in the sixty-seat Classic Studio.

FIRST-PLACE WINNERS OF THE THEODORE WARD PRIZE FOR AFRICAN AMERICAN PLAYWRITING

1986–1987   Silas Jones, *The John Doe Variations*

1987–1988   Christopher Moore, *The Last Season*

1988–1989   Jeff Stetson, *Fathers and Other Strangers*

1989–1990   No winner

1990–1991   William F. Mayfield, *Sing Black Hammer*

1991–1992   No winner

1992–1993   Chuck Cummings, *The Negro Building*

1993–1994   Gloria Bond Clunie, *North Star*

1994–1995   Charlotte A. Gibson, *The Temple*

1995–1996   Duane Chandler, *The Trees Don't Bleed in Tuskegee*

1996–1997   Charlotte A. Gibson, *Lost Creek Township*

1997–1998   David Barr, *Black Caesar*

1998–1999   Benard Cummings, *The Grandmamma Tree*

1999–2000   Javon Johnson, *Hambone*

2000–2001   Lydia Diamond, *The Gift Horse*

2001–2002   Shepsu Aakhu, *Kiwi Black*

2002–2003   Leslie Lee, *Sundown Names and Night-Gone Things*

2003–2004   Mark Clayton Southers, *Ma Noah*

2004–2005   Gloria Bond Clunie, *Sweet Water Taste*

2005–2006   Zakiyyah Alexander, *The Etymology of Bird*

2006–2007   Kara Lee Corthron, *Like a Cow or an Elephant*

SCENES AND MONOLOGUES

Sundown Names and Night-Gone Things

SCENES

9–12	African American male and female
38–40	African American male and female
40–43	African American male and female
45–47	African American males (2)
47–49	African American males (2)
52–55	African American male and female
55–58	African American male and female
74–76	African American males (2)

MONOLOGUES

48–49	African American male
55	African American female
64	African American female
72–73	African American male
73	African American male

Ma Noah

SCENES

83–85	African American females (2)
95–97	African American females (2)
115–17	African American male and female
118–20	African American females (2)
129	African American male and female

MONOLOGUES

120–21   African American female

The Diva Daughters DuPree

SCENES

151–54   Caucasian male, African American female
167–69   African American females (2)
170–74   African American females (2)
174–76   African American females (2)
181–83   African American male and female
193–95   African American male and female
195–96   African American male and female
203–5   African American females (2)

MONOLOGUES

159   African American female
191   African American female
197–98   African American male

ABOUT THE PLAYWRIGHTS

KIM EUELL is Dean's Fellow at the University of Iowa, where she is pursuing a Master of Fine Arts degree in playwriting. Her latest play, *Otto Bingo*, was presented at the Iowa New Play Festival in May 2006. She recently received the Stanley International Research Fellowship to support research in South Africa for her upcoming play *Sistern*. *The Diva Daughters DuPree* was named "Outstanding New Show of 2004" by critics at the *Minneapolis-St. Paul Star Tribune* in their year-end review. Euell has been awarded three Artist Residency Grants for playwriting by the California Arts Council. She is a company member of the Penumbra Theatre in St. Paul. Euell is also a new play dramaturge, having served on the artistic staffs of the Mark Taper Forum, Hartford Stage Company, and Sundance Institute Theatre Lab, among others.

LESLIE LEE is a full-time associate teacher in the Dramatic Writing Program at New York University. He also teaches a playwriting workshop at the Frederick Douglass Creative Arts Center in Manhattan. In addition to *Sundown Names and Night-Gone Things*, Lee has written a number of other plays. *The First Breeze of Summer*, which received an Obie Award and a Tony nomination, was produced at the Stella Adler Theatre in Los Angeles in August 2006. *Legends* was given a reading by the Producers' Club in October 2006 and was read at the Stella Adler Theatre in November 2006, directed by Adleane Hunter. *The War Party* was given a reading at New Dramatists in October 2006. *The Ninth Wave*, directed by Stephen McKinley Henderson, was scheduled for a reading in New York by early 2007. A new play, *Bitch!* was read at the Goldberg Theater at NYU and is scheduled to be produced at La MaMa Experimental Theatre Club in New York in November 2007. Lee is developing two other new plays and an idea for a television series about a black family.

MARK CLAYTON SOUTHERS is the founder and producing artistic director for the Pittsburgh Playwrights Theatre Company (also known as PPTCO). Now in its fifth season, PPTCO offers four or five mainstage productions a year as well as the Theatre Festival in Black and White, a concept that Southers formulated in which the works of five black playwrights and five white playwrights are presented, with black directors directing the white playwrights' plays and vice versa. Southers has recently returned from Ireland, where he has been working on his most recent play, *James McBride*. It is the second play in his six-play culture class series, a series of plays that introduce two different cultures onstage. The first play in the series, *Hoodwinked*, directed by Ron O. J. Parson, was produced at PPTCO in 2006. It is a tale about an elderly Jewish couple who move back into their former home in the hood. Southers's full-length play *Ashes to Africa* is part of the 2007 season at the Ensemble Theatre in Houston. Southers recently curated the Teenie Harris Collection II at the Carnegie Museum of Art in Pittsburgh, an exhibition of more than two hundred photographs spanning four decades, all of them taken by former *New Pittsburgh Courier* photographer Charles "Teenie" Harris.

Chuck Smith and Theodore Ward, 1972

CHUCK SMITH is a resident director at the Goodman Theatre in Chicago, where his productions have included *The Story, Proof, The Death of Bessie Smith, The Gift Horse, The Amen Corner, A Raisin in the Sun, Blues for an Alabama Sky, Ma Rainey's Black Bottom, A Christmas Carol,* and *The Meeting.* Smith is also a faculty member in the theater department of Columbia College Chicago. He is the editor of *Seven Black Plays: The Theodore Ward Prize for African American Playwriting.*

THEODORE WARD, the sixth of eleven children, was born in Thibodaux, Louisiana, where his father was a teacher and principal of a parish school for fifty years. At the age of thirteen he hopped a freight to Omaha and ended up in Chicago, where he lived and nurtured his playwriting gift until his death on May 8, 1983. Sharing the literary and sociopolitical vision of his contemporaries Richard Wright and Clifford Odets, Ward was one of the most significant playwrights to emerge from the Chicago chapter of the Federal Theatre Project during the mid-1930s.

Following a period of study at the University of Wisconsin as a Zona Grey fellow, Ward had his first major play, *Big White Fog,* produced in Chicago by the FTP. During the early 1940s, he became cofounder of the Negro Playwrights Company in New York and with the help of a Theater Guild scholarship developed and produced his historical play *Our Lan'* on Broadway in 1945. The author of more that twenty plays, Ward was a recipient of the John Simon Guggenheim and National Theatre fellowships for playwriting and was one of the major role models who influenced the shape of the intellectual and cultural life of Chicago's African American community.

COVER PHOTOGRAPHS

FRONT (TOP): Mark James Heath as Larry and Regina Whitehead-Mays as Rebecca in Mark Clayton Southers's *Ma Noah* (photograph by Lisa Ebright)

FRONT (MIDDLE): My-Isha Cason-Brown as Abbey, Iris Farrugia as Billie, and Sonya Carswell as Sarah in Kim Euell's *The Diva Daughters DuPree* (photograph by Rick Smith)

FRONT (BOTTOM): Inda Craig-Galvan as Mae Ann and Byron Glenn Willis as Travis in Leslie Lee's *Sundown Names and Night-Gone Things* (photograph from the collection of the Chicago Theatre Company)

BACK: Chuck Smith (photograph by Lisa Ebright)